The Case of the Turquoise Sun

A Natural History of Creation

Ev Cochrane

Zanzara Press

Zanzara Press
PO Box 5069
Madison, WI 53705-5069
USA
zanzarapress.com
editor@zanzarapress.com

Zanzara Press

THE CASE OF THE TURQUOISE SUN
2024 © Ev Cochrane

All rights reserved. No part of this work covered by the copyright hereon may be reproduced or used in any form or by any means—graphic, electronic, or mechanical, including photocopying, recording, taping, or information storage and retrieval systems—without written permission of the publisher. Neither the author nor the publisher make any representation, express or implied, with regard to the accuracy of the information contained in this book and cannot accept any legal responsibility or liability for any errors or omissions that may be made.

ISBN: 978-1-941892-81-7

Book layout and design by polytekton.com

Our books may be purchased in bulk for promotional, educational, and/or business use. Please contact your local bookseller or the Culicidae Press Sales Department at +1-515-462-0278 or by email at sales@culicidaepress.com

twitter.com/culicidaepress – facebook.com/culicidaepress
threads.net/culicidaepress – instagram.com/culicidaepress

Table of Contents

Acknowledgements	5
Preface	6
Introduction	9
01 The Ancient Sky	**14**
Suns and Planets in Prehistoric Rock Art	15
02 Solar Imagery in Ancient Mesopotamia	**21**
03 Solar Imagery in Ancient Egypt	**28**
Horus on the Lotus	30
04 The Drilling of Fire and the Origin of the Sun	**35**
Xiuhtecuhtli	37
The Vedic Fire-god Agni	38
Lord of the Four Corners	41
The Turquoise Enclosure	47
Conclusion	51
05 The Aztec Myth of Creation	**52**
Nanahuatl	59
Conclusion	63
06 The Skidi Pawnee Myth of Creation	**64**
07 The Planet Venus in Ancient Mesopotamia	**70**
The Garden of Venus	74
Conclusion	85
08 The Blossom of Creation	**86**
09 The Thundergod and Creation	**92**
Tohil	95
Tezcatlipoca	97
10 The Coupling of Heaven and Earth	**101**

11 In the Beginning: Heaven and Earth Were One	**108**
12 Zeus: Thundergod Extraordinaire	**115**
Postscript	120
13 The Primordial Earth	**124**
Reimagining Creation	129
14 The King of the Four Quarters	**135**
The Maintenance of Cosmic Order	142
15 The King's Fire	**151**
16 An Obsession with Creation	**157**
17 Conclusion	**163**
Appendix One	**166**
Appendix Two	**170**
Appendix Three	**173**
Appendix Four	**176**
Appendix Five	**178**
Appendix Six	**180**
Appendix Seven: Earthborn Zeus	**183**
Appendix Eight	**186**
Appendix Nine: The World Tree	**189**
Appendix Ten	**194**
Appendix Eleven: A Baptism by Fire	**196**
Conclusion	207
Appendix Twelve: Sky-God or Thundergod?	**209**
Conclusion	216
Bibliography	**219**
Index	**238**

Acknowledgements

It goes without saying that the thesis defended here owes much to my forty-year plus collaboration with David Talbott, author of the groundbreaking *The Saturn Myth* (1980). Dave's ingenious theory of the polar configuration and innumerable insights are evident on nearly every page of this manuscript. I have also benefited from a decades-long correspondence with my old comrade Marinus van der Sluijs, author of the most learned compendium on comparative mythology to date—*Traditional Cosmology* (2011). The physicists Anthony Peratt and Wal Thornhill were a constant source of inspiration and guidance with regard to the possible appearance and underlying plasma-based structure of the polar configuration. Throughout my long career as a researcher, I have been blessed by the friendship and intelligence of Birgit Liesching, who willingly gave of her time in translating difficult texts in German and French. With regards to the present manuscript, Kaede Mailes prepared the bibliography and helped with the final editing. A special thanks is also due to Iowa State University for granting me continuing access to their state-of-the-art Interlibrary Loan department, a veritable lifeline for an independent researcher (It was at ISU that I studied ancient Near Eastern history and Sumerian myth under Achilles Avraamides). And last but certainly not least, I owe a major debt of gratitude to my old friend Chuck Harmison, who provided me with a loan just when it was needed most, thereby allowing me to publish my Magnum Opus.

Preface

> All these facts originate from the same event in cosmic history, and so do hosts of others yet more marvelous than these. However, as this great event took place so long ago, some of them have faded from man's memory; others survive but they have become scattered and have come to be told in a way which obscures their real connection with one another. No one has related the great event of history which gives the setting of all of them; it is this event which we must now recount.[1]

To believers and non-believers alike, Creation represents the most fascinating and enduring mystery of all. Yet the circumstances attending the ordering of the world at the Time of Beginning remain as inscrutable as ever in the twenty-first century, well over four thousand years after the first written accounts purporting to describe them. Long considered the special purview of metaphysicians, new research suggests that the time has come for natural scientists to revisit the debate over origins. It is the purpose of the present monograph to investigate—and, if possible, outline and elucidate—the extraordinary natural events remembered by our forebears as "Creation."

It is our judgment that the best window into Creation is provided by the countless mythological traditions recounting it, often in surprisingly explicit detail. Typically the most treasured of cultural traditions, for untold millennia cosmogonic myths were committed to memory with each new generation and recited or acted out during all especially sacred occasions such as New Year's cel-

---

[1] *The Statesman* 269b5-c3 as translated in L. Brisson, *Plato the Mythmaker* (Chicago, 2000), p. 110.

ebrations, the coronation of a king, the founding of a new temple or township, etc.[2] Creation-accounts are common to all cultures at all times and, as a result, researchers are blessed with a vast database of evidentiary testimony to sift through and subject to forensic analysis.

Ancient myth itself was primarily concerned with describing the momentous events attending Creation. In distinct contrast to folktale—which is generally understood to be the product of creative storytelling and thus primarily fictional in nature—myth has been characterized as a sacred narrative "having to do with the gods and their actions, with creation, and with the general nature of the universe and of the earth."[3] Summarizing his principal conclusions after a lifetime of research into the fundamental purpose and meaning of myth, Mircea Eliade offered the following observation, one that we would endorse in its entirety:

> Myth narrates a sacred history; it relates an event that took place in primordial Time, the fabled time of the 'beginnings.' In other words, myth tells how, through the deeds of Supernatural Beings, a reality came into existence, be it the whole of reality, the Cosmos, or only a fragment of reality—an island, a species of plant, a particular kind of human behavior, an institution. Myth, then, is always an account of a 'creation'; it relates how something was produced, began to *be*. Myth tells only of that which *really* happened, which manifested itself completely. The actors in myths are Supernatural Beings. They are known primarily by what they did in the transcendent times of the 'beginnings.'...Because myth relates the *gesta* of Supernatural Beings and the manifestation of their sacred powers, it becomes the exemplary model for all significant human activities. When the missionary and ethnologist C. Strelow asked the Australian Arunta why they performed certain ceremonies, the answer was always: 'Because the ancestors so commanded it.'[4]

---

[2] C. Lopez-Ruiz, *When the Gods Were Born: Greek Cosmogonies and the Near East* (Cambridge, 2010), p. 184.
[3] S. Thompson, "Myth and Folktales," in T. Sebeok, *Myth: A Symposium* (Bloomington, 1955), p. 173. Alan Dundes, "Madness in Method Plus a Plea for Projective Inversion in Myth," in L. Patton & W. Doniger eds., *Myth and Method* (London, 1996), p. 147, offered the following definition: "For the folklorist, a myth is a sacred narrative explaining how the world and mankind came to be in their present form. Myths and legends (narratives told as true and set in the post-creation era) are different from folktales, which are narratives understood to be fictional."
[4] M. Eliade, *Myth and Reality* (New York, 1963), pp. 5-6.

What, then, do our ancestors have to report about the circumstances attending Creation? The first finding to emerge from our research is that myths of cosmogony have nothing whatsoever to do with the generation of the universe *ex nihilo* as in modern speculations regarding the Big Bang.[5] Rather, the traditions in question describe and encode cataclysmic natural events involving the neighboring planetary bodies, the import of which has been almost entirely overlooked by modern scholarship in general and astronomical science in particular. Paramount among these witnessed events was the prototypical appearance of the "sun," an occasion that was so awe-inspiring and terrifying that Earthlings everywhere were traumatized to the very core of their being and, in a fundamental sense, forever transformed. The cataclysmic events in question—never wholly forgotten—informed cosmogonic mythological traditions for millennia and left indelible traces in belief-systems, rituals, and languages the world over.

In the monograph to follow, we will draw upon the oldest literary texts still extant, including those from Mesopotamia, Egypt, and Vedic India. These archaic traditions, in turn, will be compared with cosmogonic traditions from ancient Greece, Israel, Mesoamerica, and elsewhere in order to clarify the nature and relative chronology of the extraordinary events in question. The reader will notice early on that, no matter which ancient culture we consult, strange tales of anomalous "suns" and amorous planets abound, hitherto dismissed as old wives' tales. By ignoring or seeking to explain away the unequivocal testimony attesting to the prominent role of planetary catastrophe during the recent prehistoric past, orthodox science has spoonfed the public a deeply flawed and impoverished version of human history, one which serves to distort and undermine the fundamental import of our entire Western intellectual heritage as bequeathed to us by Homer, Hesiod, Pindar, and Plato. In the grand scheme of things, it is difficult to conceive of a more consequential error in judgment than that.

---

[5] See the discussion in J. Westenholz, "Heaven and Earth," in J. Stackert & T. Abusch eds., *Gazing on the Deep* (Bethesda, 2010), p. 293.

Introduction

The (old) myths present a profound truth in a riddling manner.[6]

In *The Adventure of the Musgrave Ritual*, London's greatest detective Sherlock Holmes is tasked with deciphering a riddle in order to solve a missing person's case. The riddle in question, which had been handed down for centuries within the Musgrave family clan, read as follows:

> Whose was it?
> His who is gone.
> Who shall have it?
> He who will come.
> Where was the sun?
> Over the oak.
> Where was the shadow?
> Under the elm.
> How was it stepped?
> North by ten and by ten, east by five and by five, south by two and by two, west by one and by one, and so under.
> What shall we give for it?
> All that is ours.
> Why should we give it?
> For the sake of the trust.

Shortly thereafter, upon inspecting the grounds of the medieval Musgrave Manor and applying his formidable analytic skills, Holmes deduces that the rid-

---
[6] R. Seaford, *Euripides: Bacchae* (Oxford, 1996), p. 175.

dle in question represents a cryptogram encoding instructions leading to a buried family heirloom of some sort. Taking his cue from the reference to the sun, Holmes calculates the precise angle of shadow that would be cast by the giant oak tree. Orienting himself by the now missing elm and carefully following the instructions, Holmes eventually unearths King Charles I's golden crown and solves a murder in the process.

A master detective is distinguished by the ability to discern evidence-trails and patterns that were hitherto overlooked or obscured from view. In most criminal investigations it is not the discovery of some previously unknown smoking gun that turns the tide or seals the case; rather, it is the careful and painstaking analysis of human testimony or physical evidence already in hand that evokes a fresh insight or the revelation of some promising lead. Fundamental to the science of detection is the guiding principle that compelling circumstantial evidence will often suffice to make a probative case even when confronted by conflicting eye-witness testimony—and sometimes in the absence of a murder weapon or *corpus delicti*.[7]

In the present case study, we are tasked with decoding dozens of millennia-old riddles presented by humankind's earliest and most revered mythological traditions—namely, those describing the ordering of the cosmos. In the investigation to follow we will deploy the comparative method together with common sense in an attempt to discover the natural-historical origins of these ancient creation accounts.[8] Like a paleontologist sifting through a jumble of dislocated teeth and bone fragments in order to reconstruct a long extinct dinosaur, the comparativist must make do with whatever relic of myth, cultural artifact, or vestigial linguistic structure happens to come his way.[9] Critical thinking and a Holmesian eye for the odd detail is a must in this enterprise, needless to say.

Creation-accounts regularly include formulaic phraseology or riddling word-plays which provide invaluable insight into the fundamental meaning of the formative events in question.[10] In ancient Mesopotamia, for example, a proverbial saying for "in the Time of Beginning" was "When in ancient days heaven was separated from earth…"[11] Encoded in this archaic expression is the memory that Cre-

---

[7] J. Langbein, *Torture and the Law of Proof* (Chicago, 2006), p. 57.
[8] D. Ragavan, "Heaven on Earth: Temples, Ritual, and Cosmic Symbolism in the Ancient World," in D. Ragavan ed., *Heaven and Earth* (Chicago, 2013), p. 13: "Scholars have continued to argue strongly for the utility, indeed the necessity, of comparison with regard to religion in general and sacred architecture in particular."
[9] U. Strutynski, "Ares: A Reflex on the Indo-European War God?," *Arethusa* 13 (1980), p. 227: "The comparativist works as an archaeologist of ideas."
[10] See the masterful discussion in C. Watkins, *How to Kill a Dragon* (Oxford, 1995).
[11] Line 1 from "Lugalbanda in the mountain cave," in J. Black et al, *The Electronic Text Corpus*

ation was distinguished by the separation of heaven and earth and that, prior to that epochal event, the two entities were conjoined as one.[12] There is indisputable evidence, moreover, that such idiomatic expressions were preserved many centuries after their original meaning was forgotten, not unlike the Musgrave ritual.[13]

Most archaic formulaic phrases are not nearly so unambiguous and transparent as the previous example. Another proverb from ancient Mesopotamia describes the time of origins as that period "when the Sun-god was king."[14] The same basic idea is apparent in early Egypt as evidenced by the following account of creation from the *Coffin Texts*:

> I am the Sun in his first appearances…Variant: it is the beginning of the Sun appearing over the world…Who then is he? It is the Sun when he began the reign he has exercised. It is the Sun's beginning to appear in the kingship he has exercised, when Shu's uplifiting had not yet occurred.[15]

But what can it mean that the Sun was king? What, exactly, was it the king of? As we intend to document, the answer to this query has the potential to serve as something of a Rosetta Stone in pointing the way to a successful decipherment of ancient cosmogonic myth and, at the same time, exposing a watershed event in human history.

A common refrain in modern criminological investigations is "to follow the money." In the present case study in comparative mythology we will heed Paul McCartney's advise and follow the Sun, a strategy forced upon us by the fact that it is the sun-god who, in addition to being a prominent figure in ancient pantheons, is the prime mover in numerous cosmogonic traditions. Remarkably, however, in the earliest literature the Sun is described in a fashion that is impossible to square with present reality. Of the numerous texts that could be cited in this regard, the following Sumerian incantation to the sun-god is representative in nature: "As my king [Utu] comes forth, the heavens tremble before him and the

---

of Sumerian Literature (http://www-etcsl.orient.ox.ac.uk/) (Oxford, 1998). Hereafter *ETCSL*.
[12] J. Westenholz, "Heaven and Earth," in J. Stackert & T. Abusch eds., *Gazing on the Deep* (Bethesda, 2010), p. 304: "Creation began with the separation of heaven and earth."
[13] G. Selz, "Early Dynastic Vessels in 'Ritual' Contexts," *Wiener Zeitschrift für die Kunde des Morgenlandes* 94 (2004), p. 277 observed: "Sumerian and Akkadian proverbial sayings, which reflect and perpetuate cultural values and were copied in scribal classrooms almost verbatim for millennia…"
[14] Line 14 from "Enmerkar and Ensuhgirana," as translated in H. Vanstiphout, *Epics of Sumerian Kings* (Leiden, 2004), p. 29.
[15] Spell 335 as translated in J. Allen, *Genesis in Egypt* (New Haven, 1988), p. 32.

earth shakes before him."[16] Elsewhere in the same hymn Utu is described as follows: "The lord, the son of Ningal…thunders over the mountains like a storm."[17] Now I ask: Does this sound like a realistic description of the modern experience of sunrise? In what sense is the solar epiphany ever accompanied by thunder or the shaking of heaven and earth?

Early artworks allegedly depicting the sun are equally difficult to reconcile with the familiar solar orb. As we will argue in the chapters to follow, a proper interpretation of these artworks portends a revolution in our understanding of the solar system's recent history.

Before commencing with our analysis, a word or two is in order with regards to the nature of the comparative enterprise. What is true of the master detective is also true of the adept practitioner of comparative mythology: Those who make the greatest contributions—scholars like Jacob Grimm, Wilhelm Roscher, Georges Dumézil, Walter Burkert, Jaan Puhvel, Calvert Watkins, Gregory Nagy and Roger Woodard—have the requisite training and analytical skills to discern the underlying thematic patterns or linguistic relationships that remain obscure to other researchers. The end result of their investigations into ancient myth and religion, if successful, is the revelation of historical connections hitherto overlooked and, not infrequently, additional insight into problems that had previously seemed intractable.

The present exercise in comparative mythology is distinguished from previous researches by our reliance upon archaic artworks such as petroglyphs and cylinder seals. It is our opinion that the testimony of cosmogonic myth is often complemented and clarified by prehistoric artworks, the latter of which offer researchers a rich iconic compendium by which to examine and crosscheck humankind's earliest beliefs regarding the nature of the cosmos and the fundamental essence of the divine. By juxtaposing and comparing the testimony transmitted by ancient artworks and cosmogonic myth we will attempt to reconstruct the natural history behind the manifold Creation-accounts, arguing that they are best understood as inspired by extraordinary astronomical events of a cataclysmic nature. If the former exercise properly belongs to comparative mythology and will be perfectly familiar to other scholars working in the field, the emphasis on cataclysmic natural events is tantamount to virgin territory and, as such, is likely to spark some controversy and blowback.[18] So be it: The diligent researcher of ancient lore must

---

[16] Lines 13-14 from "A hymn to Utu (Utu B)," *ETCSL*.

[17] Line 28. See also lines 3-4 in "An adab (?) to Utu for Shulgi (Shulgi Q)," *ETCSL*: "Hero emerging from the holy interior of heaven, storm whose splendour covers the Land and is laden with great awesomeness."

[18] See now the voluminous evidence collected in M. van der Sluijs, *On the Origin of Myths in*

follow Ariadne's clew wherever it might lead, even if that involves an occasional foray into hitherto uncharted or forbidden territory and runs counter to prevailing scholarly opinions. As Holmes himself was known to observe: "Once you eliminate the impossible, whatever remains, no matter how improbable, must be the truth."

Catastrophic Experience, Vol. 1 (Vancouver, 2019).

01 The Ancient Sky

The earliest home of the gods that we can discern is the sky.[19]

The sky has long been a source of wonder and fascination for Earthlings everywhere. Even today, on those rare occasions when we leave the city lights behind and venture out into a natural setting offering an unobstructed vision of the heavens, the majestic splendor of the night sky and its myriad of stars and constellations is a treasure to behold. Those of us who have been fortunate enough to witness the spectacular fireworks presented by a total eclipse, passing comet, or auroral display can appreciate how such astronomical phenomena might well elicit sudden stirrings of powerful emotions ranging from the sublime to utter dread. There is much reason to believe, in fact, that it was precisely such visceral responses to awe-inspiring events that were the wellsprings of religion, as argued most forcefully by Rudolph Otto and Thorkild Jacobsen:

> "Basic to all religion—and so also to ancient Mesopotamian religion—is, we believe, a unique experience with power not of this world. Rudolph Otto called this confrontation 'Numinous' and analyzed it as the experience of *mysterium tremendum et fascinosum*, a confrontation with a 'Wholly Other' outside of normal experience and indescribable in its terms: terrifying, ranging from sheer demonic dread through awe to sublime majesty; and fascinating, with its irresistible attraction, demanding unconditional allegiance. It is the positive human response to this experience in thought (myth and theology) and action (cult and worship) that constitutes religion."[20]

---

[19] E. Hornung, *Conceptions of God in Ancient Egypt* (Ithaca, 1982), p. 227.
[20] T. Jacobsen, *Treasures of Darkness* (New Haven, 1976), p. 3.

The Sun is far and away the most conspicuous star in today's sky. Few things in life are more familiar or predictable than the solar orb's appearance each morning from the eastern horizon. Indeed, the Sun's diurnal journey across the heavens has long been a proverbial symbol of the solar system's seemingly perfect regularity, order, and stability. That said, there is reason to believe that this much-vaunted stability is of relatively recent origin and that, well within the memory of humankind, the familiar Sun was not the primary focus of sky-watchers' attention. Instead, a different "sun" altogether formerly dominated the sky together with other long since vanished structures. If this point can be established—the primary thesis of the book at hand—it stands to reason that a scientific revolution is in order the likes of which promises to make that sparked by Copernicus's revelations look meager by comparison.

In order to develop this radical hypothesis, it will be necessary to examine humankind's earliest historical records to learn what they have to say about the Sun and other prominent celestial bodies. References to an active and volatile "sun" occur in the earliest literary records attested—those from ancient Mesopotamia and Egypt—and these will feature prominently in the analysis to follow.

Archaic artworks likewise provide a wealth of important testimony regarding the appearance of the ancient sky and its manifold structures. Already during the prehistoric period sky-watchers were recording their impressions of the sky and its most prominent denizens on cave walls and other media. So, too, symbols of a sun-like object and other stellar bodies are ubiquitous in ancient religious iconography, not only in Mesopotamia and Egypt, but around the globe as well. Yet the earliest artworks purportedly depicting the "sun" reveal a startling anomaly: They bear virtually zero resemblance to the appearance of the current solar orb.

In the next three chapters we will offer a brief review of the evidence bolstering this claim, much of which has been presented elsewhere in more detail. This background material, in turn, will serve as a recurring point of reference in the chapters to follow.

Suns and Planets in Prehistoric Rock Art

The discovery in 1879 of spectacular paintings in the caves of Altamira (northern Spain) was initially met with disbelief and ridicule, so radical was the idea that artwork of such beauty and sophistication could have been created by people living in the Stone Age. It was only after the discovery of similar finds in France, Portugal, and elsewhere in Europe that the scientific community was forced to accept the reality of Paleolithic rock art. In the meantime, it has been documented that rock art is present upon all inhabited continents and spans a period of time measured in millennia (the paintings of Altamira and Lascaux are typically dated to circa 15-35,000 BCE).[21]

During the Paleolithic Age, rock art was devoted primarily to the naturalistic depiction of various forms of wildlife, presumably objects of the hunt or associated in some way with rites of sympathetic magic.[22] Paintings of horses and wisent—the great bison that once roamed the steppes of Europe—are especially common, although mammoths, woolly rhinoceroses, and other long extinct fauna also appear. Paintings of the Sun, Moon, or celestial structures such as the Milky Way are notably absent from these earliest artworks. Indeed, so far as we can tell, out of the many thousands of paintings from the Paleolithic Age there is not a single clearly discernible image of the Sun or Moon.[23]

It was during the subsequent Neolithic Age, apparently, that artists first began recording their impressions of celestial phenomena through paintings and petroglyphs (incised images in rock). Not unlike fossilized bones, which provide paleontologists with a rich vein with which to reconstruct the precise structure and relative abundance of prehistoric fauna, rock art represents a tangible record of humankind's enduring interest in the stars and, as such, offers a vast library of images upon which to test reconstructions of the solar system's recent history.

Among the most common petroglyphs are those interpreted as early images of the Sun. Included here are relatively simple images featuring a circular disc from which "rays" emanate in all directions (see figure one).[24] Certainly this is how one might expect our Neolithic forebears to depict the current solar orb.

Figure one

---

[21] A. Willcox, *The Rock Art of Africa* (Kent, 1984), pp. 1-5.
[22] H. Breuil & H. Obermaier, *The Cave of Altamira* (Madrid, 1935), p. 12; F. Windels, *The Lascaux Cave Paintings* (London, 1949), p. 137.
[23] G. Curtis, *The Cave Painters* (New York, 2006), p. 17.
[24] This image is adapted from figure 17 in P. Harper et al eds., *The Royal City of Susa* (New York, 1992), p. 44. It dates to the Susa I period circa 4000 BCE.

Other images, however, are more difficult to explain by reference to the familiar Sun. Consider the image in figure two, depicting what would appear to be a circular disc with a smaller orb set within its center.[25] Of this particular image, the Italian archaeologist Emmanuel Anati remarked:

> This kind of symbolic representation of the sun is common to many primitive societies and ancient civilizations. It occurs in the ancient Near East, in the Far East, as well as in Europe and elsewhere.[26]

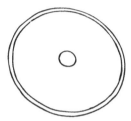

Figure two

Even more difficult to explain is the image in figure three, showing a flower-like object set within the center of a disc (the fact that the image in question occurs together with other "solar" images confirms its celestial provenance).[27] Although less common than the image represented in figure two, this particular petroglyph also has precise parallels around the globe.[28]

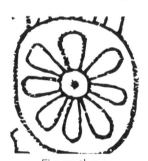

Figure three

---

[25] This image is reproduced from E. Anati, *Camonica Valley* (New York, 1961), p. 162. Analogous images occur in R. Heizer & C. Clewlow, *Prehistoric Rock Art of California* (Ramona, 1973), figure 329.
[26] E. Anati, *op. cit.*, p. 47.
[27] This image, taken from Cairn T of Lough Crew, forms figure 235 in E. Twohig, *The Megalithic Art of Western Europe* (London, 1981).
[28] See figure 438 of B. Teissier, *Ancient Near Eastern Cylinder Seals* (Berkeley, 1984), p. 225. For a parallel from the New World, see R. Heizer & C. Clewlow, *op. cit.*, figure 85.

Consider also the image illustrated in figure four.[29] How is it possible to explain the peculiar wheel-like "spokes" radiating outwards across the disc by reference to the familiar solar orb?[30] Most perplexing, perhaps, is the fact that such petroglyphs occur in Neolithic contexts and thus predate by several millennia the actual invention of spoked wheels: "The wheel-like symbols cannot *be* wheels since passage grave art appeared some millennia before the spoked wheel came into being in these regions."[31]

Figure four

Other petroglyphs depict what appear to be ladder-like structures projecting from the so-called solar image (see figure five).[32] Here, too, we are dealing with a petroglyph of widespread distribution, one typically interpreted as the sun with "rays."

Figure five

---

[29] This image is adapted from Cairn U at Loughcrew. See M. Brennan, *The Stones of Time* (Rochester, 1994), p. 160. The very same image appears in abundance at Val Camonica. For an analogue from Africa, see figure 8:4 from A. Willcox, *The Rock Art of Africa* (Kent, 1984). For an analogue from the New World, see figure 47w from R. Heizer & C. Clewlow, *Prehistoric Rock Art of California* (Ramona, 1973).
[30] Of these wheel-like forms, E. Anati, *Camonica Valley* (New York, 1961), p. 163 observes: "A number of hypotheses have been advanced in an attempt to explain them, but none is truly satisfactory."
[31] M. Green, *The Sun-Gods of Ancient Europe* (1991), p. 25.
[32] Adapted from figure 253 in R. Heitzer & C. Clewlow, *Prehistoric Rock Art of California*, Vol. 2 (Ramona, 1973). See also the discussion in E. Cochrane, "Ladder to Heaven," *Aeon* 6:5 (2004), pp. 55-76.

Although the aforementioned "sun-images" occur in a wide variety of artistic contexts and media, it is not uncommon to find them associated with scenes of apparent worship and ritual. In some engravings, for example, people are depicted "offering salutations" to the sun with upraised arms. In Camonica Valley (northern Italy), one of the richest and most thoroughly explored petroglyph sites in the world, Anati reported: "The carvings of the first period are limited to the depiction of one person praying, facing the sun—which is drawn as a disc with a dot in the center."[33] Such scenes, coupled together with abundant evidence suggesting that the sun featured prominently in ancient religions, have led scholars to assume that the petroglyphs in question served some sort of religious purpose for the Stone Age artists and their communities.[34]

Reviewing the aforementioned images, it is evident at once that they have no obvious counterpart in the present skies. How, then, are we to interpret them? As mere random doodlings? As the product of drug-induced hallucinations of shamans and cave men as per the speculations of modern scholars? For Miranda Green, author of *The Sun-Gods of Ancient Europe*, the artworks in question are a product of creative imagination: "The pictures do not describe reality."[35] The same author elsewhere adds the curious observation:

> Man did not simply look at the sun and copy what he saw to the best of his ability. He went further and interpreted and superimposed new images of the sun which were not based entirely on his visual perception.[36]

Such interpretations are entirely baseless and wrongheaded, in our opinion. The mere fact that analogous images are attested around the globe suffices to discredit Green's claim. From our vantage point there is no more reason to question the realism of these so-called solar petroglyphs than the prehistoric paintings of horses and bison at Altamira and Lascaux. No one would ever think of dismissing the latter artworks as a product of creative imagination, fantasy, or hallucination. Why, then, should the anomalous celestial petroglyphs be dismissed out of hand as nonrepresentational simply because they fail to conform with the present skies and preconceptions about the appearance of the ancient sun? For us it makes more sense to interpret both types of artworks as representational in nature—as rela-

---

[33] E. Anati, *op. cit.*, p. 47.
[34] *Ibid.*, p. 230. See also M. West, *Indo-European Poetry and Myth* (Oxford, 2007), p. 198.
[35] M. Green, *The Sun-Gods of Ancient Europe* (1991), p. 76.
[36] *Ibid.*, p. 33. Elsewhere, p. 20, the same author writes: "The artist, even of a veristic image, is unable to transcribe exactly what he sees."

tively faithful attempts to convey the actual experience and natural world of the prehistoric cave artists. Yet once you open your mind to this possibility, it becomes very difficult to put the genie back in the bottle, for the simple willingness to take the ancient artists' testimony at face value naturally prioritizes the question as to how to explain the peculiar forms displayed in the manifold celestial iconography.

In the chapters to follow we will be discussing a plethora of different "solar" images, all of which are anomalous by reference to the prevailing skies. It is our contention that each of these images has its own story to tell—one directly tied to the unfolding of Creation. In order to advance the scientific study of archeoastronomy, the way forward must commence by first journeying backwards in time, to the very origins of civilization in ancient Mesopotamia and Egypt. A survey of the earliest artworks and cosmogonic traditions of these two civilizations, in turn, will reveal one glaring anomaly after another, each pointing to a radically different solar system, hitherto overlooked by all scholars.

02 Solar Imagery in Ancient Mesopotamia

We may consider the ancients' perception of the stars in the sky a pure metaphor but for many of them it had apparently empirical reality, it was simply what they saw.[37]

Mesopotamian man lived in a concrete world that he experienced directly.[38]

A basic understanding of how the cosmos is organized appears to have survived unchanged throughout the entire span of the cuneiform civilization.[39]

Mesopotamia is rightly renowned as the birthplace of astronomical science. From time immemorial, Babylonian sky-watchers scanned the sky for signs of impending disaster and ominous portents, eventually collecting their observations and omens together in a series of texts known as the *Enuma Anu Enlil*, compiled during the second millennium BCE. It was these particular omen texts that Ptolemy consulted when attempting to place Greek astronomical methods on a rational scientific foundation (Babylonian astronomi-

---

[37] G. Selz, "The Tablet with 'Heavenly Writing', or How to Become a Star," in A. Panaino ed., *Non licet stare caelestibus* (Milano-Udine, 2014), p. 55.
[38] A. Oppenheim, "Man and Nature in Mesopotamian Civilization," in C. Gillispie ed., *Dictionary of Scientific Biography, Vol. 15* (New York, 1981), p. 634.
[39] P. Steinkeller, "Of Stars and Men," in W. Moran & A. Gianto eds., *Biblical and Oriental Essays in Memory of William L. Moran* (Rome, 2005), p. 18.

cal practices were early on diffused abroad and influenced the development of the physical and mathematical sciences in China, India, and Arabia). As John Steele pointed out in a recent survey of scientific methodology, astronomy itself is largely dependent on the use of past observations:

> Astronomy always has been and still is a science that relies on the use of past observations. Unlike most sciences, astronomy can never be truly experimental: astronomers can only observe the astronomical phenomena that present themselves…Perhaps uniquely in the sciences, astronomers, therefore, are forced to rely upon empirical data collected by their predecessors.[40]

Given the unrivaled antiquity and broad scope of their observations, the Mesopotamian astronomical records and traditions remain indispensable for the modern scholar attempting to piece together humankind's earliest conceptions associated with the Sun, stars, and planets.

Complementing the astronomical texts are various artworks such as the so-called cylinder seals, engravings cut into various types of stone that originally served as signs of property ownership. Deriving from earlier stamp seals, cylinder seals first appeared in the mid-fourth millennium BCE and are generally regarded as among the "high points of Mesopotamian craftmanship."[41] Early cylinder seals commonly depict images believed to represent familiar celestial bodies. Figure one, for example, is universally held to depict the sun.[42] Why Mesopotamian artists would select this particular image to serve this function remains unclear, as the current solar orb does not display a central dot. That said, the very same image is ubiquitous around the globe, occurring in both historic and prehistoric contexts.[43] In the earliest pictographic scripts in Egypt and China, moreover, this very sign served as an ideogram for "sun."

---

[40] J. Steele, *Ancient Astronomical Observations and the Study of the Moon's Motion* (1691-1757) (London, 2012), pp. 3-4.

[41] C. Fischer, "Twilight of the Sun-God," *Iraq* 64 (2002), p. 125. See also O. Topcuoglu, "Iconography of Protoliterate Seals," in C. Woods ed., *Visible Language* (Chicago, 2015), p. 29.

[42] Adapted from figure II:8 in L. Werr, *Studies in the Chronology and Regional Style of Old Babylonian Cylinder Seals* (Malibu, 1988). See also P. Amiet, *La glyptique mésopotamienne archaique* (Paris, 1961), figure 1641.

[43] E. Cochrane, "Suns and Planets in Neolithic Rock Art," in *Martian Metamorphoses* (Ames, 1997), pp. 194-214.

Figure one

Similar questions arise with regard to the image depicted in figure two, which shows a solar disc with an eight-pointed star inscribed in its center.[44] In Mesopotamian iconography, the eight-pointed star is known to represent the planet Venus.[45] How, then, are we to explain the fact that early cylinder seals seemingly depict the Venus-star as superimposed on the "sun"-disc and enclosed within a "lunar" crescent? Dominique Collon—a leading authority on Mesopotamian cylinder seals—offered the following opinion on this remarkable state of affairs:

> From Ur III times onwards, however, the crescent is also often combined with a disc inscribed with a star which is placed within it (star-disc and crescent…). This could either be explained as different phases of the moon or, more likely, is a shorthand for the principal celestial bodies, sun (and star?) and moon.[46]

---

[44] Adapted from figure III:5 in L. Werr, *Studies in the Chronology and Regional Style of Old Babylonian Cylinder Seals* (Malibu, 1988).

[45] F. Rochberg, "Heaven and Earth," in S. Noegel & J. Walker eds., *Prayer, Magic, and the Stars in the Ancient and Late Antique World* (University Park, 2003), pp. 174-176 writes: "The association of the heavenly bodies with certain deities seems to go back to the very beginnings of Mesopotamian civilization and persists as well to the end. Astral emblems, such as the lunar crescent (Akk. *uškaru*) for Sin, the eight-pointed star for Ištar, and the solar disc (Akk. *šamšatu*) for Šamaš, are a regular feature of Mesopotamian iconography throughout its history. These divine symbols can be traced on cylinder seals as early as the Early Dynastic period and as late as the Neo-Babylonian."

[46] D. Collon, "Mond," *RA* 8 (Berlin, 1993-1997), p. 357.

Figure two

At this point the open-minded researcher must confront certain fundamental questions of common sense and logic: How likely is it that the most sophisticated astronomers of the ancient world would have insisted upon depicting the three most prominent celestial bodies in astronomically impossible positions (the present sun cannot appear within a crescent and Venus does not appear superimposed on the Sun)? Was it sheer perversity alone that inspired the ancient artists to reproduce these particular images again and again across millennia?

Gennadij Kurtik is one of the few scholars to even address the jarring anomaly presented by these archaic sun-discs with the Venus-star depicted in the center. Yet his explanation of the hybrid celestial symbol amounts to little more than a wild guess:

> Since the period of the Akkade Dynasty (XXIV-XXII centuries BC), …the astral symbol of Inanna (an eight-pointed star) was frequently found inscribed in a circle. Why? The answer is probably in some poetic texts of the New-Sumerian period (XXII-XXI centuries BC); for example, in the hymn by Iddin-Dagan devoted to Inanna her shining in the night is compared with the light of day or the Sun…the attribute of being solar is transferred to Inanna, therefore the solar disk is becoming her symbol.[47]

Kurtik and Collon are seemingly unaware of the fact that artworks depicting "stars" set within the center of a "sun"-disc are to be found around the globe. Witness the African image depicted in figure three.[48] Here, too, the mere fact that

---

[47] "The Identification of Inanna with the Planet Venus," *Astronomical and Astrophysical Transactions* 17 (1999), p. 508.
[48] Adapted from figure 21 in G. Williams, *African Designs* (New York, 1971).

analogous images are commonplace on other continents as well suffices to rule out the manifestly ad hoc explanations offered by Collon and Kurtik, which would interpret the anomalous "solar" images as the product of imaginative musings unique to ancient Mesopotamia.

Figure three

As we have documented elsewhere, a survey of the Mesopotamian cylinder seals will reveal dozens of anomalous "suns," none of which bears any resemblance to the current solar orb.[49] In numerous representations of the ancient sun, for example, the eight-pointed star presents a wheel-like appearance (see figure four).[50]

Figure four

An equally common symbol on Mesopotamian cylinder seals finds the central star being depicted as a four-rayed or diamond-shaped form (figure five depicts a

---

[49] E. Cochrane, "Anomalies in Ancient Descriptions of the Sun-God," *Chronology & Catastrophism Review* (2016), pp. 3-12.
[50] Adapted from figure V:9 in L. Werr, *Studies in the Chronology and Regional Style of Old Babylonian Cylinder Seals* (Malibu, 1988).

so-called "sun"-image from the Akkadian period, thought to originate from around 2300 BCE).[51] Here, too, however, virtually identical images will be found around the globe, thereby supporting the conclusion that these particular images depict a conspicuous celestial object or constellation, albeit one unknown to modern astronomical science. Figure six features a similar image from an Egyptian bowl dating to the predynastic period (circa mid-4th millennium BCE).[52] Figure seven, finally, depicts a stellar form common throughout the American Southwest.[53]

Figure five

Figure six

---

[51] Adapted from figure IV:4 in L. Werr, *op. cit.* See also J. Black & A. Green, *Gods, Demons and Symbols of Ancient Mesopotamia* (London, 1992), p. 168: "The disc with four-pointed star and three radiating wavy lines between each of the points occurs from the Akkadian down to the New Babylonian Period. It almost invariably stands as a symbol of the sun god Šamaš (Utu)."
[52] Eva Wilson, *Ancient Egyptian Designs* (London, 1986), figure 8.
[53] Adapted from Barton Wright, *Pueblo Shields* (Flagstaff, 1976), p. 50. It will be noted that the same basic image denoted "sun" in the Nahuatl pictographic script. See M. León-Portilla & E. Shorris, *In the Language of Kings* (New York, 2001), p. 4.

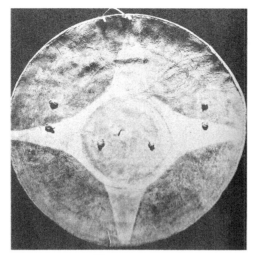
Figure seven

The similarity between these three images is evident at once, as is the fact that they bear no discernible resemblance to the appearance of the present solar orb. How, then, are we to account for their origin and former prevalence? The fact that analogous artworks will be found around the globe and share a number of distinct structures in common suggests that we have to do here with relatively faithful depictions of a former "sun" or constellation and *not* with any arcane "shorthand" or metaphorical process peculiar to the Mesopotamian mindset. Yet historians of ancient art never consider the possibility that these iconic symbols might faithfully represent the appearance of a lost "sun."

03 Solar Imagery in Ancient Egypt

Egyptian interest in nature and the resulting style of cognition and theorizing was religious in its orientation; put more precisely, it was a solar theology. The actual locus of Egyptian 'natural history' and cosmography was the cult of the sun.[54]

Horus was the power of kingship. To the Egyptians this was as much a force of nature as those embodied in the other gods. It was manifest in two phenomena: the sun, the most powerful force in nature; and the pharaoh, the most powerful force in human society).[55]

Whoever wishes to understand ancient Egyptian culture, and especially its religion and way of thinking, must learn the language of images.[56]

The great gods confront us already at the dawn of history. The Egyptian Horus is a case in point, his cult being prominent already in predynastic times. Rulers from the Naqada I period (circa 4000-3500 BCE), for example, worshipped the falcon-god prior to the unification of Egypt.[57]

The pharaoh himself was considered to be the earthly embodiment of the god, a belief-system reflected in the so-called Horus names borne by Egyptian rulers

---

[54] J. Assmann, *The Search for God in Ancient Egypt* (Ithaca, 2001), p. 55.
[55] J. Allen, *Middle Egyptian* (Cambridge, 2010), p. 148.
[56] E. Hornung, "Ancient Egyptian Religious Iconography," in J. Sasson ed., *Civilizations of the Ancient Near East, Vol. 3/4* (Farmington Hills, 1995), p. 1729.
[57] J. Assmann, *The Mind of Egypt* (Cambridge, 1996), p. 33.

from the first dynasty on.[58] Yet if it is commonly acknowledged that Horus represents the quintessential Egyptian god, there is little agreement as to his origins or fundamental nature.[59] That he was a celestial power all authorities concur. The question, however, is which celestial body best explains Horus's manifold functions in Egyptian religion?

From the earliest funerary traditions in the Pyramid Texts in the third millennium BCE to the inscriptions adorning the walls of the Horus-temple at Edfu constructed during the Ptolemaic period, Horus is described as a nascent "sun" who appeared at the time of Creation—*zp tpj*. A passage from the *Book of the Dead* is representative in this regard:

> When thou appearest in the horizon of heaven, hymns to thee are in the mouths of everyone, thou being beautiful and youthful in the sun-disk within the arms of thy mother Hathor. How thou shinest in every place, thy heart rejoicing forever…How thou shinest in the horizon of heaven. Thou hast strewn the Two Lands with turquoise.[60]

Evident here is the idea that the epiphany of the Horus-star was distinguished by a spectacular "greening" (*mkf3t*) of the cosmos—this in striking contradiction to present empirical reality. The same basic story is reiterated in text after text. During the momentous natural events remembered as Creation, the Horus-star radiated a beautiful greenish color: "Der am Anbeginn erzeugte, der alles Seiende enstehen liess durch seinen Samen, schöne Sonne aus Türkis (*jtn nfr n mfk3t*), der Himmel und Erde erfüllt mit seinem Glanz (*m j3mw.f*), starker Horus."[61]

The primal sun is explicitly described here as a "sun of turquoise." Indeed, as Jan Zandee pointed out in his commentary on this hymn, turquoise was deemed to be the very substance of which the sun was composed.[62]

The cult of the sun reached its greatest heights during the New Kingdom (1500-1200 BCE). "Hail to you who rises in Turquoise" (*jnf ḥr.k wbnw m mfkt*) reads one solar hymn.[63] Such imagery is so commonplace in the solar hymns that

---

[58] H. Frankfort, *Kingship and the Gods* (Chicago, 1948), p. 39. See also T. Wilkinson, *Early Dynastic Egypt* (London, 1999), p. 184: "The most fundamental aspect of kingship was the ruler's embodiment of Horus, the supreme celestial deity."
[59] H. Frankfort, *op. cit.*, p. 37: "Pharaoh is Horus, and of this god little enough is known."
[60] H. Stewart, "Traditional Egyptian Sun Hymns of the New Kingdom," *Bull. Inst. Arch.* 6 (1967), p. 52.
[61] J. Zandee, *Der Amunshymnus des Papyrus Leiden I 344 verso, Vol. 1* (Leiden, 1992), p. 363.
[62] *Ibid.*, p. 362: "Türkis ist die Substanz, aus der die Sonne selbst zusammengesetzt ist."
[63] TT 53 as translated in J. Assmann, *Egyptian Solar Religion in the New Kingdom* (London,

Egyptologists readily concede the point even though it stands in stark contradiction to empirical reality. Joris Borghouts emphasized the point: "In certain hymns the sun is said to strew the sky with turquoise."[64] Jan Zandee, who devoted a fair amount of ink to the subject, concluded: "In vielen Belegstellen hängt 'Türkis' besonders mit der aufgehenden Sonne zusammen."[65]

How are we to understand this greening effect associated with the sun-god's epiphany?[66] Egyptologists assure us that this language is simply a metaphorical description of the familiar sunrise. It is our position, in contrast, that the formulaic language in question has nothing whatsoever to do metaphor or poetic license. Rather, the ancient Egyptian accounts of a turquoise sun offer a remarkably precise and coherent description of *extraordinary* natural events attending the prototypical sunrise, a nova-like explosion of turquoise-colored radiation the likes of which were never experienced before or since. We know this to be the case because the Egyptian testimony has striking parallels in Mesoamerica and other cultures (see below). If this claim can be substantiated, it is fair to say that the archaic traditions describing a turquoise "sun" represent the all-important smoking gun that researchers and detectives are always seeking but rarely find—in this case, compelling circumstantial evidence that the primal "sun" of cosmogonic myth must be distinguished from the present Sun.

Horus on the Lotus

To add to the mystery, Egyptian mythological traditions report that Horus appeared atop a lotus flower at the time of Creation. Thus it is that a passage from the *Coffin Texts* describes the god's inaugural appearance during the tumultuous natural events attending the primeval separation of heaven and earth, a pivotal juncture in cosmogonic myths around the globe: "The earth opens its mouth, Geb throws open his jaws on my account, and I will raise up Horus pre-eminent in Pe on to his lotus-flowers…"[67]

The nascent sun's appearance atop the lotus is celebrated again and again in Egyptian texts, albeit always in allusive terms. A hymn from the post-Ama-

---

1995), p. 15.
[64] J. Borghouts, *Book of the Dead [39]: From Shouting To Structure* (Wiesbaden, 2007), p. 52, citing Budge *Book of the Dead* 11.10.
[65] J. Zandee, *op. cit.*, p. 364.
[66] E. Brunner, "Die Grüne Sonne," in M. Görg & E. Pusch eds., *Festschrift Elmar Edel* (Wiesbaden, 1979), pp. 54-59 would explain the imagery as reflecting "einer physiologischen Besonderheit des menschlichen Auges zu erklären versuchte, namlich mit dem sog. Nachbild in der jeweiligen Komplementärfarbe."
[67] *CT* VI:95 as translated in R. Faulkner, *The Ancient Egyptian Coffin Texts* (Oxford, 1973), p. 184. Hereafter *CT*.

rna period invokes the Horus-child as follows: "Greetings, boy from the womb, Child, who ascends in the lotus flower, Beautiful youth, who comes from the land of light, And illuminates the [Two Lands] with his light."[68] The fact that the very same idea is alluded to in the following text from Edfu inscribed nearly two millennia later attests to the stubborn conservativeness of Egyptian religion: "Conceived in the ocean, born in the flood, a lotus came forth in which was a beautiful child who illumines this land with his rays."[69]

Plutarch drew attention to the Egyptian sun-god's intimate connection to the lotus of the Beginning several millennia ago. Anticipating the *communis opinio* of modern Egyptologists, he sought to explain it as the product of allegorical reasoning and metaphor: "Nor, again, do they believe that the sun rises as a newborn babe from the lotus, but they portray the rising of the sun in this manner to indicate allegorically the enkindling of the sun from the waters."[70]

The Horus-child atop a lotus flower represents a popular theme in Egyptian religious iconography as well (see figure one).[71] According to Erik Hornung, the dean of Egyptologists: "The sun-god on a lotus-blossom…was an image of the first emergence of shapes at the creation."[72] James Allen offered a very similar assessment of the archaic traditions attached to the lotus: "One of the images of the first place in which the sun rose."[73] Yet why an infant child sitting atop a lotus should be an archetypal symbol of Creation is rarely addressed by Egyptologists and has never received a satisfactory answer. At no point is the elephant in the room addressed—namely: Where in all of heaven is a lotus-like flower to be found in the immediate vicinity of the Sun?

---

[68] J. Assmann, *Egyptian Solar Religion in the New Kingdom* (London, 1995), p. 45, citing CP. Berlin 3002.

[69] Edfu R. I, 289 as translated in P. Boylan, *Thoth: The Hermes of Egypt* (Oxford, 1922), p. 117.

[70] *On Isis and Osiris* 355c.

[71] W. Waitkus: "Die Geburt des Harsomtus aus der Blüte," *SAK* 30 (2002), p. 377: "Der Sonnengott des Morgens aus einer Lotusblüte geboren wird."

[72] E. Hornung, "Ancient Egyptian Religious Iconography," in J. Sasson ed., *Civilizations of the Ancient Near East, Vol. 3/4* (Farmington Hills, 1995), p. 1717.

[73] J. Allen, *Genesis in Egypt* (New Haven, 1988), p. 69. He offered a similar assessment in "The Celestial Realm," in D. Silverman ed., *Ancient Egypt* (London, 1997), p. 120: "It was from this flower that the sun could blossom into the world."

Figure one

Yet if we take our cue from ancient artworks purportedly depicting the Sun an obvious answer presents itself: The lotus likely has reference to the petaloid forms associated with the "sun" in iconic images around the globe, many of which occur in prehistoric contexts. Consider the Syrian cylinder seal depicted in figure two, which shows what appears to be a four-petaled "sun."[74]

Figure two

This four-petaled sun, in turn, finds an iconic parallel in the Egyptian *wn(b)*-flower depicted in figure three. According to the Coffin Texts, the *wnb*-flower appeared together with Re at the time of Creation: "I am the *wnb*-flower which issued from Rēʿ, the ʿʒʿ-flower which issued from the horizon, I am the œåb-flower which issued from the garden."[75] It is commonly acknowledged, moreover, that the *wnb*-flower is to be identified with the lotus of the Beginning: "The *wnb*

---

[74] Adapted from figure 80 from B. Teissier, *Egyptian Iconography on Syrian-Palestinian Cylinder Seals of the Middle Bronze Age* (Fribourg, 1996), p. 67.
[75] VI:198.

flower is none other than the primordial lotus from which the sun emerges at dawn in the east."⁷⁶

Flower
Phonetic value *wn*.

Figure three

Our hypothesis receives a significant measure of corroboration from the fact that analogous conceptions are evident in pre-Columbian Mesoamerica. The most common name for "sun" in the Mayan language was *kin*, the hieroglyph for which depicts a four-petaled flower (see figure four).⁷⁷ Such imagery is perfectly familiar to all Mayanists: "In Maya iconography and epigraphy it [the sun] was conventionally represented as a four-petaled flower, sometimes infixed with the T533 NIK or 'flower' glyph."⁷⁸

Although Maya mythology is poorly represented in comparison to that from the Old World, it is significant to find that it preserves a distinct memory of the primal sun as formerly residing within a flower. According to *The Book of Chilam Balam of Chumayel*, the sun-god (*Ah Kin Xocbiltun*) was described as follows: "Four-fold [or four-branched] was the plate of the flower, and Ah Kin Xocbiltun [the sun god] was set in the center."⁷⁹ Here the Mayan sun-god is explicitly described as dwelling at the center of a four-petaled flower.⁸⁰

---

⁷⁶ T. Schneider, "Das Schriftzeichen 'Rosette' und die Göttin Seschet," *Studien zur Altägyptischen Kultur* 24 (1997), p. 249: "La fleur *wnb* n'est autre quile lotus primordial dont emerge le soleil de l'aube, a l'Orient." Translation courtesy of Birgit Liesching.
⁷⁷ M. León-Portilla, *Time and Reality in the Thought of the Maya* (Norman, 1998), p. 18: "The most common [glyph signifying kin] is the one simulating a flower with four petals."
⁷⁸ M. Looper & J. Kappelman, "The Cosmic Umbilicus in Mesoamerica: A Floral Metaphor for the Source of Life" *Journal of Latin American Lore* 21 (2000), p. 14.
⁷⁹ R. Roys, *The Book of Chilam Balam of Chumayel* (Washington D.C., 1933), p. 105.
⁸⁰ See the discussion in K. Taube, "At Dawn's Edge: Tulúm, Santa Rita, and Floral Symbolism…," in G. Vail & C. Hernández eds., *Astronomers, Scribes, and Priests* (Washington, D.C., 2010), p. 162.

Figure four

Considered in isolation, the Mayan traditions with respect to a four-petaled "sun" can only appear as incongruous and alien in nature, divorced as they are from our own experience, where flower-like forms are nowhere to be found in the immediate vicinity of the Sun. Yet when viewed in light of the cylinder seals from the ancient Near East depicting a four-petaled "sun" they suddenly take on profound significance. Can anyone doubt that, were such a constellation to present itself in the sky, traditions of a four-petaled "sun" would be certain to follow? Yet so far as I'm aware, not a single Mayanist, Egyptologist, or Sumerologist has ever entertained the possibility that the artworks and hieroglyphs in question might faithfully reflect the Sun's visual appearance at some point during the distant past as suggested by traditions such as those from the *Pyramid Texts* and *The Book of Chilam Balam of Chumayel*.

04 The Drilling of Fire and the Origin of the Sun

The making of fire is tantamount to creation and birth.[81]

Fire seems to have been the oldest, or one of the oldest, gods of center place in Mesoamerican cosmology.[82]

Fire was widely considered to be of divine or celestial origin.[83]

Festivals of new fire are among the most common folk customs all over the world; striking parallels have been adduced from the Red Indians as well as from East Indian Burma; and one could refer to the Incas as well as to the Japanese.[84]

Those readers who have viewed Mel Gibson's thrilling epic *Apocalypto* will have some idea of the abject horror which likely gripped the captive warrior who, upon being outfitted with a crown of feathers and paraded forth before a throng of frenzied villagers calling for his sacrifice, was led up to the Hill of the Star on a pitch-black night in 1507 and, after being forcibly splayed out upon a blood-stained rock, had his heart ripped out to appease the Aztec god of fire (Xiuhtecuhtli). Immediately after extracting the valiant warrior's still-beating heart, the priest presiding over the gruesome ceremony solemnly drilled a fire in the vic-

---

[81] K. Taube, "The Turquoise Hearth," in D. Carrasco ed., *Mesoamerica's Classic Heritage* (Boulder, 2000), p. 292.
[82] D. Carrasco, *City of Sacrifice: The Aztec Empire and the Role of Violence in Civilization* (Boston, 1999), p. 103.
[83] J. Gonda, *Some Observations on the Relations Between "Gods" and "Powers" in the Veda* ('s-Gravenhage, 1957), p. 38.
[84] W. Burkert, "Jason, Hypsipyle, and New Fire at Lemnos," *Classical Quarterly* 20 (1970), p. 4.

tim's now-empty chest cavity, his every movement being monitored by a crowd of anxious onlookers, all of whom were convinced that the world would come to a sudden end should the new fire fail to be generated. According to the eye-witness account of the Franciscan Friar Bernardino de Sahagún, arguably history's first ethnographer of Amerindian culture:

> At nightfall, from here in Mexico, they departed. All the fire priests were arranged in order, arrayed in and wearing the garb of the gods…And the one who was the fire priest of Copulco, who drew new fire, then began there. With his hands he proceeded to bore continuously his fire drill…And when it came to pass that night fell, all were frightened and filled with dread. Thus it was said: it was claimed that if fire could not be drawn, then [the sun] would be destroyed forever; all would be ended; there would evermore be night. Nevermore would the sun come forth. Night would prevail forever, and the demons of darkness would descend, to eat men…[85]

In order to make sense of such primal and deep-rooted fears it is essential to recognize the fundamental affinity between the new fire and the "sun" which it represented.[86] For the one belief is impossible to understand apart from the other. The decisive key to deciphering the archaic belief-system in question is the previously quoted statement recorded by Sahagún: "It was claimed that if fire could not be drawn, then [the sun] would be destroyed forever; all would be ended; there would evermore be night."

By all accounts, the New Fire ceremony was the most important religious ritual in Mesoamerica.[87] Commonly believed to reenact the central events of the Aztec Creation myth—specifically, the creation of the sun through the self-immolation of Nanahuatl[88]—it was typically held after a period of 52 years had elapsed:

> The Aztecs conceived of the end of the fifty-two-year cycle as a commemoration of the world's creation and would celebrate it by

---

[85] *The Florentine Codex: Book 7* (Santa Fe, 1953), p. 27.
[86] M. Izeki, *Conceptions of 'xihuitl': History, Environment and Cultural Dynamics in Postclassic Mexica Cognition* (Oxford, 2008), p. 34 writes: "The sun was regarded as the celestial fire by the Mexica." See also R. Hall, *An Archaeology of the Soul* (Urbana, 1997), p. 194: "The hearth fire was regarded as an earthly representation of the sun in much Indian belief."
[87] D. Carrasco, *City of Sacrifice* (Boston, 1999), pp. 90-105.
[88] K. Taube, "The Turquoise Hearth," in D. Carrasco ed., *Mesoamerica's Classic Heritage* (Boulder, 2000), p. 315: "The new fire rites reenacted the birth of the sun at Teotihuacan."

destroying their household items and extinguishing their fires. The rekindling of the new fire symbolized the creation of the sun and the beginning of time.[89]

How is it possible to explain the origin of such bizarre belief-systems and religious rituals? In what sense could the drilling of fire have anything to do with the origin of the Sun, much less with Creation or the end of the world? In order to address such questions, it is instructive to examine the cult of Xiuhtecuhtli in greater detail.

Xiuhtecuhtli

The fire-god Xiuhtecuhtli is generally recognized as one of the most important gods in the Aztec pantheon. A prayer recorded by Sahagún in the 16th century reports that the god dwelled within the center of the hearth:

> Ueueteotl [the old god, i.e., Xiuhtecuhtli], who is set in the center of the hearth, in the turquoise enclosure.[90]

The hearth is here explicitly identified with a turquoise enclosure (*xiuhtetzaqualco*). A related passage from elsewhere in the same book of Aztec prayers reveals additional information of interest:

> The father of the gods [Xiuhtecuhtli], who resideth in the navel of the earth, who is set in the turquoise enclosure, [enclosed] with the waters of the lovely cotinga, enclosed with clouds—Ueueteotl, he of Ayamictlan, Xiuhtecuhtli.[91]

It will be noted that the Aztec fire-god is represented as residing in the navel of the earth (*tlalxicco*)—hence the god's epithet *Tlalxictentica*, "He Who Is in the Earth's Navel."[92] The navel in question, moreover, is identified as a "circle of turquoise."

In addition to his role as Father of the Gods, the Aztec fire-god was also celebrated as the "archetype of all rulers." Henry Nicholson emphasized this aspect of the god's cult:

---

[89] A. Headrick, "Gardening with the Great Goddess at Teotihuacan," in A. Stone ed., *Heart of Creation* (Tuscaloosa, 2002), pp. 88-89.
[90] *Florentine Codex: Book 6* (Santa Fe, 1969), p. 41.
[91] *Ibid.*, p. 89.
[92] B. Sahagún, *Book 4—The Soothsayers* and *Book 5—The Omens* (Santa Fe, 1979), p. 87.

Conceived as the eldest of the gods (*Huehueteotl*), *Xiuhtecuhtli* also served as the archetype of all rulers, who were preferably consecrated and confirmed in their public offices on his special calendric sign, 4 *Acatl* (Sahagún, 1950-69, bk. 4, p. 88; 1956, I:352).[93]

As is evident from Sahagún's testimony, the ruler's fundamental affinity with the ancient fire-god forms a cornerstone of Aztec religion.[94] Indeed, the Aztec king was believed to actually incarnate the fire-god: "The new ruler was thought to serve as substitute of the deity and called 'the precious turquoise.'"[95] In perfect keeping with this symbolism, Moteuczoma (also spelled Moctezuma)—the Aztec ruler at the time of the Conquest—had himself depicted as Xiuhtecuhtli.[96]

The vagaries of Aztec royal ideology prompt questions at every turn. How is it possible to understand Xiuhtecuhtli's status as the archetype of rulers by reference to fire's role in the natural world? Why would fire be associated with the origin of kingship and archaic conceptions of sovereignty? For possible answers to these questions, we pivot to briefly consider the cult of the fire-god in ancient India.

The Vedic Fire-god Agni

The first verse of the *Rig Veda*, the oldest collection of religious texts in India, attests to the veneration formerly accorded fire: "Agni do I invoke—the one placed to the fore."[97] According to tradition the sacred fire must be generated in the ancient manner, which is to say by means of a fire-drill employing two sticks of wood, known as *arani*. In India, as in the New World, the fire-churning (*agni manthana*) was likened to sexual intercourse, with the two fire-sticks being conceptualized as male and female.[98] This archaic symbolism is evident in the following Vedic hymn: "Bring here the clanlord's lady Let us churn Agni in the ancient

---

[93] H. B. Nicholson, "Religion in Pre-Hispanic Central Mexico," in R. Wauchope ed., *Handbook of Middle American Indians, Vol. 10* (Austin, 1971), p. 413.

[94] J. Olko, *Turquoise Diadems and Staffs of Office* (Warsaw, 2005), p. 128: "There is no doubt that the fire god Xiuhtecuhtli was a special patron of Aztec rulers."

[95] M. Izeki, *Conceptions of 'xihuitl': History, Environment and Cultural Dynamics in Postclassic Mexica Cognition* (Oxford, 2008), p. 36, citing Sahagún, Book 6, 17.

[96] As in the *Codex Borbonicus*, for example. See the discussion in P. Hajovsky, *On the Lips of Others: Moteuczoma's Fame in Aztec Monuments and Rituals* (Austin, 2015), p. 88.

[97] *RV* 1.1.1. Note: All translations from the *Rig Veda* are from S. Jamison & J. Brereton, *The Rigveda* (Austin, 2014) unless otherwise indicated.

[98] S. Jamison & J. Brereton, *op. cit.,* p. 503: "This process of churning out the fire was regularly identified in the Rgvedic hymns with sexual intercourse, and this repeated image presents the upper fire-churning stick as the father…and the lower fire-churning stick as the mother of fire."

way."⁹⁹ The word translated as "lady" here, *vispátni*, denotes the flat wooden board upon which the fire was drilled.

The sacred fire itself was identified with Agni and conceptualized as the prototypical masculine power. It was Agni whom women beseeched to implant an embryo (*garbha*) within their womb.[100]

The hearth-like *vedi*, in turn, was conceptualized as the archetypal female power. According to Mircea Eliade, the union of male and female powers inherent in the drilling of fire was a dominant theme in Vedic symbolism:

> In Vedic India the sacrificial altar (*vedi*) was looked upon as female and the fire (*agni*) as male and 'their union brought forth offspring.' We are in the presence of a very complex symbolism which cannot be reduced to a single plane of reference. For, on the one hand, the *vedi* was compared to the navel (*nabhi*) of the Earth, the symbol *par excellence* of the 'centre'. But the *nabhi* was also established as being the womb of the Goddess (cf. Shatapatha-Brahmana, I, 9, 2, 21).[101]

Evident here is the idea that the *vedi* (altar, hearth) symbolized the navel of the Earth. The Vedic Agni, like the Aztec fire-god Xiuhtecuhtli, resided within this navel, the latter conceptualized as the center of the cosmos.[102] A hymn from the *Rig Veda* alludes to this symbolism:

> As he was being born in the highest distant heaven, Agni became manifest to Matarisvan. By the resolve and might of him as he was kindled, his blaze illuminated heaven and earth...The all-possessor whom the Bhrgus have aroused upon the navel of the earth.[103]

In ancient India, as in pre-Columbian Mexico, the ritual landscape was purposefully organized in order to reproduce or model the cosmos.[104] The local hearth

---

[99] *RV* 3:29:1.
[100] *RV* 10:184:2-3. See also the discussion in A. Parpola, *The Roots of Hinduism* (Oxford, 2015), p. 284.
[101] M. Eliade, *The Forge and the Crucible* (New York, 1962), p. 39.
[102] A. Coomaraswamy, "An Indian Temple," in R. Lipsey ed., *Coomaraswamy: Selected Papers* (Princeton, 1977), p. 7: "The sacred hearth, is always theoretically at the center of navel of the earth."
[103] *Rig Veda* 1:143:2-4.
[104] S. Jamison & J. Brereton, *The Rigveda* (Oxford, 2014), p. 401: "[The net effect of identifying Agni with the fire] is to concentrate all of the cosmos into this small space, the sacrificial

and central fire, according to this archaic ideology, mirrored and symbolized the celestial hearth and its stellar fire—namely, the primal sun, as evidenced by the following Vedic hymn: "The sun became visible when the fire was born."[105] As Eliade pointed out with great insight and erudition, the ritual drilling of fire was commonly believed to reenact Creation *in illo tempore*. And insofar as fire was to be found at the center of the world, it follows that Creation proceeded from the *nabhi* (=*vedi*) outwards:

> It is from a 'centre' (navel) that the creation of the world starts and, in solemnly imitating this primary model, every 'construction', every 'fabrication', must operate from a starting 'centre'. The ritual production of fire reproduces the birth of the world.[106]

In addition to his status as the Prime Mover in Creation, the Vedic fire-god was intimately associated with ancient conceptions of kingship and sovereignty.[107] Thus it is that the *Rig Veda* invokes him as follows:

> You, o Agni, the sovereign king over the peoples…Shine as a herdsman of truth in your house…You rule in every direction.[108]

Such conceptions prompted Jan Gonda to offer the following summary of Agni's cult in ancient India, one that we would endorse in its entirety:

> In India and elsewhere this idea of fire was expanded to gigantic proportions, the element becoming a paramount deity, a universally vivifying power, a fundamental principle, supporting mankind and the universe; seated on the back of the earth, Agni fills the air with his shine, props the sky with his light, upholding the quarters by his lustre (cf. *Vaj.S.* 17, 72). His is universal sovereignty (*samrajya- Sat.Br.* 9,3,4,17), through whom everything exists (*Sat.Br* 8,1,1,4)….[109]

---

ground, and this single entity, the sacrificial fire—indeed making the sacrificial microcosm the equivalent of the macrocosm."

[105] *RV* 4:3:11.

[106] M. Eliade, *The Forge and the Crucible* (Chicago, 1978), pp. 39-40.

[107] S. Jamison & J. Brereton, *op. cit.*, p. 175 speak simply of "the identification of Agni as king."

[108] *RV* 3:10:1-7.

[109] J. Gonda, *Some Observations on the Relations Between "Gods" and "Powers"* ('S-Gravenhage, 1957), p. 44.

To summarize: In Vedic India, as in indigenous Mexico, the fire-god was intimately associated with ancient conceptions of Creation and sovereignty and, as such, was localized at the navel of the earth. Insofar as not one of these symbolic associations finds a rational explanation by reference to fire's role in the familiar natural world, the question arises as to how to understand the origin of these particular belief-systems?

The answer proposed here is that Xiuhtecuhtli represents the Celestial Fire—i.e., the primal Sun of Creation—the natural-historical prototype for kings around the globe (see appendix one).[110] Recall again the Sumerian and Egyptian references to the Time of Beginning "when the Sun-god was king."[111] That Xiuhtecuhtli represented the primal Sun is not only evident in the symbolism attached to the New Fire ritual, wherein the new fire represents the sun, it is encoded in his name, which translates as "Turquoise Lord," a patent reference to the greening of the cosmos attendant upon the "birth" of the prototypical sun.[112] Thus it is that the very first line of Sahagún's seventh book invokes the Sun as *xippilli*, "Turquoise Prince": "The sun: the soaring eagle, the turquoise prince, the god."[113]

Armed with this hypothesis, we turn to consider other equally incongruous elements of the Fire-god's cult.

Lord of the Four Corners

A recurring theme in the Aztec traditions identifying the navel as the center of the world is the idea that it was the source of all life and vital energy (*elan vital*).[114] Such conceptions feature prominently in Xiuhtecuhtli's cult. Consider the cosmogram depicted in *Codex Fejervary-Mayer*, wherein Xiuhtecuhtli is pictured at the center of the cosmos (see figure one). With regards to the symbolism depicted in this artwork, David Carrasco offered the following observation:

> At the heart of the universe stands the body of Xiuhtecuhtli, the Fire God. From his body flow four streams of blood into the four quarters of the universe, giving them energy and life.[115]

---

[110] S. Jamison & J. Brereton, *The Rigveda* (Oxford, 2014), p. 41 observe: "As a god he [Agni] is often identified with the sun, the celestial form of fire."
[111] Line 14 from "Enmerkar and Ensuhgirana," as translated in H. Vanstiphout, *Epics of Sumerian Kings* (Leiden, 2004), p. 29.
[112] See M. Aguilar-Moreno, *Handbook to Life in the Aztec World* (Oxford, 2006), p. 208: "The Sun was considered to be the Shining One, the Precious Child, the Jade, and Xiuhpiltontli (Turquoise Child)."
[113] *The Florentine Codex: Book 7* (Santa Fe, 1953), p. 1. See also J. Bierhorst, *A Nahuatl-English Dictionary and Concordance to the Cantares Mexicanos* (Stanford, 1985), p. 390.
[114] J. Maffie, *Aztec Philosophy* (Boulder, 2014), p. 107.
[115] D. Carrasco & S. Sessions, *Daily Life of the Aztecs* (London, 1998), p. 53.

Figure one

The epithet *Nauhyotecuhtli*, "Lord of the Four," evidently encodes Xiuhtecuhtli's intimate relation with the four corners.[116] Eduard Seler doubtless had it correct when he identified Xiuhtecuhtli as the "Lord of the four quarters; he is not only *Tlalxictentica*, but also *Nauhyo teuctli*."[117] So, too, Miguel León-Portilla, pointing to Sahagún's statement that Xiuhtecuhtli resided at the center of the earth, observed: "From his position on the navel of the earth, the text implies, [Xiuhtecuhtli] sustains the world from its very center, at the mid-point of the four cardinal directions."[118]

Xiuhtecuhtli's connection with the four directions is also suggested by his association with the so-called quincross (Maya Kan cross), one of the most com-

---

[116] L. Lujan, *The Offerings of the Templo Mayor of Tenochtitlan* (Albuquerque, 2005), p. 147: "The Nahua invoked Xiuhtecuhtli by saying, '*Tlalxitenticae, Nauhiotecatlé*,' that is, 'he who fills the navel of the earth, he of the group of four'." See also B. Brundage, *op. cit.*, p. 226.
[117] E. Seler, *Codex Fejérváry-Mayer* (Berlin, 1901/2), p. 5.
[118] M. León-Portilla & E. Shorris eds., *In the Language of Kings: An Anthology of Mesoamerican Literature* (New York, 2001), p. 32.

mon symbols in Mesoamerican culture (see figure two, wherein the god's headgear displays a number of quincrosses).[119] Typically painted a luminous turquoise color, the cross in question is widely believed to represent "the four world directions and corners."[120]

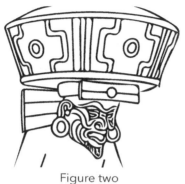

Figure two

A closely related symbol is the quincunx (see figure three). According to Karl Taube, the quincunx was a symbol of fire and signified the center of the world.[121] Yet the quincunx also symbolized turquoise: "For the Aztecs, the quincunx represented turquoise, *xiuitl*, an important morpheme in the name Xiuhtecuhtli."[122]

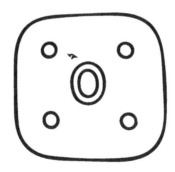

Figure three

---

[119] Adapted from K. Taube, *The Major Gods of Ancient Yucatan* (Washington D.C., 1992), p. 125. D. Carrasco, *City of Sacrifice* (Boston, 1999), p. 103, similarly, noted that "we can see this god as lord or center of the sacred number (groups) four (the cosmic directions)."
[120] K. Taube, "Structure 10L-16 and Its Early Classic Antecedents," in E. Bell et al eds., *Understanding Early Classic Copan* (Philadelphia, 2004), p. 266.
[121] K. Taube, "The Turquoise Hearth," in D. Carrasco ed., *Mesoamerica's Classic Heritage* (Boulder, 2000), pp. 312-316.
[122] K. Taube, *The Major Gods of Ancient Yucatan* (Washington D.C., 1992), p. 125. See also P. Hajovsky, *On the Lips of Others: Moteuczoma's Fame in Aztec Monuments and Rituals* (Austin, 2015), p. 94.

A quincunx-like image—the so-called Lamat sign, or T-510, is intimately associated with the Morning Star in various Maya codices (see figure four).[123] When coupled together with the T-109 prefix *chac*, the phrase in question is known to denote "Great or Red" Star—i.e., the Morning Star.[124]

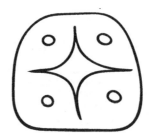

Figure four

This image, in turn, bears a close resemblance to the image depicted in figure five, believed to represent the Morning Star as the "Great Star" in the American Southwest.[125] In addition to presenting a cross-like form, the "Great Star" image features a dark "sun" at the center of a four-fold star whose "rays" extend outwards towards the four cardinal directions.[126]

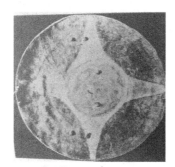

Figure five

---

[123] Adapted from M. Macri & M. Looper, *The New Catalog of Maya Hieroglyphs* (Norman, 2003), p. 229.

[124] D. Tedlock, *2000 Years of Mayan Literature* (Berkeley, 2010), p. 203. See also B. Stross, "Venus and Sirius: Some Unexpected Similarities," *Kronos* XII:1 (1987), pp. 26-27.

[125] J. Carlson, "Transformations of the Mesoamerican Venus Turtle Carapace War Shield," in V. del Chamberlain, J. Carlson, & M. Young eds., *Songs From the Sky* (Washington, D.C., 2005), p. 115. See also E. Cochrane, *On Fossil Gods and Forgotten Worlds* (Ames, 2010), pp. 124-138.

[126] For an early example of the star in question see the La Venta colossal head 1 dating to the Olmec period. See here figure 4.12 in F. Reilly, "The Landscape of Creation," in A. Stone ed., *Heart of Creation* (Tuscaloosa, 2002), p. 58. For a close parallel from the ancient Near East, see plate 3 in Grace White, "The Religious Iconography of Cappadocian Glyptic in the Assyrian Colony Period..." Dissertation for the University of Chicago (1993), p. 432.

With regards to the cruciform appearance of the Lamat sign and quincross, it is significant to note that Amerindian tribes across the North American continent represented fire as a cruciform structure. Such was the case with the Osage, for example.[127] Other Amerindian tribes preserved comparable belief-systems. Among the Cheyenne, for example, the sacred fireplace was purposefully designed as a cruciform structure:

> A fireplace is sometimes dug somewhat in the form of an equal-armed cross, the arms pointing in the four cardinal directions (*nivstanivoo*). This term is constantly used for the four directions.[128]

Analogous traditions are commonplace throughout the American Southwest. The Navaho, like the Aztecs, were keen observers of the sky and stellar imagery is ubiquitous in their sacred iconography and artworks.[129] For the Navaho the stellar cross represented fire: "The cross also represents other things including fire and the four directions."[130] Now here is an idea not readily explained by reference to the present sky: Why would fire, of all things, be compared to a cruciform structure or related to the four cardinal directions?

According to Taube, Xiuhtecuhtli's placement at the nexus of a cruciform structure in Aztec cosmology is a product of metaphor—namely, the location of the hearth in the terrestrial dwelling: "This middle place of fire clearly relates to the cosmological metaphor of the four-sided house, here in terms of the central hearth."[131] The possibility that the Aztec cosmogram accurately reflects the appearance of the prehistoric sky is never considered. Yet it is our opinion that this explanation is the only one consistent with the evidence.

If Xiuhtecuhtli's association with the four quarters is to be traced to a specific celestial prototype, it stands to reason that analogous traditions should be associated with fire gods in other cultures far removed from Mesoamerica.[132] Such is the case with regards to the Vedic Agni, who was expressly associated with the four quarters of the cosmos in the *Taittiriya Samhita*: "Seated on the back of the

---

[127] J. Dorsey, "Indian Names for the Winds and Quarters," *The Archaeologist* 2 (1894), p. 247.
[128] G. Grinnell, *The Cheyenne Indians* (Bloomington, 2008), pp. 67-68.
[129] See the frontispiece in B. Haile, *Starlore Among the Navaho* (Santa Fe, 1947).
[130] V. del Chamberlain & P. Schaafsma, "Origin and Meaning of Navajo Star Ceilings," in V. del Chamberlain, J. Carlson, & J. Young eds., *Songs From the Sky* (Washington D.C., 1987), p. 91.
[131] K. Taube, "Creation and Cosmology: Gods and Mythic Origins in Ancient Mesoamerica," in D. Nichols & C. Pool eds., *The Oxford Handbook of Mesoamerican Archaeology* (Oxford, 2012), p. 745.
[132] V. Straizys & L. Klimka, "The Cosmology of the Balts," *Journal of the History of Astronomy* 22 (1997), p. 66 document that fire is depicted as a cross in Baltic artworks much like the sun.

earth, Agni fills the air with his shine, props the sky with his light, upholding the quarters by his lustre (cf. *Vaj.S.* 17, 72)."¹³³ The god's epithet *caturanga* evidently encodes the idea: "In RV 10.92.11, the term *caturanga*, 'four-limbed', is used as an epithet of Agni Narasamsa, naming him after his capacity to fill out, as fire, in the four directions."¹³⁴

Similar conceptions are attested in ancient Mesopotamia. In a hymn to the ancient sun-god Shamash, the god's fire is said to illuminate the four quarters:

> Light of the great gods, light of the earth, illuminator of the four quarters…Your [rising] is blazing fire (literally: Girra).¹³⁵

The Akkadian phrase translated as "four quarters" here is *kibrat erbetti*, the standard term for the earth's four quadrants in Mesopotamian cosmic geography.¹³⁶ Although scholars have been hard-pressed to explain the origin of such widespread conceptions—one cannot see the world directions, after all—a perfectly logical solution was provided by David Talbott who, in *The Saturn Myth*, argued that the four directions of cosmogonic myth trace to the four streamers shown radiating outwards from the central "sun" in ancient Mesopotamian pictographs (see figure thirteen).¹³⁷ A similar pictograph from Amerindian culture (Middle Mississippi Valley Group) is depicted in figure fourteen.¹³⁸

Figure thirteen

---

¹³³ J. Gonda, *Some Observations on the Relations Between 'Gods' and 'Powers' in the Veda* ('S-Gravengage, 1957), p. 44.

¹³⁴ D. Srinivasan, *Many Heads, Arms and Eyes* (Leiden, 1997), p. 31.

¹³⁵ J. Polonsky, *The Rise of the Sun-God and the Determination of Destiny in Ancient Mesopotamia*. Ph.D. dissertation, University of Philadelphia (2002), p. 536.

¹³⁶ W. Horowitz, *Mesopotamian Cosmic Geography* (Winona Lake, 1994), p. 298.

¹³⁷ Adapted from figure 16 in A. Jeremias, "Schamasch," in W. Roscher ed., *Ausführliches Lexikon der griechischen und römischen Mythologie, Vol. 4* (Leipzig, 1965), col. 555. See also the discussion in W. Gaerte, "Kosmische Vorstellungen im Bilde prähistorischer Zeit: Erdberg, Himmelsberg, Erdnabel und Weltenströme," *Anthropos* 9 (1914), pp. 978-979.

¹³⁸ Adapted from M. Naylor ed., *Authentic Indian Designs* (New York, 1975), p. 14. For a close variant see R. Heizer & C. Clewlow, *Prehistoric Rock Art of California* (Ramona, 1973), figure 312b.

Figure fourteen

Given the fact that analogous images can be found around the globe, often in prehistoric (i.e., Neolithic) contexts, it is plausible to conjecture that they describe some empirically observed celestial reality, whether a temporary apparition or, more likely, a sustained stellar structure of some sort, such as a conjunction of stars or a particularly spectacular nova. Granted this proposition, can it be doubted that if a prehistoric sky-watcher were to behold such a celestial apparition he would conceptualize the four radiating structures as four "streams" of "fire" or as four "winds" extending to the four corners of the universe? To merely pose this hypothetical question is to know the answer: The interpretation of the central orb's radiating streamers as four fires/winds would not only be a perfectly natural and rational idea; it would be predictable (see Appendix 2).

The Turquoise Enclosure

The sacred traditions of the Aztecs identify a turquoise enclosure as the dwelling-place of the archaic fire-god Xiuhtecuhtli—"the archetype of all rulers"—and describe it as a cosmic hearth. A turquoise enclosure is also identified as the locus of sunrise—specifically, as the birthplace of Nanahuatl as the fifth sun. Such convergent traditions naturally beg the question: How are we to understand this turquoise enclosure from the perspective of celestial topography?

If the Aztec traditions reference a tangible celestial structure and encode actual historical events, as we believe to be the case, it stands to reason that other cultures around the globe must have preserved analogous traditions with respect to a turquoise enclosure associated with the primal sun. Perhaps the most instructive parallel to Xiuhtecuhtli's turquoise enclosure is provided by the Egyptian *shen*-bond, commonly held to depict the sun within a turquoise-colored band—this despite the fact that a turquoise-colored structure is nowhere to be found in the immediate vicinity of the current solar orb (see figure six).[139] Explicitly identified as a "circle in the sky," the shen-bond was early on assimilated with the *akhet*, the

---

[139] W. Barta, "Der Königsring als Symbol zyklischer Wiederkehr," *Zeitschrift für Ägyptische Sprache und Altertumskunde* 98 (1970), pp. 5-13.

locus of sunrise.¹⁴⁰ At the same time, the shen bond was a popular symbol of royalty otherwise known as the ring of sovereignty.¹⁴¹

Figure six

The Egyptian shen-bond, in turn, finds an iconic parallel in the *kippatu*-ring, a prominent item of royal insignia presented to the king in Mesopotamian coronation scenes (see figure seven).¹⁴² The ring in question is explicitly represented as a rope and typically appears together with a rod.¹⁴³

Figure seven

---

¹⁴⁰ C. Müller-Winkler, "Schen-Ring," *Lexikon der Ägyptologie V* (Wiesbaden, 1984), col. 578, notes: "Gewisse formale und inhaltliche Assoziationen mit dem Achet-Amulet (Horizont) sind nachweisbar."

¹⁴¹ S. Quirke, *Ancient Egyptian Religion* (London, 1992), p. 62. See also A. Sugi, "The Iconographical Representation of the Sun God in New Kingdom Egypt," in Z. Hawass ed., *Egyptology at the Dawn of the Twenty-first Century, Vol. 2* (Cairo, 2003), p. 515.

¹⁴² J. Scurlock, "Images of Dumuzi," in J. Hill et al eds., *Experiencing Power, Generating Authority* (Philadelphia, 2013), p. 173: "The symbols of Assyrian kingship frequently shown in the process of being handed over by Ashur or other gods were a rod (*ḫattu*) and a ring (*kippatu*)."

¹⁴³ K. Slanski, "The Mesopotamian 'Rod and Ring'," *Proceedings of the British Academy* 136 (2007), p. 41 writes as follows of the ring depicted on the Ur-Nammu stela: "The 'ring' appears clearly as a braided rope coiled into a circle."

The *kippatu* is elsewhere described as encircling the Sun.[144] As the "circle of heaven" (*kippat šamê*), the ring appears in the following hymn invoking the Sun: "You are their (mankind's) light in the circle of the distant heavens."[145] So, too, the great Shamash hymn describes the sun-god as follows: "You (Shamash) hold the totality of the countries from the center of the sky as if suspended [*kip-pat* KUR.KUR *ina qereb šamê šaqlata*]."[146] Evident here is the idea that the Sun rules from within the *kippatu*-band in middle of the sky (*qereb šamê*).

Mesopotamian texts explicitly link the *kippatu* with the locus of sunrise and, as a result, the term is attested in phrases conventionally translated "horizon" in modern commentaries. Wayne Horowitz documented this point in his *Mesopotamian Cosmic Geography*: "Other idioms referring to the horizon include…*kippat matati* 'circle of the lands', *kippat erṣeti* 'circle of earth', *kippat tubuqat erbetti* 'circle of the four corners', *kippat šar erbetti* 'circle of the four (regions)'."[147] Here there can be little question that a clearly visible celestial structure is being described.

As for how we are to understand this celestial bond or "circle" from an astronomical standpoint, scholars have offered nary a clue. From our vantage point, however, the answer is readily deducible: The rope-like bond has reference to the turquoise-colored band that formerly encircled the primal sun (see appendix three).[148] Here, too, ancient pictographs point the way to an evidence-based conclusion. Consider the image depicted in figure three above: In the center of the quincunx one finds an inner orb encircled by a band of some sort.[149] This, in our view, is the natural-historical prototype for the Egyptian shen-bond featuring a turquoise-colored band encircling an inner "sun." In fact, Mesoamerican codices depict red sun-like orbs encircled by a turquoise band (see figure eight).[150] Analogous images are evident in the sacred artwork of the Plains Indians (see figure nine). The resemblance to the Egyptian shen-sign is evident at once and indisputable.

---

[144] A. George, *Babylonian Topographical Texts* (Leuven, 1992), p. 429.

[145] W. Horowitz, *Mesopotamian Cosmic Geography* (Winona Lake, 1994), p. 264

[146] "kippatu," in A. L. Oppenheim et al eds., *The Assyrian Dictionary, Vol. K* (Chicago, 1971), p. 399.

[147] C. Woods, "At The Edge of the World," *JANER* 9:2 (2009), p. 186.

[148] E. Cochrane, *On Fossil Gods and Forgotten Worlds* (Ames, 2010), pp. 101-123.

[149] It will be noted that two celestial bodies in conjunction would produce the same image if the closer orb was slightly smaller than the more distant orb.

[150] Adapted from page 34 of the *Codex Borgia*.

Figure eight

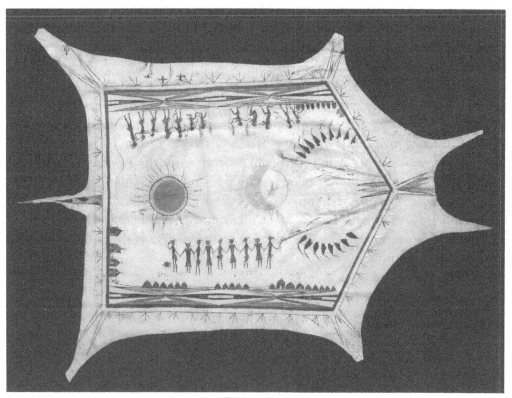

Figure nine

If figure three represents the nascent sun nestled within the turquoise band, figure four represents the kindling or flaring up of the central fire (=primal sun). As the central sun flared up, sending its fiery rays to the four corners of the cosmos, it presented a cruciform appearance (see also figure five depicting a central "sun" within a star-like body). Hence, we would understand the otherwise inexplicable relationship between fire, a cross, and the four cardinal directions.

Conclusion

The foregoing analysis of Xiuhtecuhtli's cult has revealed that the Aztec fire-god was conceptualized as residing within a turquoise enclosure at the navel of the earth, wherefrom he ruled over the four quarters of the universe. In addition to being the patron god of Aztec rulers and archetypal king par excellence, Xiuhtecuhtli also presided over the New Fire rites believed to commemorate Creation and signal a new year.

As first documented here, the Aztec traditions attached to Xiuhtecuhtli find a remarkable parallel in ancient India, where the Vedic fire-god Agni was conceptualized as residing in a hearth at the navel of the earth (see appendix four). Like Xiuhtecuhtli, Agni was regarded as the divine prototype of rulers and believed to reside at the nexus of the four quarters of the cosmos. The numerous correspondences between the disparate cults of Xiuhtecuhtli and Agni detailed here attest to the fundamental coherence and likely empirical nature of such archaic mythological structures.

05 The Aztec Myth of Creation

> The very existence of the Mesoamericans presupposed observation of the sky. Without sky-watchers, the ethos of this people, its distinguishing spirit, its genius would have developed along very different lines, if it had developed at all.[151]

In the Aztec myth of Creation, it is the leprous god Nanahuatl who sacrifices himself on a divine hearth in order to generate the "sun." This myth is told in a number of different indigenous sources, typically in a frustratingly fragmentary fashion.[152] According to the account preserved by Sahagún, Nanahuatl [Nanauatzin] eventually succeeded in bringing light to a darkened world through an act of self-sacrifice in the Time of Beginning:

> It is told that when yet [all] was in darkness, when yet no sun had shone and no dawn had broken—it is said—the gods gathered themselves together and took counsel among themselves at Teotihuacan. They spoke; they said among themselves: 'Come hither, o gods! Who will carry the burden? Who will take it upon himself to be the sun, to bring the dawn?'…None dared; no one else came forward [apart from Tecuciztecatl]. Everyone was afraid; they [all] drew back…Then the gods called to this one. They said to him: 'Thou shalt be the one, O Nanauatzin.'… And then, also, at this time, the fire was laid. Now it burned, there in the hearth…And when this was done, when midnight had come, all the gods proceeded to encircle the hearth, which

---

[151] M. León-Portilla & E. Shorris, *In the Language of Kings* (New York, 2001), p. 22.
[152] O. Mazariegos, *Art and Myth of the Ancient Maya* (New Haven, 2017), pp. 167-168.

was called *teotexcalli*, where for four days had burned the fire…
[Tecuciztecatl fails to throw himself on the fire out of fear]…
And Nanauatzin, daring all at once, determined…All at once he
quickly threw and cast himself into the fire; once and for all he
went. Thereupon he burned; his body crackled and sizzled. And
when Tecuciztecatl saw that already he burned, then, afterwards,
he cast himself upon [the fire]. Thereupon he also burned…And
after this, when both had cast themselves into the flames, when
they had already burned, then the gods sat waiting [to see] where
Nanauatzin would come to rise—he who first fell into the fire—
in order that he might shine [as the sun]; in order that dawn
might break…And when the sun came to rise, when he burst
forth, he appeared to be red; he kept swaying side to side. It was
impossible to look into his face; he blinded one with his light.
Intensely did he shine. He issued rays of light from himself; his
rays reached in all directions; his brilliant rays penetrated everywhere…They could only remain still and motionless [i.e., the
two celestial lights Nanauatzin and Tecuciztecatl]…Here endeth
this legend and fable, which was told in times past, and was in
the keeping of the old people.[153]

The report that Nanahuatl's auto-sacrifice by fire occurred during a period when all "was in darkness" is one of several clues that suggests we are likely dealing with an archaic account of Creation, inasmuch as the cosmogonic myths of cultures around the globe typically place the inaugural appearance of light—the prototypical Dawn—in a general context of apocalyptic Darkness.[154] Indeed, the prototypical "sun" is widely reported to have originated from a "house" or place of darkness.[155]

If this much is clear, it is less obvious what natural events or associative learning response might have inspired the Aztec sky-watchers to recognize a fundamen-

---

[153] B. de Sahagún, *The Florentine Codex: Book 7* (Santa Fe, 1953), pp. 1-8.
[154] According to the account of Creation in *The Florentine Codex: Book 3* (Santa Fe, 1978), p. 1: "the time was when there still was darkness." See also E. Cochrane, *On Fossil Gods and Forgotten Worlds* (Ames, 2010), pp. 231-244. See also H. Ringgren, "Light and Darkness in Ancient Egyptian Religion," in *Liber Amicorum* (Leiden, 1969), pp. 144-145: "The victory of light at creation, however, is not a final one. Darkness is not defeated once and for all, it has only been pushed back and surrounds this world of light, continuously threatening to encroach upon its dominion…Consequently, darkness has to be repelled constantly. Every sunrise is a repeated defeat of chaos and darkness or, if you like, a new creation."
[155] E. Cochrane, *Phaethon: The Star That Fell From Heaven* (Ames, 2017), pp. 117-119.

tal affinity between the sacred fire and the sun. That just such an association was made is evident—hence their belief that if the fire were allowed to go out the sun would be extinguished. The same conclusion is supported by the fact that a very similar belief system prevailed in Vedic India. Witness the following hymn to Agni from the *Rig Veda*, wherein the Angirases perform the archetypal deed traditionally ascribed to the Vedic Thundergod Indra—namely, cleaving the primeval rock that proved to be the origin of all things:

> By truth they threw open the rock, having split it. The Angirases roared along with the cows. For blessing the men besieged the dawn; the sun became visible when the fire was born.[156]

Here, too, the appearance of the first dawn and prototypical "sun" is expressly analogized to the generation of fire. Indeed, a recurring theme in the *Rig Veda* holds that the appearance of the sun is contingent upon the kindling of Agni.[157]

If an inherent logical connection between the ritual drilling of fire and the generation of the sun can be recognized in ancient Vedic and Aztec lore—and it is quite impossible to deny such a connection in light of the cosmogonical traditions adduced above—it stands to reason that the Aztecs' anxiety regarding the ominous effects that would befall the world were the New Fire not to be drilled might be related to analogous fears attached to solar eclipses. For much as was the case with the Aztecs' beliefs regarding the extinction of the perpetual fire, numerous cultures feared that a permanent "Night" might ensue every time the sun was eclipsed. Sahagún himself provides ample evidence of this particular belief-system in ancient Mexico:

> Then [upon an eclipse of the sun] there were a tumult and disorder. All were disquieted, unnerved, frightened. There was weeping. The common folk raised a cry, lifting their voices, making a great din, calling out, shrieking. There was shouting everywhere. People of light complexion were slain [as sacrifices]; captives were killed. All offered their blood…And in all the temples there was the singing of fitting chants; there was an uproar; there were war cries. It was thus said: 'If the eclipse of the sun is complete, it will

---

[156] *RV* 4:3:11.
[157] *RV* 5:6:4. See especially the discussion in G. Nagy, *Greek Mythology and Poetics* (Ithaca, 1990), p. 147: "The macrocosmic principle inherent in Agni, god of sacrificial fire, is anchored in a belief that the rising of the sun is dependent on the kindling of the sacrificial fire."

be dark forever! The demons of darkness will come down; they will eat men!'[158]

It is exceedingly difficult to explain such mass hysteria by reference to the familiar natural world, inasmuch as solar eclipses are never accompanied by cosmic disaster. Nor, for that matter, are solar eclipses permanent or even prolonged in nature, lasting for a few minutes at most. How, then, are we to explain such stubbornly held beliefs—beliefs which, it must be emphasized, are commonplace among indigenous cultures on every inhabited continent?[159]

Equally incongruous is Sahagún's reference to the "demons of darkness" that were thought to descend from the sky during an eclipse, wreaking havoc and destruction. The demons in question are the Tzitzimime, falling stars elsewhere described as being long-haired agents of destruction.[160] Here, too, the mere mention of disaster-bringing stars is enough to confirm that Sahagún's indigenous informants were not describing a run-of-the-mill solar eclipse—rather, an apocalyptic catastrophe threatening the world with destruction.

Sahagún's statement that an eclipse might lead to permanent darkness is especially telling, for it suggests that the Aztecs' obsessive fears about solar eclipses, like their sense of dread regarding the extinction of the perpetual fire at the end of their sacred Calendar Round, can only be properly understood by reference to the Aztec myth of Creation, wherein a prolonged period of darkness forms a central theme.

According to Sahagún's eye-witness testimony, once the new fire was generated all the local villagers put on new clothes and replaced their hearths and pestles, which had been intentionally destroyed at the outset of the ritual. With the generation of fire and the dawning of the New Year, the threat of apocalyptic darkness and assault at the hands of pestilence-causing demons was effectively averted:

---

[158] B. Sahagún, *Florentine Codex: Book 7* (Sante Fe, 1953), p. 2.

[159] J. Grimm, *Teutonic Mythology, Vol. 2* (Gloucester, 1976), p. 706: "One of the most terrific phenomena to heathens was an *eclipse* of the sun or moon, which they associated with a destruction of all things and the end of the world." The following report from the Amazonian region not only recalls Sahagún's report; it is representative of analogous traditions that recur around the globe: "[Upon a solar eclipse] it is then feared that the epoch of chaos will return and monsters and demons will come from the jungle and rivers to attack people." See G. Reichel-Dolmatoff, *Amazonian Cosmos* (Chicago, 1971), p. 72.

[160] Eduard Seler, *Codex Vaticanus No. 3773* (Berlin, 1903), p. 172 doubtless had it right when he described Tzitzimime as "*stellar deities* who became demons of darkness." See also B. Brundage, *The Fifth Sun* (Austin, 1979), pp. 62-64.

Thus it was said that truly the year newly started. There was much happiness and rejoicing. And they said: 'For thus it is ended; thus sickness and famine have left us.'[161]

Such ideas find striking parallels in the Old World. In ancient Rome, for example, the Old Year was banished with the extinction of all fires; the New Year, in turn, was marked by the generation of a new fire on March first in the temple of Vesta, the latter representing a renewal of the generative forces of nature.[162] So, too, in ancient Greece the new fire generated at Delphi was "a signal of a new beginning."[163]

For one reason or another, the peculiar superstitions and ominous portents surrounding the end of the year have received relatively little attention from scholars—this despite their seemingly universal distribution and the profound significance they held within indigenous cultures in general. A notable exception in this respect is the Dutch scholar Arent Wensinck. As Wensinck discerned many years ago, traditions regarding the potential disasters attending the turning of the Year reflect archaic conceptions regarding Creation, wherein it was commonly believed that an all-engulfing Darkness threatened to destroy the world:

> This material speaks for itself; not only is each New Year a memorial of the creation but it is a repetition of it, and the creation itself is regarded as a kind of New Year. Indeed, the last expression is the right one. New Year belongs to cosmogony, New Year and creation are the reflection one of the other…Finally we come to the relation between New Year and the chaos that precedes the cosmos and without which the latter cannot come into existence… Only when the Tehom is beaten back, or—in mythological language—when Tiamat is defeated, does the world order begin…It is a struggle of life and death between the powers of darkness and light, of confusion and order, of Evil and Good… The end of the cosmos is seen in an eclipse of the sun, when the very existence of the god of order is threatened and the world is abandoned to the powers of darkness.[164]

---

[161] B. Sahagún, *Florentine Codex: Book 7* (Sante Fe, 1953), p. 31.
[162] Ovid *Fasti* 3, 141-144. See also G. Dumézil, *Archaic Roman Religion, Vol. 1* (Baltimore, 1966), p. 322.
[163] H. S. Versnel, "Apollo and Mars One Hundred Years After Roscher," *Visible Religion* IV/V (1985/6), p. 154. See also W. Kristensen, *The Meaning of Religion* (The Hague, 1960), p. 139, who points out that "new life" began on Lemnos with the generation of the New Fire.
[164] A. J. Wensinck, "The Semitic New Year and the Origin of Eschatology," *Acta Orientalia* 1

Mircea Eliade, doubtless influenced by Wensinck's groundbreaking study, also called attention to the apocalyptic fears attending the end of the Year. In a discussion of the ritualized drilling of the new fire, he offered the following observation:

> The ritual production of fire reproduces the birth of the world. Which is why at the end of the year all fires are extinguished (a re-enactment of the Cosmic night), and rekindled on New Year's Day (this is an enactment of the Cosmogony, the rebirth of the world.)[165]

At this point in our analysis we are finally in a position to identify the probable natural-historical basis for the Aztecs' seemingly irrational fears surrounding the drilling of the new fire and solar eclipses: It was precisely because the Aztec priests *knew* that the world had previously been brought to the very brink of extinction when a former "sun" had been blotted out that they had reason to fear that such terrifying conditions might return were the present Sun to become eclipsed or—in what amounts to the same thing—were the perpetual fire allowed to die out. Indeed, it is our opinion that this particular phobia can only be fully understood by reference to a collective memory of an extraordinary cataclysm preceding the First Dawn, during which a former "sun" *was* eclipsed and an apocalyptic Darkness threw the cosmos into chaos and confusion (see the discussion in chapter X).[166]

Such archetypal fears, in turn, are inextricably bound up with Aztec traditions of multiple suns. As is well known, it was a central tenet of Aztec cosmology that previous suns had come and gone amidst terrifying catastrophic disasters of one form or another.[167] Nor were the Aztecs alone in this belief: "This belief that the sun was not eternal was shared by other American Indian tribes so widely that we consider it must have been part of their belief long before any high culture had arisen in the Americas."[168]

(1923), p. 169.

[165] M. Eliade, *The Forge and the Crucible* (Chicago, 1962), pp. 39-40. See also W. Kristensen, *The Meaning of Religion* (The Hague, 1960), p. 139 who wrote as follows with respect to the renewal of the Vestal fire: "The idea at the basis of this custom is that the yearly renewal of the life of nature is not a natural event that occurs automatically; it is a miracle, the repetition of the miracle of the original Creation."

[166] E. Cochrane, *On Fossil Gods and Forgotten Worlds* (Ames, 2021), pp. 179-187.

[167] H. B. Alexander, "Latin American Mythology," in L. Gray ed., *The Mythology of All Races* (New York, 1964), p. 85 observes: "The earlier world-epochs, or 'Suns,' as the Mexicans called them, are commonly four in number, and each is terminated by the catastrophic destruction of its Sun and of its peoples, fire and flood overwhelming creation in successive cataclysms."

[168] C. Burland, *The Gods of Mexico* (New York, 1967), p. 140.

Equally deeply ingrained and widespread were archaic traditions telling of a "Long Night" or an extended period of Darkness that had gripped the world during a previous Age.[169] If these traditions of a Primeval Darkness have an historical basis, as we believe to be the case, it follows that the Aztecs' fears regarding eclipses and the extinction of the perpetual fire originated in witnessed natural events of a catastrophic nature and are thus fundamentally rational in origin, albeit induced by traumatic experiences and regularly reinforced by mimetic rituals further bolstering collective hysteria and PTSD. That we have to do here with *remembered* events of a catastrophic nature—racial and cultural memories, as it were, rather than figurative language run amok—is rendered virtually certain by the manifold ancient traditions reporting that the prototypical "sun" of Creation must be distinguished from the present Sun. Alas, such traditions have been almost uniformly ignored by scholars of comparative myth—this despite the fact that they are surprisingly commonplace.[170]

As it turns out, some of the most compelling testimony in this regard comes from pre-Columbian Mesoamerica. The K'iche' Maya *Popol Vuh* offers the following account of the "dawning" of the prototypical sun:

> Like a man was the sun when it showed itself, and its face glowed when it dried the surface of the earth. Before the sun rose, damp and muddy was the surface of the earth, before the sun came up; but then the sun rose, and came up like a man. And its heat was unbearable. It showed itself when it was born and remained fixed [in the sky] like a mirror. Certainly it is not the same sun which we see, it is said in their old tales.[171]

Yet if it was not the current sun that formed the subject of the K'iche' account of Creation, which sun was it?[172] The unbearably intense "heat" of the former sun, together with its "fixed" or motionless nature, offers a decisive clue and recalls Sahagún's description of Nanahuatl's "sun" in the Aztec myth of Creation:

---

[169] E. Cochrane, *On Fossil Gods and Forgotten Worlds* (Ames, 2010), pp. 233-236.
[170] See now M. van der Sluijs, *Traditional Cosmology, Vol. 5* (Vancouver, 2018), pp. 3-8.
[171] M. León-Portilla & E. Shorris, *In the Language of Kings* (New York, 2001), p. 447.
[172] Comparable traditions will be found around the globe. Witness the following Desana tradition from the Amazonian Region reported by G. Reichel-Dolmatoff, *Amazonian Cosmos* (Chicago, 1971), p. 41: "The Sun Creator, nevertheless, was not the same sun that now illuminates our earth." See the discussion in E. Cochrane, *On Fossil Gods and Forgotten Worlds* (Ames, 2010), pp. 42-43.

> And when the sun came to rise, when he burst forth, he appeared to be red; he kept swaying side to side. It was impossible to look into his face; he blinded one with his light. Intensely did he shine. He issued rays of light from himself; his rays reached in all directions; his brilliant rays penetrated everywhere…When both appeared [over the earth] together, they could, on the other hand, not move or follow their paths. They could only remain still and motionless [i.e., the two celestial lights Nanauatzin and Tecuciztecatl]…

However such traditions are to be explained from the standpoint of modern astronomical science, it seems obvious that the peculiar stories surrounding Nanahuatl hold the key to sorting out the Aztec belief-systems linking the drilling of fire with the origin of the sun. Yet despite his central role in Aztec cosmogonical traditions, the archaic god in question has received relatively little attention from modern scholars.

Nanahuatl

To my knowledge, the most comprehensive and insightful analysis of Nanahuatl's mythology was that offered by B. C. Brundage. This vastly underrated historian summarized the god's myth as follows:

> One of the more enigmatic figures in Mesoamerican mythology is the diseased god Nanahuatl. The name itself is curious. Nanahuatl is the word for afflictions of the skin, generally running or pustulous sores. The god's name is thus simply the name of a disease, and he may be considered to be the god who sends the disease and who can also cure it. Human sacrifices made to him in fact were chosen from among those who suffered from his diseases. He is thus the 'disease' Quetzalcoatl. He must have been a very old god, for he appears to have had a limited cult at the time of the Spanish entry, yet he is the central figure in the myth of the five suns that originated in the days of Teotihuacan. His name also appears as Nanahuatzin or Nanahuaton, both translated as Little Nanahuatl, the implication being that he was a dwarf or was thought to be strikingly small in stature. He appears among the Quichés as Nanahuac and is one of their early creator gods, along with Gukumatz (Quetzalcoatl), and he is called by them 'dwarf,' or 'green,' that is, young.[173]

---

[173] B. Brundage, *The Fifth Sun* (Austin, 1979), pp. 224-225.

What are we to make of this curious collage of traditions? As is evident from Brundage's summary, Nanahuatl is literally defined by his pustulous sores. Yet here, too, scholars have been virtually silent about what this particular trait could signify or reference. Michel Graulich, in his discussion of this core Mesoamerican myth, could only muster the following admission of befuddlement:

> What are the gods doing on earth and in darkness? Why are they material and why is one of them bubonous?[174]

As we have argued elsewhere, the fact that the Morning Star was commonly conceptualized as suffering from "sores" or skin eruptions by indigenous cultures throughout North and South America provides an apparent clue to understanding the mythological traditions under review here.[175] A myth from the Sikuani of South America is instructive in this regard:

> In those days the sun and the moon and everyone were human beings and lived on this earth. Sun had a son who had sores all over his body; he was the morning star.[176]

Analogous traditions are attested in Mesoamerica. According to the Mixe-Popoluca of Oluta, the Creator Viejito was a dwarfish being beset by skin eruptions or pimples:

> The Mixe-Popoluca of Oluta and Sayula, in the Veracruz Isthmus region, view the morning star as an old man, *El Viejo* or *Viejito*, and the east is described as the 'place of the Old Man's house'… Viejito is alone, not married. Viejito has a ragged shirt, white is his hair…long is his hair. He is frail, he walks with his staff, dirty little breeches, long is his white beard, his body has pimples all over…[177]

If we are to take our cue from these Amerindian traditions describing the Morning Star as covered with sores, it stands to reason that the Aztec Nanahuatl is to be identified with that same celestial body.[178] This identification is further bol-

---

[174] M. Graulich, "Aztec Human Sacrifice as Expiation," in J. Bremmer ed., *The Strange World of Human Sacrifice* (Leuven, 2007), p. 15.
[175] E. Cochrane, *Starf*cker* (Ames, 2010), pp. 56-72.
[176] J. Wilbert & K. Simoneau, "Sun and Moon," in *Folk Literature of the Sikuani Indians* (Los Angeles, 1992), pp. 25-28.
[177] Quoted from I. Sprajc, "The Venus-Maize Complex in the Mesoamerican World View," *Journal of the History of Astronomy* 24 (1993), pp. 35-36.
[178] E. Cochrane, *Starf*cker* (Ames, 2006), pp. 111-114.

stered by the fact that native sources identify Nanahuatl with Quetzalcoatl. Thus it is that the so-called *Legend of the Suns* (1558) describes the former god as follows:

> The name of this sun is 4 Motion. This is now our sun, the one under which we live today. This is its figure, the one here, because his sun fell into the fire at the sacred hearth in Teotihuacan. It is the same sun as that of Topiltzin, 'Our Beloved Prince' of Tollan, Quetzalcoatl. Before becoming this sun, its name was Nanahuatl, who was of Tamoanchan.[179]

That Quetzalcoatl himself is to be identified with the Morning Star is well-known. On this matter, the indigenous sources speak as if with one voice (see below). Not unlike Nanahuatl, Quetzalcoatl was described as hideously ugly in appearance, his face being distinguished by warts and other swellings: "His face all heavily pockmarked and furrowed; he was a monstrous sight."[180] Indeed, the god was so closely connected with skin diseases that he was deemed to be an advocate for human beings similarly afflicted:

> The annual ceremony to Quetzalcoatl here is also described, which featured dancing by the merchants and lords and comic impersonations of deformed and diseased individuals and animals on a large platform in the patio of the temple. These had serious ritualistic overtones, for Quetzalcoatl was held to be *'abogado de las bubas y del mal de los ojos y del romadico y tosse.'* During their mimic performances, the participants uttered pleas to this god for health, while sufferers from these afflictions came to his temple with prayers and offerings.[181]

As the buboes-laden god who became a "sun" and ushered forth a new age, Quetzalcoatl is evidently the same celestial figure as Nanahuatl.

At this point it will no doubt appear that we have wandered far afield from our original subject matter—namely, the Aztec cult of Xiuhtecuhtli. Yet Xiuhtecuhtli himself was expressly identified with the Morning Star in the *Dresden Codex*.[182] There the god's name was spelled CHAK-xi-wi-te-'i. According to Erik Book:

---

[179] Quoted from the translation in M. León-Portilla & E. Shorris eds., *In the Language of Kings: An Anthology of Mesoamerican Literature* (New York, 2001), p. 58.
[180] *Ibid.*, p. 188.
[181] H. Nicholson, *Topiltzin Quetzalcoatl* (Boulder, 2001), p. 107.
[182] See page 49 of the Codex as illustrated in C. & J. Villacorta, *The Dresden Codex* (Walnut Creek, 1930), p. 98. See also S. Milbrath, "The Many Faces of Venus in Mesoamerica," in G. Villalobos & D. Barnhart eds., *Archaeoastronomy and the Maya* (Oxford, 2014), p. 126.

This spelling can be transliterated *chak xiwte'e'i* ['] and it is probably the Mayanized approximation of the Náhuatl name Xiuhtecuhtli (or *xiw te-kuh-tli*) 'Fire Lord.' The Maya rendition of the name opens with *chak*, a word with the meaning 'red, great' and a common part of the Maya name for the planet Venus, Chak Ek' 'Red/Great Star' (which follows each of the god names in this section).[183]

There are additional reasons to suspect a fundamental affinity between Xiuhtecuhtli and Nanahuatl. It will be remembered that the Aztec fire-god was conceptualized as dwelling within a turquoise enclosure, the latter explicitly identified with the cosmic hearth. Yet the turquoise enclosure in question, according to Sahagún, was the very place associated with the birth of the Nanahuatl. Witness the following account of the generation of the fifth sun:

> This is its [the sun's] story. It is said that when the god was made, when the god was formed, in the time of darkness...it is said, a very great fire was laid in a place called the god's hearth, the turquoise enclosure...But he dared not do it [i.e., leap into the fire]; he feared the fire...But little Nanauatl had already dared; he thereupon leaped into the fire. Thus he became the sun.[184]

Nanahuatl, not unlike Xiuhtecuhtli, was "born" from the turquoise hearth—hence the inherent connection between the drilled fire and the new-born "sun." And much as Xiuhtecuhtli was remembered as the archetypal sovereign, the *Leyenda* reports that, after suffering immolation on the hearth and transforming into a sun during a time of oppressive darkness, Nanahuatl became the ruler of the world (native sources describe him as being installed upon the celestial throne).[185] Indeed, Nanahuatl is remembered as the "king star."[186]

Nanahuatl's post-mortem enthronement, moreover, mirrors the mythical biography of Quetzalcoatl who, according to the *Codex Chimalpopoca*, was first established on the throne *after* immolating himself on a great funeral pyre and becoming transformed into the Morning Star:

---

[183] E. Boot, "Loanwords, 'Foreign Words,' and Foreign Signs in Maya Writing," in A. de Voogt & I. Finkel eds., *The Idea of Writing* (Leiden, 2010), p. 156.
[184] B. Sahagún, *op. cit.*, p. 84.
[185] M. Graulich, "Aztec human sacrifice as expiation," *History of Religions* 39:4 (2000), pp. 356-357 writes: "In the *Leyenda*, when he reaches the sky, the supreme creators solemnly enthrone him."
[186] F. Olquin, "Religion," in E. Moctezuma & H. Burden eds., *Aztecs* (London, 2002), p. 225.

> He set himself on on fire, he offered himself up in flame…And it is said that even as he burned, his ashes emerged and arose… And when the ashes were extinguished, then arose his heart, the quetzal bird itself; they saw it. And so they knew he had entered the sky within the sky. The old ones used to say he was transformed to the dawn star; thus it is said that when Quetzalcoatl died this star appeared, and so he is named Tlahuizcalpanteuctli, 'Lord of the Dawn House.' They used to say that when he died he did not appear for four days; he went to live in Mictlan, the Nether World, they said. And also in another four days he made for himself arrows. So in eight days appeared the great star which was named Quetzalcoatl, and this, they said, is when he was enthroned as Lord.[187]

As the legendary first ruler of Tula, Quetzalcoatl was regarded as the exemplary model for all future Mexican rulers. And much like Xiuhtecuhtli, Quetzalcoatl ruled from within a turquoise house. Witness the following prayer addressing the Mexican god: "The turquoise house, the serpent house, you built them here in Tollan where you came to rule."[188]

Conclusion

The peculiar details of the Aztec New Fire ritual can only be properly understood by reference to the extraordinary celestial events referenced in cosmogonic myth. The ritual called for the extinguishing of all fires precisely because Creation had occurred in the wake of an apocalyptic Darkness that had occluded a former "sun." The mass hysteria that greeted the extinction of fires associated with the New Fire ritual, in this sense, is functionally identical with the mass hysteria occasioned by solar eclipses since time immemorial. The absence of the perpetual fire, like the absence of the solar orb during eclipse, portended a return to the apocalyptic Darkness and chaos that threatened to destroy the world in the fabled Time of Beginning.[189] The drilling of the New Fire—in reality, the generation of a new "sun"—served to dispel such fears while signaling a return to order and normalcy.

---

[187] *Codex Chimalpopoca* 11 as translated in M. León-Portilla & E. Shorris, *In the Language of Kings* (New York, 2001), pp. 191-192.
[188] As translated in J. Bierhorst, *Four Masterworks of American Indian Literature* (Tucson, 1974), p. 65.
[189] J. Zandee, *Der Amunshymnus des Papyrus Leiden I 344 verso, Vol. 1* (Leiden, 1992), p. 310: "Finsternis und Tod sind gleich eng miteinander verbunden wie Licht und Leben."

06 The Skidi Pawnee Myth of Creation

No other primitive people has such an extensive and accurate record of its myths, tales, and legends as the North American Indian.[190]

Mythology occupies a vital place in the worldview of most people, particularly among those without written traditions. Mythology was essentially indistinguishable from what modern people might call 'reality' or 'history.' Often tied to religious belief, mythology can be a window into the past and the means by which people make sense of the present.[191]

In the creation story, fruitfulness and light had come into the world because Morning Star and his realm of light had conquered and mated with Evening Star in her realm of darkness.[192]

In theory the Skidi Pawnee ceremonies all have as their object the performance either through drama or through ritual of the acts which were performed in the mythologic age. The ritual is a formal method of restating the acts of the supernatural beings in early times…[193]

---

[190] S. Thompson, *Tales of the North American Indians* (Bloomington, 1966), p. xvi.
[191] B. Pritzker, *A Native American Encyclopedia* (Oxford, 2000), p. xi.
[192] G. Weltfish, *The Lost Universe* (New York, 1965), p. 106.
[193] James Dorsey as cited by R. Linton, "The Origin of the Skidi Pawnee Sacrifice to the Morning Star," *American Anthropologist* 28 (1928), p. 461.

How and when the Americas were first settled is lost in the mists of prehistory and remains a matter of controversy and on-going investigation. Whether the earliest emigrants trekked across the Bering land-bridge which formerly connected Siberia with western North America or arrived in several waves by way of canoes or make-shift rafts, will not concern us here. What is certain is that shortly after their arrival from distant continents, the ancestors of the Amerindians set about expanding into the furthest outreaches of North and South America. Some, like those who settled along the northwest coast of Canada and North America, adopted a relatively sedentary lifestyle marked by fishing and farming. Others, like the Plains Indians, eventually pursued a more nomadic lifestyle, following the thundering buffalo herds wherever they might lead them.

Among the indigenous tribes that Lewis and Clark encountered during their epic trek across the heartland of North America were the Skidi Pawnee, who had settled along the Platte and Loup Rivers in what is now central Nebraska. The Skidi made their living hunting buffalo, raising corn, and raiding their neighbors.[194]

The Skidi comprise one of the four major bands of the Pawnee and are thought to have immigrated to the Midwestern plains from the deep South, likely preserving religious practices otherwise characteristic of the cultures of Mesoamerica and the American Southwest. They speak a Caddoan language.

At the time of their first encounter with Europeans—Spanish and French trappers—the tribe is thought to have numbered around 10,000. Within one century after the visit by Lewis and Clark, the Skidi were reduced to some 600 individuals living on the brink of starvation and extinction.[195]

The Skidi were inveterate sky-watchers. Indeed, it has been said that they were "obsessed with the planets" and had "a sky-oriented theology perhaps without parallel in human history."[196] The planet Venus was conceptualized as a beautiful woman by the name of *cu-piritta-ka*, which translates literally as "female white star."[197] The anthropologist James Murie, himself of Skidi blood, summarized the lore surrounding this planet as follows:

> The second god Tirawahat placed in the heavens was Evening Star, known to the white people as Venus…She was a beautiful woman. By speaking and waving her hands she could perform wonders.

---

[194] For a general overview of their history, see B. Pritzker, *op. cit.*, pp. 350-352.
[195] *Ibid.*, p. 351.
[196] V. Del Chamberlain, *When Stars Came Down to Earth* (College Park, 1982), pp. 29, 82.
[197] J. Murie, "Ceremonies of the Pawnee," *Smithsonian Contributions to Anthropology* 27 (Cambridge, 1981), p. 39.

> Through this star and Morning Star all things were created. She is the mother of the Skiri [Skidi]. Through her it is possible for people to increase and crops to mature.[198]

It is to be noted that the planet Venus was explicitly distinguished from the "Morning Star." In fact, the Skidi identified the mythical "Morning Star" with the planet Mars, the latter envisaged as a powerful warrior of irascible disposition. Murie offered the following summary of the sacred traditions surrounding the Morning Star:

> The first one he placed in the heavens was the morning star…This being was to stand on a hot bed of flint. He was to be dressed like a warrior and painted all over with red dust. His head was to be decked with soft down and he was to carry a war club. He was not a chief, but a warrior.…This is Mars, *u-pirikucu?* (literally, 'big star'), or the god of war.[199]

Like numerous other indigenous cultures, the Skidi traced their origins to events involving the respective planets. The central act of Skidi cosmogony described the Martian warrior's pursuit and eventual conquest of the planet Venus. Creation itself unfolded as a direct result of their sexual union. In summarizing the events in question, Ralph Linton stated simply "The Morning Star married the Evening Star."[200]

The *hieros gamos* between Mars and Venus was ritually reenacted during especially sacred celebrations. On rare occasions, or in the face of some perceived threat—the appearance of a meteor, an epidemic, or some other portent—the Pawnee offered a human sacrifice to the Morning Star, usually in the years when Mars appeared as a morning star.[201] Here a band of warriors would accompany a man impersonating the Morning Star in raiding a neighboring campsite, where they sought to kidnap a young woman of choice. Along the way there was much singing and dancing, during which the mythological deeds of the Martian warrior were recounted and celebrated. Upon capturing a suitable victim, the war party returned to the Skidi village where several months might elapse while the priests

---

[198] *Ibid.*
[199] *Ibid.*, p. 38.
[200] R. Linton, "The Sacrifice to Morning Star by the Skidi Pawnee," *Leaflet Field Museum of Natural History, Department of Anthropology* 6 (1923), p. 5
[201] R. Linton, "The Origin of the Skidi Pawnee Sacrifice to the Morning Star," *American Anthropologist* 28 (1928), p. 457. See also the detailed analysis by Von Del Chamberlain, *When Stars Came Down to Earth* (College Park, 1982).

prepared for the sacrifice and awaited signs for the most propitious time. The culmination of the rite saw the young woman—representing Venus—being painted head to toe and outfitted with a curious fan-shaped headdress. The victim was then led to a scaffold specially erected for the occasion whereupon, after mounting the final rung, she was shot through the heart by an arrow from the bow of the man impersonating Morning Star. The priests in charge of the gruesome rite took great care to ensure that the girl's blood was directed to a cavity below the scaffold. This pit was lined with white feathers and was held to represent the sacred garden of the planet-goddess: "The pit symbolized the Garden of the Evening Star from which all life originates."[202]

Successful completion of the sacrifice was greeted with great rejoicing throughout the Skidi village. According to Gene Weltfish's account, the men and women danced and "there was a period of ceremonial sexual license to promote fertility."[203]

As bizarre as this rite appears to the modern reader, anthropologists are generally agreed that its fundamental purpose was to reenact and commemorate the principal events of Creation. Ralph Linton's opinion is representative in this regard:

> The sacrifice as a whole must be considered as a dramatization of the overcoming of the Evening Star by the Morning Star and their subsequent connection, from which sprang all life on earth. The girl upon the scaffold seems to have been conceived of as a personification or embodiment of the Evening Star surrounded by her powers. When she was overcome, the life of the earth was renewed, insuring universal fertility and increase.[204]

The primeval conjunction of Mars and Venus featured prominently in numerous different aspects of Pawnee religion. In a ritual that will assume a central role in this particular study, the *hieros gamos* or "marriage" between the planets Mars and Venus was invoked every time a new fire was drilled. In Skidi cosmology the drilling fire stick was identified with the prototypical masculine power (Mars as the "Morning Star") while the hearth symbolized the female power (Venus as the "Evening Star"):

> The Skiri also conceive of the firesticks as male and female. The idea is that the kindling of fire symbolized the vitalizing of the

---

[202] G. Weltfish, *The Lost Universe* (New York, 1965), p. 112.
[203] *Ibid.*, p. 114.
[204] R. Linton, "The Sacrifice to Morning Star by the Skidi Pawnee," *Leaflet Field Museum of Natural History, Department of Anthropology* 6 (1923), p. 17.

world as recounted in the creation. Specifically, the hearth represents the Evening Star and the drill the Morning Star in the act of creation.[205]

It will be noted that the Skidi sky-watchers identified the hearth—the matrix of Creation—with the planet Venus. The prototypical fire-drill, on the other hand, was identified with the planet Mars. For the Skidi, as for indigenous cultures around the globe, the drilling of fire was conceptualized as a sexual act between cosmic powers.[206] Thus it is that, from a functional and symbolic standpoint, the ritual drilling of fire is analogous to a *hieros gamos* between Mars and Venus *in illo tempore*.[207]

The Skidi traditions with respect to Venus and Mars raise a number of intriguing questions. How are we to explain the origin of such peculiar ideas and practices? The simplest explanation, as well as the most logical, is to trace the mythological traditions to objective events involving Venus and Mars. We would thus endorse the opinion expressed by the astronomer Ray Williamson: "The care with which the Pawnee observed the sky and noted the celestial events suggests that the story of Morning Star and Evening Star, in addition to serving as an explanation of the original events of the Pawnee universe, might also reflect actual celestial occurrences."[208]

It was the astronomer Von Del Chamberlain who conducted the most extensive investigation into the historical basis of the Skidi traditions.[209] He, too, concluded that astronomical events inspired the sacred traditions in question: "The conjunctions of Venus and Mars do seem to be the key to the Skidi concept of celestial parentage."[210] As for how these "conjunctions" were to be understood from an astronomical standpoint, Von Del Chamberlain opined that they had reference to Mars' periodic migration from the morning sky to the western evening sky whereupon, on very rare occasions,

---

[205] J. Murie, "Ceremonies of the Pawnee: Part I: The Skiri," *Smithsonian Contributions to Anthropology* 27 (1981), p. 40.
[206] R. Hall, *An Archaeology of the Soul* (Chicago, 1997), p. 98: "The drilling of fire by friction for the New Fire ceremony also symbolized the sexual union of Morning and Evening Star. The lower board or hearth board in such cases represented the Evening Star; the fire drill symbolized Morning Star." See also J. Frazer, *Myths of the Origin of Fire* (London, 1930), pp. 26ff.
[207] The firesticks are addressed as follows: "You are to create new life even as Morning Star and Evening Star gave life to all things."
[208] R. Williamson, *Living the Sky* (Norman, 1984), p. 225.
[209] V. Del Chamberlain, *When Stars Came Down to Earth* (College Park, 1982).
[210] *Ibid.*, p. 84.

it would conjoin with Venus. Other astronomers have since endorsed Chamberlain's interpretation.[211]

Granted that "actual celestial occurrences" are encoded in the Skidi myth of Creation, it remains far from obvious how it is possible to understand the origin of the specific motifs surrounding the respective planets given Von Del Chamberlain's hypothesis. Why was Venus conceptualized as the prototypical female power? Why was Mars viewed as masculine in nature or identified as Morning Star? Why would the periodic, relatively mundane conjunction of these two particular planets be linked to Creation, the origin of life, and ideas of universal fertility? Not one of these questions finds a satisfactory explanation under the thesis advanced by Von Del Chamberlain.

An important question facing students of cosmogonic myth is the following: Do the Skidi myths with respect to Venus and Mars have an historical or observational basis? Stated another way: Are the sacred traditions in question to be understood as reliable memories regarding the recent history of the solar system, or are they a product of creative storytelling and thus unique to that particular culture?

In order to investigate whether there was a celestial prototype for the *hieros gamos* described by Skidi mythmakers, it is instructive to deploy the comparative method to determine whether analogous ideas are evident in other cultures, ideally far removed from the North American heartland. The archaic cultures of Mesopotamia produced the most skilled astronomers in the Old World and thus they would appear to offer the perfect control study for our comparative enterprise, especially as there is no evidence of any direct influence of their astronomical traditions on those of the American Plains.

---

[211] E. Krupp, *Beyond the Blue Horizon* (New York, 1991), pp. 189-192.

07 The Planet Venus in Ancient Mesopotamia

The very ancient rite of the sacred marriage was of the utmost importance, if not the essential and pivotal element of Babylonian religion.[212]

The nature of a ritual of kingship known as the 'Sacred Marriage' has long puzzled scholars.[213]

The belief that the king could in some sense actually have sexual intercourse with the goddess is intimately connected to the belief in the divinity of the kings of this period [Isin].[214]

If we survey the whole of the evidence on this subject…we may conclude that a great Mother Goddess, the personification of all the reproductive energies of nature, was worshipped under different names but with a substantial similarity of myth and ritual by many peoples of Western Asia; that associated with her was a lover, or rather series of lovers, divine yet mortal, with whom she mated year by year, their commerce being deemed essential to the propagation of animals and plants, each in their several kind; and further, that the fabulous union of the divine pair was simulated and, as it were, multiplied on earth by the real, though temporary, union of the human sexes at the sanctuary of the goddess for the

---

[212] E. van Buren, "The Sacred Marriage in Early Times in Mesopotamia," *Orientalia* 13 (1944), p. 1.
[213] K. McCaffery, "The Sumerian Sacred Marriage: Texts and Images," in H. Crawford, *The Sumerian World* (New York, 2013), p. 227.
[214] J. Black et al, *The Literature of Ancient Sumer* (Oxford, 2004), p. 89.

sake of thereby ensuring the fruitfulness of the ground and the increase of man and beast.[215]

Veneration of the planet Venus under the guise of the goddess Inanna is ubiquitous in the earliest temples yet excavated in Mesopotamia. At Uruk, the oldest urban site in the ancient Near East, offerings to Inanna/Venus far outnumber those of any other deity.[216] In strata conventionally dated to the late fourth millennium BCE (Uruk IV-III), the planet-goddess is already associated with a number of symbols that would characterize her later cult (the eight-pointed star, rosette, and reed bundle, among others).[217]

The Sumerian cult of Inanna, upon being assimilated with that of the Semitic goddess Ishtar, would dominate the religious landscape of Mesopotamia for well over two thousand years. As our earliest historical testimony documenting the worship of the planet Venus, the literary hymns extolling Inanna and Ishtar must figure prominently in any systematic study of astral myth.

The oldest extant literary texts from Mesopotamia date from the Early Old Babylonian period (ca. 2000-1800 BCE).[218] Included among these early texts are several royal hymns describing the so-called sacred marriage ritual, deemed to be among the most important religious celebrations in the Mesopotamian cultural sphere.[219] Of untold antiquity—a vase recovered from the Protoliterate period at Uruk (ca. 3100 BCE) is thought to depict the marriage of Inanna and Dumuzi[220]—the ritual appears to have died out after the Old Babylonian period.[221]

In the ceremony in question a "flowered bed" would be prepared, whereupon the king would have intercourse with a woman representing Inanna.[222] Douglas Frayne offered the following summary of the rite:

---

[215] J. Frazer, *Adonis, Attis, Osiris* (New Hyde Park, 1961), p. 39.

[216] K. Szarzynska, "Offerings for the goddess Inana," *Revue d'assyriologie et d'archéologie orientale* 87 (1993), p. 7.

[217] K. Szarzynska, "Cult of the Goddess Inana in Archaic Uruk," in *Sumerica* (Warsaw, 1997), p 147: "The second symbol of Inana was the rosette."

[218] J. Hayes, *A Manual of Sumerian Grammar and Texts* (Malibu, 2000), p. 394.

[219] E. van Buren, "The Sacred Marriage in Early Times in Mesopotamia," *Orientalia* 13 (1944), p. 1.

[220] H. Frankfort, *The Art and Architecture of the Ancient Orient* (1954), pp. 25-27. See also G. Selz, "Five Divine Ladies," *NIN* 1 (2000), p. 31.

[221] R. Kutscher, "The Cult of Dumuzi/Tammuz," in J. Klein ed., *Bar-Ilan Studies in Assyriology* (New York, 1990), p. 41. Although references to a sacred marriage rite are to be found in the letters of Esarhaddon and Assurbanipal, human beings no longer take an active role in consummating the marriage of the goddess and her consort. See also D. Frayne, "Notes on The Sacred Marriage Rite," *Bibliotheca Orientalis* 42:1/2 (1985), cols. 11, 22.

[222] See here the discussion in D. Frayne, *op. cit.*, cols. 14, 21.

It is clear that the central purpose of the Sacred Marriage Rite was to promote fertility in the land. The rationale of the ceremony was that by a kind of sympathetic act involving the sexual union of the king, playing the role of the *en* [typically personifying Dumuzi] with a woman, generally referred to simply as Inanna, the crops would come up abundantly and both the animal and human populations would have the desire and fertility to ensure that they would multiply.[223]

In ancient Mesopotamia, as elsewhere, the ritual *hieros gamos* formed a prominent feature of the New Year's celebrations. By all accounts it was a particularly joyous occasion, marked by a period of feasting and revelry following consummation of the royal marriage:

The glad news of the successful accomplishment of the long rite having been communicated to the people who had been waiting in anxious expectation to learn the issue, there was an outburst of exultation and thanksgiving, followed by a great feast of which all partook, the newly-wedded pair, the visiting divinities, the whole multitude who, in gratitude for the fertility which was now assured, raised jubilant hymns to the sound of the lyre, flutes and drums.[224]

The single most important source describing the archaic ritual is the marriage hymn of Iddin-Dagan, the third king of the First Dynasty of Isin (ca. 1974-1954 BCE). The text begins by invoking Inanna as the planet Venus:

I shall greet her who ascends above…I shall greet the great lady of heaven, Inana! I shall greet the holy torch who fills the heavens, the light, Inana, her who shines like the daylight, the great lady of heaven, Inanna! I shall greet the Mistress, the most awesome lady among the Anuna gods; the respected one who fills heaven and earth with her huge brilliance…Her rising is that of a warrior.[225]

---

[223] *Ibid.*, col. 6.
[224] E. van Buren, "The Sacred Marriage in Early Times in Mesopotamia," *Orientalia* 13 (1944), p. 34.
[225] Lines 1-18 as quoted from "A *šir-namursaga* to Ninsiana for Iddin-Dagan (Iddin-Dagan A)," *ETCSL*. See also D. Reisman, "Iddin-Dagan's Sacred Marriage Hymn," *Journal of Cunei-*

It will be noted that Venus is described as filling heaven and earth with her huge brilliance, hardly a realistic judgment of that planet's current appearance in the dawn or evening sky, where it is simply one bright star amongst numerous others. The fact that the planet is conceptualized as a "warrior" is equally incongruous given its present tranquil behavior and appearance.

In the subsequent lines of the hymn there are scattered allusions to various offerings given to Inanna. After the goddess bathed herself, a bed is set up for her and the king to share. Upon being properly prepared, the king—in the guise of Dumuzi, here addressed by the epithet Ama'ušumgalanna—approaches the bed:

> On New Year's Day, the day of ritual, They set up a bed for my lady. They cleanse rushes with sweet-smelling cedar oil, They arrange them (the rushes) for my lady, for their (Inanna and the king) bed…My lady bathes (her) pure lap, She bathes for the lap of the king…The king approaches (her) pure lap proudly, Ama'ušumgalanna lies down beside her, He caresses her pure lap…She makes love with him on her bed, (She says) to Iddin-Dagan: 'You are surely my beloved.'…The palace is festive, the king is joyous, The people spend the day in plenty. Ama'ušumgalanna stands in great joy. May he spend long life on the radiant throne![226]

The most comprehensive study of the sacred marriage rite in ancient Mesopotamia is that by Pirjo Lapinkivi.[227] She posed the following question:

> The language of most of the sacred marriage texts is so explicitly sexual that it seems beyond question that they describe a sexual union between the king and the goddess Inanna, the consummation of their marriage. The crucial question, however, is, *why*? Why did this union take place, and why was it performed ritually…?[228]

Lapinkivi then proceeds to answer her own question—the historical origins and fundamental purpose of the sacred marriage rite remain unknown:

---

form Studies 25 (1973), pp. 186-191.
[226] Lines 175-215 from "A *šir-namursaga* to Ninsiana for Iddin-Dagan (Iddin-Dagan A)," as translated in D. Reisman, *op. cit.*, pp. 190-191.
[227] See also the wide-ranging Master's thesis of S. Beaulieu, *Eve's Ritual: The Judahite Sacred Marriage Rite* (Montreal, 2007).
[228] P. Lapinkivi, *The Sumerian Sacred Marriage* (Helsinki, 2004), p. 14.

> Despite all the various suggestions reviewed above, no scholarly consensus has been reached regarding this basic question. While the importance of the sacred marriage for the Sumerians is obvious, it has remained enigmatic to the modern scholars.[229]

There is a very simple reason why scholars have failed to discern the original significance of the sacred marriage rite: They have all but ignored the decisive role played by planets in the genesis of ancient myth and religion. Thus it is that Venus's primacy in the sacred marriage rite has been essentially overlooked. The fact that most scholars have eschewed a comparative approach has also proven myopic and prevented them from discovering that analogous traditions surround the same planet in other cultures. Modern prejudices notwithstanding, *the very fact that the Skidi Pawnee likewise associated the planet Venus with a sacred marriage associated with Creation* should prompt Sumerologists to consider the possibility that Inanna's sacred marriage rite has celestial determinants.

The Garden of Venus

> Plautus speaks of gardens being under the guardianship of Venus.[230]

> Previous studies of the Sumerian sacred marriage have almost exclusively sought to explain it on the basis of the Sumerian evidence alone. As already noted, this approach has resulted in a plethora of mutually contradictory or problematic explanations, none of which has won general acceptance.[231]

Venus has been associated with gardens from time immemorial. The question is why this should be the case. Why would a distant, barren planet be linked to a garden of verdant greenery and abundance?

The idea is attested already in the earliest literary texts from ancient Mesopotamia. In several royal hymns describing the *hieros gamos* between Inanna and Dumuzi it is reported that a glorious garden burgeoned forth in the immediate aftermath of their sexual union.[232] The following Sumerian hymn alludes to this general theme:

---

[229] *Ibid.*, p. 14.
[230] Pliny, *Natural History* XIX.xix.20.
[231] P. Lapinkivi, "The Sumerian Sacred Marriage and Its Aftermath in Later Sources," in M. Nissinen & R. Uro eds., *Sacred Marriages* (Winona Lake, 2008), p. 14.
[232] P. Steinkeller, "Priests and Sacred Marriage," in K. Watanabe ed., *Colloquium on the Ancient Near East* (Heidelberg, 1999), p. 136 notes that: "quite a few sources" dealing with the sacred marriage emphasize "that through the performance of that ritual great abundance immediately followed."

> The holy embrace. Fresh fruits (?) and shoots…As she arises from the king's embrace, the flax rises up with her, the barley rises up with her. With her, the desert is filled with a glorious garden.[233]

How are we to understand such traditions? Why would a profusion of vegetation or verdant greenery be associated with the sexual union between a Sumerian king and the planet Venus?

Floral imagery is also conspicuous in literary descriptions of the *locus amoenus*. Sumerian hymns routinely describe Inanna's marriage bed as flower-like in appearance or as generously laden with herbs and other greenery. As a case in point, witness the following hymn describing Dumuzi's temple in Badtibira:

> O house where lustrous herbs are strewn upon the flowery bed, the bed-chamber of holy Inana, where the lady of the plain refreshes herself! Brick-built E-muš (House which is the precinct), is flowery and holy….[234]

Inanna's bed is described here as girin, denoting flowery or "blossoming." Yet as Herman Vanstiphout has pointed out, there is reason to believe that the "bed" in question was also conceptualized as the planet-goddess's womb:

> The term used here for the bed (^{giš}nu$_2$ girin-a) is well known from sacred marriage texts. It is sometimes translated neutrally as 'splendid,' but 'flowery' or 'blossoming' seems to be much nearer the mark…It can be defended that it is also a transparent metaphor for Inana's vulva.[235]

It was Elizabeth van Buren, perhaps, who came the closest to capturing the essense of the vegetative symbolism associated with the sacred marriage rite. As she pointed out many years ago, Inanna herself was analogized to a green garden and the king to a "gardener":

---

[233] Lines C 7-11 from "A balbale (?) to Inana (Dumuzid-Inana P)," *ETSCL*.
[234] Lines 210-213 from "The temple hymns," *ETCSL*.
[235] H. Vanstiphout, *Epics of Sumerian Kings* (Leiden, 2004), pp. 46-47. See also G. Leick, *Sex and Eroticism in Mesopotamian Literature* (London, 1994), p. 53: "Although the garden is a popular locale for amorous encounters, and a metaphor for the female genitals…"

Deified kings who enacted the role of the bridegroom were said to be placed 'in the holy garden'. By analogous symbolism the divine bride was compared to a green garden.[236]

The modern scholar who has done the most to elucidate the manifold imagery attached to the sacred marriage rite is Yitzhak Sefati. Sefati underscored the symbolic importance of the garden and the attendant floral-imagery in the sacred marriage between the goddess Baba and the storm-god Ningirsu referenced in Gudea's inscriptions:

> The comparison of Baba to a beautiful garden is a simile found frequently in the Dumuzi-Inanna songs. The description of flowering and abundance accompanying the [sacred marriage] and the reference to the decreeing of fates, are all an implicit indication of the couple's union.[237]

Sefati's erudite commentary is marred, unfortunately, by the fact that he virtually ignores Inanna's identification with the planet Venus. At no point does he ever seek to explore the possible celestial determinants of the sacred marriage rite—this despite the fact that Iddin-Dagan's marriage hymn explicitly identifies the goddess as planetary in nature. Nor, for that matter, does he ever consider the possibility that the goddess's verdant green garden had a tangible, concrete reference in the natural world—i.e., in the celestial landscape.

Sefati is not alone in this regard—far from it, in fact. Conventional scholarship routinely disavows the possibility that celestial phenomena could have played a significant role in Mesopotamian myth or religion. Wolfgang Heimpel's categorical denial is representative in this regard:

> The plots of myths provide clear evidence that the primary concern of myth was with the great stages of human life, and that astral connections and allegorization cannot have shaped the myths in a fundamental way.[238]

---

[236] E. van Buren, "The Sacred Marriage in Early Times in Mesopotamia," *Orientalia* 13 (1944), p. 31. See also G. Selz, "Plant Metaphors: On the Plant of Rejuvenation," in S. Gaspa et al eds., *From Source to History* (Munster, 2014), p. 664: "It is a well attested though underestimated fact that in Ancient Near Eastern thought the fields of vegetable and sexual fertility were strictly intertwined."

[237] *Love Songs in Sumerian Literature* (Jerusalem, 1998), p. 34.

[238] W. Heimpel, "Mythologie A.1," in E. Ebeling & B. Meissner, *Reallexikon der Assyriologie*, Vol. 8 (Berlin, 1993-1997), p. 539. See also B. Pongratz-Leisten, "When the Gods are Speak-

Such learned interpretations of Mesopotamian myth and religion are so wide of the mark as to be essentially worthless. The earliest Sumerian texts themselves leave absolutely no doubt that Inanna herself was unequivocally celestial in nature and thus it stands to reason that there might be an astronomical basis for some of the imagery attending the sacred marriage rite. In the epic tale *Enmerkar and the Lord of Aratta*, for example, the planet Venus is described as the "splendor" (giri$_{17}$-zal) of An (Heaven).[239] In the passage in question, the planet-goddess appears in her familiar role as the consort of Dumuzi, here invoked by his epithet Ama-ušumgal-ana: "Thereupon the splendor of holy An, the lady of the mountains, the wise, the goddess whose kohl is for Ama-usumgal-ana, Inana, the lady of all the lands, called to Enmerkar…"[240]

Here, then, is explicit testimony that Inanna's "splendor" is celestial in nature and intimately associated with the planet Venus (the Sumerian logogram AN can be read alternately as "heaven" or as the god An).[241] Yet the very epithet identifying the planet Venus as the "heavenly splendor"—giri$_{17}$-zal—is elsewhere employed to describe the verdant greenery of the garden that springs up as a result of the *hieros gamos* with Inanna/Venus. Thus, the phrase translated above as "glorious garden" is ^{giš}kiri$_6$ giri$_{17}$-zal-gin$_7$, wherein ^{giš}kiri$_6$ denotes garden. The modifying phrase giri$_{17}$-zal, denoting "slendor, joy, prosperity," is also spelled kiri$_3$-zal and thus forms an apparent cognate of the Sumerian word for garden, kiri$_6$.[242] Encoded in both of these words is the idea of a brilliant greening effect characteristic of luxuriant verdure:

> Giri$_x$-zal would correspond to *tašiltu*, the exact meaning of which is not established, here denoting the splendor of vegetation; in this context I refer to *tašiltu=urqitu* 'herbs and plants, verdure, green in a list of synonyms.[243]

---

ing," in M. Köckert & M. Nissinen eds., *Propheten in Mari, Assyrien, und Israel* (Göttingen, 2003), p. 144: "All these roles, tropes or concepts connected with the topic of female deities forming alliances with a king or crown prince originate in the human social system: one is the role of the beloved of the king in the trope of the 'sacred marriage.'"

[239] Line 65 from "Enmerkar and the lord of Aratta," *ETCSL*

[240] Lines 65-68 from "Enmerkar and the lord of Aratta," *ETCSL*.

[241] H. Vanstiphout, *op. cit.*, p. 59, translates the first clause as follows: "Thereupon the splendor in the sacred sky…"

[242] J. Halloran, *Sumerian Lexicon* (Los Angeles, 2006), p. 145. See also the discussion in M. Cohen, *An Annotated Sumerian Dictionary* (University Park, 2023), pp. 489, 780.

[243] Å. Sjöberg, "Hymns to Meslamtaea, Lugalgirra and Nanna-Suen in Honour of King Ibbisuen (Ibbisin) of Ur," *OrSuec* 19-20 (1970-71), p. 169.

In addition to the evidence adduced above, Sumerian Temple Hymns reference a divine garden in the sky. Thus it is that the third-millennium Keš Temple Hymn begins by invoking Enlil as follows: "The four corners of heaven became green for Enlil like a garden."[244] Here, then, is compelling testimony that a verdant garden-like structure was a conspicuous feature of the Mesopotamian sky and somehow associated with the four corners of heaven.

A luxuriant garden also features prominently in an early account of Creation preserved in the Sumerian hymn *Enki and the World Order*. In the hymn in question, luminous greenery sprouts forth at the god's ordering of the cosmos:

> He raised a holy crown over the upland plain. He fastened a lapis-lazuli beard to the high plain, and made it wear a lapis-lazuli headdress. He made this good place perfect with greenery in abundance.[245]

The phrase translated as "greenery in abundance" here—u_2-šim $giri_{17}$-zal-am_3—includes the same epithet used to describe Inanna's garden *and* the planet-goddess herself.

In order to determine if there was a celestial prototype for the Venus-garden described in early Sumerian literature, it is necessary to investigate whether analogous ideas are attested among other cultures. As documented in a previous chapter, the Skidi Pawnee held that Creation resulted from a sacred marriage between the planet Venus—conceptualized as the archetypal mother goddess—and Mars, the latter identified as the prototypical masculine power. The female star, in turn, was renowned for her celestial garden that was said to be "ever growing and ever green."[246] Thus, Skidi hymns invoked Venus as follows:

> She maintained a garden in the west in which there were fields of ripening corn and many buffalo, and from which sprang all streams of life.[247]

Venus's verdant, life-bearing garden is a central leitmotif in Skidi religious rituals. In the human sacrifice reenacting the *hieros gamos* between Mars and Venus, as noted previously, the Skidi priests were careful to ensure that the victim's blood

---

[244] Line 6 from "The Keš temple hymn," *ETCSL*.
[245] Lines 349-351 from "Enki and the world order," *ETCSL*.
[246] N. Curtis, *The Indians' Book* (New York, 1907), p. 102.
[247] R. Linton, "The Thunder Ceremony of the Pawnee," *Field Museum of Natural History* (1922), p. 5.

was channeled to a shallow pit below the scaffold.[248] The cavity in question was held to represent Venus's garden: "The pit symbolized the Garden of the Evening Star from which all life originates."[249]

The mere fact that the planet Venus was associated with a life-bearing garden by cultures in the New World as well as the Old should suffice to force comparativists to wake up to the reality that astral elements feature prominently in these archaic cosmogonic traditions. Especially significant is the fact that the Skidi sky-watchers, like those from Mesopotamia, described the planet Venus as a prototypical female power *and* as a participant in a sacred marriage of sorts, the successful performance of which was believed to promote fertility and prosperity throughout the land. Such converging thematic patterns, in our opinion, constitute compelling evidence that the Sumerian traditions attached to Inanna/Venus were directly inspired by memorable celestial events and thus empirical in nature.

But there is more. Inanna's bed, it will be remembered, was strewn with flowers and associated with garden-like imagery. Analogous conceptions are evident in traditional Skidi lore, wherein Venus's garden was specifically compared to a "bed":

> The pit symbolized the Garden of the Evening Star from which all life originates. The pit was called *Kusaru*, which in Pawnee simply means bed.[250]

And as Vanstiphout pointed out, Inanna's bed was also conceptualized as her womb. Here, too, it is possible to point to a precise parallel in Skidi myth. According to Linton, the pit identified as Venus's garden was also identified as her womb: "This pit was called *kusaru*, and represented the garden which the Evening Star kept in the west, or, according to another account, the reproductive organs of the Evening Star."[251]

Such widespread traditions beg the following question: Why would the planet Venus, or its extraterrestrial "garden," be likened to a womb or sexual organs? The probable answer is that Venus was conceptualized as a womb-like matrix whence all life originated—hence the Skidi tradition marking Venus as the source of "all

---

[248] V. del Chamberlain, *When Stars Came Down to Earth* (Los Altos, 1982), p. 65: "A few drops of the girl's blood would be allowed to drip into this symbolic garden."
[249] G. Weltfish, *The Lost Universe* (New York, 1965), p. 112.
[250] *Ibid.*, p. 112. See also R. Hall, *An Archaeology of the Soul* (Urbana, 1997), pp. 97-106.
[251] R. Linton, *op. cit.*, pp. 31-32.

life."²⁵² While such traditions have no conceivable reference in the present skies, the fact remains that analogous conceptions are attested in the Old World as well. Thus, an early epithet of the Venus-star among Mesopotamian sky-watchers was ^{d}ti-mu$_2$-a, "the divine source of all life."²⁵³

The same symbolism is attested at the very dawn of human civilization. Already in the third millennium BCE the Sumerian king Gudea can be found celebrating the sacred marriage, wherein the participating goddess (Bau) is invoked as "a green garden bearing fruit."²⁵⁴ Yet elsewhere in the very same inscription we read that: "Bau is the life source of Gudea."²⁵⁵

In perfect keeping with the symbolism associated with the Venusian garden, the *hieros gamos* between Inanna and the king credits her with being a source for new "life." In the following Sumerian hymn celebrating the sacred marriage of Ißme-Dagan, for example, Inanna's womb is extolled as a locus of life:

> Give him Inana your beloved daughter as a spouse. May they embrace each other forever! May the days of delight and sweetness last long in her holy embrace full of life!²⁵⁶

The word translated as "life" here is nam-ti. In the Sumerian language the prefix nam is employed to denote an abstract or collective noun and hence it serves to emphasize that whatever word it is combined with is the supreme manifestation of the power in question (nam-lugal, for example, denotes "kingship"). In the aforementioned passage, therefore, nam-ti denotes something like "Life" or "life-giving."²⁵⁷ The basic idea expressed here, evidently, is that Inanna's "lap" or womb represents the *fons et origo* of all life.²⁵⁸

The very same phrase is employed to denote the sacred temple wherein Inanna and Dumuzi reside as wife and husband: E-namtila. Described as a place of abundance and "long life," the temple is recalled as "the amazing source of the Land's radiance."²⁵⁹

---

²⁵² The fact that Venus served as the primordial hearth or *materia* (*mater*=mother) whereupon fire was drilled by the Martian warrior also contributed to this idea, needless to say.

²⁵³ F. Bruschweiler, *Inanna la déesse triomphante et vaincue dans la cosmologie sumérienne* (Leuven, 1988), p. 112. See also B. Hruška, "Das spätbabylonische Lehrgedict 'Inannas Erhöhung," *Archiv Orientalni* 37 (1969), p. 482, who observes: "In der sumerischen Zeile wird ^{d}ištar-kakkabi mit dem Namen ti-mú-a 'Leben erzeugende' wiedergeben."

²⁵⁴ Line 924 from "The building of Ningirsu's temple (Gudea, cylinders A and B)," *ETCSL*.

²⁵⁵ Line 654.

²⁵⁶ Lines 92-95 from "Išme-Dagan and Enlil's chariot: a *tigi* to Enlil (Išme-Dagan I)," *ETCSL*.

²⁵⁷ J. Hayes, *A Manual of Sumerian Grammar and Texts* (Malibu, 2000), p. 73.

²⁵⁸ Note the close parallel in Skidi lore: "Through her [Venus] it is possible for people to increase and crops to mature."

²⁵⁹ Lines C 31 from "A balbale (?) to Inana (Dumuzid-Inana P)," *ETSCL*.

Granted that the Sumerian Inanna-hymns treated above have some reference to the planet Venus, how is it possible to visualize or reconstruct the floral imagery from an astronomical perspective? Mesopotamian artworks depicting Inanna/Venus offer a wealth of insight: Thus early cylinder seals represent Inanna/Venus by an eight-pointed rosette (see figure one).[260] A close variation on this symbol appears in Mesopotamian artworks supposedly depicting the Sun (see figure two), thereby confirming its celestial provenance.[261] Certainly it must be admitted that, were the planet Venus to present such a form in the ancient sky, its conception as a "blossoming" flower or "garden" would be perfectly understandable.

Figure one

Figure two

Other early artworks help flesh out our understanding of the garden-imagery attached to Venus. Figure three depicts a stellar object as a four-spoked "wheel"-like form.[262] Early exemplars of this image have been discovered in the prehistoric

---

[260] Adapted from figure 8 in U. Moortgart-Correns, "Die Rosette—ein Schriftzeichen?" in *Altorientalische Forschungen* 21 (1994), p. 369. See also E. van Buren, "The Rosette in Mesopotamian Art," *Zeitschrift für Assyriologie XI* (1939), pp. 99-107.
[261] Adapted from BM 22963 in D. Collon, *First Impressions* (London, 1987), p. 42.
[262] Adapted from figure 84 in B. Teissier, *Egyptian Iconography on Syro-Palestinian Cylinder Seals of the Middle Bronze Age* (Fribourg, 1996), p. 67.

strata at Susa, conventionally dated to *circa* 4000 BCE (figure four).[263] As Petr Charvát pointed out in his discussion of these archaic artworks, there is good reason to believe that they inform the much later Mesopotamian representations of the Sun and Venus:

> Halaf pottery has other patterns that can also be interpreted as referring to later written and pictorial (iconographic) sources of ancient Mesopotamia. These patterns are a rosette, usually eight-pointed, and a four-pointed star. Both patterns are so similar that we could consider them as variations of one and the same graphic element.[264]

Figure three

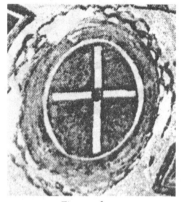

Figure four

It is to be noted that, in his discussion of these cruciform stellar images depicted on Susa pottery, Charvát suggested that they likely have reference to the world and its four quarters or cardinal directions. We would endorse this opinion,

---

[263] See the discussion in P. Harper et al eds., *The Royal City of Susa* (New York, 1992), p. 34ff.
[264] P. Charvát, *The Birth of the State* (Prague, 2013), p. 79.

provided that by "world" we understand the celestial landscape or "cosmos" as experienced by prehistoric sky-watchers around the globe. In this sense, then, the stellar image depicted in figure four should rightly be understood as a cosmogram illustrating the visual appearance of the prehistoric sky.[265]

Although the stellar form depicted in figure four does not have a recognizable counterpart in the present skies, it is possible to find virtually identical artworks in the New World as well. As a case in point, consider the glyph depicted in figure five.[266] Often described as a "quartered circle," the sign in question is known to denote the concept "turquoise" among various indigenous cultures of Mesoamerica.[267] According to the anthropologist Robert Hall, the glyph has reference to the four quarters of the world:

> This glyph is a circle divided into quarters, often with a central circle as a fifth element that makes the total design a 'quincunx'. Beyond the Mixtecs the quincunx was used by the Maya as a symbol of the earth divided into four quarters.[268]

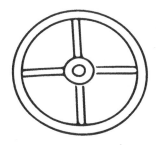

Figure five

Among the neighboring Aztecs a very similar sign is held to represent *tonalli*, a turquoise-colored "life force" imparted to humans at the moment of Creation (see figure six).[269] The word *tonalli* derives from the root *tona*, denoting the vital

---

[265] D. Talbott, *The Saturn Myth* (New York), pp. 120-144. K. Bassie-Sweet, *Maya Sacred Geography and the Creator Deities* (Norman, 2008), p. 61 observes: "The Maya cosmogram comprised four roads radiating from the center of the world to each of the four directional mountains."
[266] Adapted from Figure 12:2 in R. Hall, *An Archaeology of the Soul* (Urbana, 1997), p. 99. This is T-721 in J. Thompson's *A Catalog of Maya Hieroglyphs* (Norman, 1962), p. 309.
[267] E. Baird, "Stars and War at Cacaxtla," in R. Diehl & J. Berlo eds., *Mesoamerican After the Decline of Teotihuacan*…(Washington D.C., 1989), p. 117.
[268] R. Hall, *op. cit.*, pp. 98-99.
[269] Adapted from M. Graulich, *Myths of Ancient Mexico* (Norman, 1997), p. 48. See also the

energy radiating outwards from the Sun, the latter known as *Tonatiuh*, "he who goes forth radiating *tonalli*."[270] As James Maffie pointed out in his recent book on Aztec philosophy, the *tonalli* was intimately associated with Native American ideas regarding the four corners of heaven:

> In sum, *tonalli* diffuses over the earth's surface and its inhabitants, and in doing so energizes and influences them. Tlaltecuhtli [the earth mother] is constantly bathed and infused with heat-life energy coming from Tonatiuh and the four corners, and consequently contains a vast reserve of *tonalli*.[271]

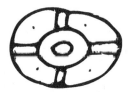

Figure six

Although the archaic images depicted in figures two through four can only be described as anomalous by reference to the present sky, the very fact that analogous images of the primal "sun" can be found around the globe strongly suggests that they accurately represent a unique astronomical constellation as witnessed by prehistoric humans.[272] Yet once grant this possibility and the various shards of cosmogonic myth suddenly begin to fall into place like the pieces of a jigsaw puzzle. Recall again the archaic Sumerian tradition likening Enlil's verdant garden to a greening of the four corners of heaven: "The four corners of heaven became green for Enlil like a garden."[273] Can there be any question that such traditions would be explained at once by the former presence of a constellation like that represented in figures five and six, each of which was expressly connected with the four quarters of the cosmos and turquoise?

---

discussion in M. León-Portilla & E. Shorris, *In the Language of Kings* (New York, 2001), pp. 21-22.

[270] J. Maffie, *Aztec Philosophy* (Boulder, 2014), p. 212. See also M. Izeki, *Conceptionualization of 'xihuitl'* (Oxford, 2008), p. 34, who defines *tona* as "the vital energy necessary for all life, especially to ripen plants."

[271] *Ibid.*, p. 272.

[272] For a precise counterpart from Bronze Age Old Europe, see M. Green, *The Sun-Gods of Ancient Europe* (London, 1991), p. 70.

[273] Line 6 from "The Keš temple hymn," *ETCSL*.

Conclusion

Venus has been associated with gardens since time immemorial. Already at the dawn of history in Mesopotamia, Sumerian hymns told of a sacred marriage between Venus and Dumuzi that produced a wondrous garden of verdant greenery. So, too, the Skidi Pawnee of the North American Plains held that Creation was sparked by a *hieros gamos* between the planets Venus and Mars and that a verdant life-giving garden was associated with the former planet. Such traditions did not originate by mere happenstance or allegorical speculation; rather, they are best explained by independant observations of an extraordinary celestial landscape, long since disappeared.

The perennial search for Venus's elusive paradisal garden will inevitably lead to a celestial configuration like that depicted in figure four above. As evidenced by the Sumerian tradition celebrating Enlil's garden, the garden in question presented a turquoise-green color and was intimately associated with the four corners of heaven. The rich green color of the celestial garden, in turn, gave rise to the conception that it was a locus of verdant greenery and fertility—indeed, the source of all life, a belief-system echoed in the epithets describing Inanna/Venus as the "divine source of all life." The Skidi report that Venus' garden was "ever growing and ever green" and the locus "from which sprang all streams of life" conforms with this archetypal memory.

08 The Blossom of Creation

> One-sentence myths and allusions have as much importance as lengthy epic-style narratives.[274]

> The beauty of vegetation as an image of human beauty is frequent in Sumerian poetry; indeed, it appears to be archetypal.[275]

An archaic Sumerian kenning for the Time of Beginning was "since the day when the (first) blossom came forth."[276] Like so many idiomatic expressions, this kenning contains a number of clues pointing to lost worlds and long-forgotten traditions of planetary gods in full bloom.

The word translated as "blossom" here is ul. As Gebhard Selz pointed out in an important study, the same word also denotes rosette or flower:

> The Sumerian word for the 'rosette' is ul. The most common usage of the word is in the phrase 'since time immemorial', in Sumerian u_4-ul-li-a-ta, which should be analyzed as *u_4-ul-é-a-ta, literally 'since the day when the (first) blossom came forth'. Thus the rosette refers to the beginning of life, the creation of the world.[277]

Why a rosette should be linked to Creation or the origin of life is never addressed by Selz nor by any other scholar, so far as I know. Yet the obvious

---

[274] W. Lambert, "Kosmogonie," in E. Ebeling & B. Meisnner eds., *Reallexikon der Assyriologie, Vol. 6* (Berlin, 1980-1983), p. 219.
[275] J. Black, *Reading Sumerian Poetry* (London, 1998), p. 128.
[276] Å. Sjöberg, "In the Beginning," in T. Abusch ed., *Riches Hidden in Secret Places* (Winona Lake, 2002), p. 238.
[277] G. Selz, "Early Dynastic Vessels in 'Ritual' Contexts," *Wiener Zeitschrift für die Kunde des Morgenlandes* 94 (2004), p. 201. See also Å. Sjöberg, *op. cit.*, p. 238.

similarity to the Egyptian traditions attached to Horus and the lotus of Creation suggests that a natural-historical explanation might be in order.

An important clue to the symbolism in question is presented by the fact that, in addition to the meanings "rosette," "flower," and "to blossom," ul also denotes "star."[278] Is it possible that the Sumerian kenning preserves a riddling allusion to a stellar flower?

It is well-documented that the planet Venus, as Inanna, was specifically identified with the rosette already in the earliest pictographic system from Uruk III (circa 3000 BCE).[279] The rosette served as Inanna's special standard throughout the third millennium as evinced by Gudea's royal inscriptions: "And he placed the rosette, the standard of Inanna, in front of them."[280] Rosettes, in fact, are ubiquitous in the prehistoric iconography attached to Inanna/Venus, as noted by Elizabeth Simpson:

> It appears on vessels, in inlay, and on wall decorations from the Eanna precinct of Inanna at Uruk, as well as on related seals. These early rosettes commonly had eight petals, with pointed ends.[281]

Yet here, too, questions abound: Why would the planet Venus be identified with a rosette-like form? This question, in turn, is indissolubly related to another question of fundamental import to a proper understanding of Mesopotamian religion: What is the relationship between the eight-petalled rosette and the eight-rayed star that eventually came to serve as a symbol of Venus?

The simplest answer is to view the two signs as mere variations upon a common celestial prototype—in this case, something about the former appearance of the planet Venus.[282] The esteemed historian of Sumerian art, Elizabeth van Buren, drew a similar conclusion nearly a century ago: "The eight-pointed star of Istar, frequently illustrated on monuments of the second and first millennia, was an

---

[278] P. Steinkeller, "On Stars and Stripes in Ancient Mesopotamia," *Iranica Antiqua* 37 (2002), p. 363: "The essential identity between 'star' (and therefore deity') and 'flower' on the level of symbolic representation continued to be recognized by artists down to the very end of the ancient Mesopotamian civilization."

[279] E. van Buren, "The Rosette in Mesopotamian Art," *Zeitschrift für Assyriologie XI* (1939), pp. 99ff. See also U. Moortgat-Correns, "Die Rosette—ein Schriftzeichen?" *Altorientalische Forschungen* 21 (1994), pp. 359-371.

[280] Line 385 from "The building of Ningirsu's temple (Gudea, cylinders A and B)," *ETCSL*.

[281] E. Simpson, *The Gordion Wooden Objects, Vol. 1* (Leiden, 2010), p. 88.

[282] P. Steinkeller, "On Stars and Stripes in Ancient Mesopotamia," *Iranica Antiqua* 37 (2002), p. 362 notes that the Mesopotamians regarded the star and rosette "to be essentially identical."

adapted form of the archaic rosette as may be clearly seen from the star carved on top of a kudurru from Susa."[283]

Granted this explanation of the evidence, we must reckon with the possibility that the planet Venus formerly presented the appearance of an eight-rayed star or eight-petalled rosette. If so, we would have a ready explanation for the otherwise anomalous Mesopotamian artworks referenced in chapter one, wherein Venus was depicted as an eight-pointed star in conjunction with the sun (see figure two in that chapter). The fact that other so-called "sun"-glyphs substitute a rosette for the eight-pointed star supports this deduction (see figure one below).

Figure one

It is notable that the word ul was employed to characterize Inanna/Venus in the specific context of her sexual union with Dumuzi. Witness the following Sumerian hymn describing the sacred marriage rite:

> Young lady, the kohl of the king, Inanna, the kohl of Dumuzi, Blossoming one, adorned with charm—To the shepherd in the stall she goes, To Dumuzi, in the sheepfold she goes… Dumuzi [came forth] like the daylight.[284]

In the passage in question, the epithet "Blossoming one" (=ul) is a patent reference to the glorious beauty of the planet-goddess.[285] Indeed, the same term

---

[283] E. van Buren, "The Rosette in Mesopotamian Art," *Zeitschrift für Assyriologie XI* (1939), p. 105. E. Simpson, *The Gordion Wooden Objects, Vol. 1* (Leiden, 2010), p. 88 has recently defended a similar position: "These early rosettes commonly had eight petals, with pointed ends, a feature that may have led to the star-like rosette of Ishtar in later periods."

[284] Lines 1-15 from "A song of Inana and Dumuzid (Dumuzid-Inana V)," as translated in Y. Sefati, *op. cit.*, p. 257.

[285] Jeremy Black, in his translation of this text, renders the phrase as "full of joy, adorned in loveliness."

is used to describe Inanna/Venus in the following passage as well: "Lady [Inanna] whom Ningal has joyously made attractive with beauty."[286]

The statement that "Dumuzi [came forth] like the daylight" warrants additional scrutiny. The word translated as "daylight" here is UD, a logogram denoting "sun," "day," and the sun-god Utu. Although most scholars have been inclined to see metaphor at work here—hence the translation "daylight"—we would suggest that a more literal interpretation is in order and that Dumuzi is here being described as a celestial body. Is there any evidence, then, that Dumuzi had a celestial dimension?

In fact, the evidence is unequivocal: Dumuzi was early on conceptualized as a star.[287] For our purposes here it is telling that Iddin-Dagan's marriage hymn likens the king, as Dumuzi, to a "sun-like" body during his union with the planet Venus (as Inanna):

> She embraces her beloved spouse, holy Inana embraces him. She shines like daylight on the great throne dais and makes the king position himself next (?) to her like the sun.[288]

Here, then, is compelling testimony that Dumuzi was conceptualized as a sun while embraced by Inanna/Venus.[289] Yet despite the fact that Iddin-Dagan's marriage hymn evidently describes a conjunction of planetary bodies, this particular passage and its attendant celestial symbolism has elicited virtually no discussion from scholars.

Additional insight into the archaic symbolism in question is provided by the royal inscriptions of Gudea. According to this king's brief allusion to the sacred marriage between the storm-god Ningirsu and the mother goddess Bau it was marked by the rising of the sun:

> Upon entering her women's chamber, Lagaš was filled with bounty, the day shone bright and the 'sun of Lagaš' (i.e., Utu) raised his head in the land.[290]

---

[286] Line 1 from "A *tigi* to Inana (Inana E)," *ETCSL*.

[287] D. Foxvog, "Astral Dumuzi," in M. Cohen ed., *The Tablet and the Scroll* (Bethesda, 1993), pp. 103-108. See also E. Cochrane, *Starf*cker* (Ames, 2007), pp. 28-37.

[288] Lines 199-202 as translated in J. Black et al, *The Literature of Ancient Sumer* (Oxford, 2004), p. 267. P. Jones, "Mesopotamian Sacred Marriage Hymn Iddin-Dagan A," *Journal of the American Oriental Society* 123:2 (2003), p. 295 translates as "Shining sunnily, the king, like the Sun-god, sat down next to her on the throne."

[289] See C. Woods, "Sons of the Sun: The Mythological Foundations of the First Dynasty of Uruk," *JANER* 12 (2012), p. 90 on Dumuzi's identification with the Sun.

[290] Lines 925-928 from "The building of Ningirsu's Temple (Gudea, cylinders A and B)," as

What is merely implicit in Iddin-Dagan's hymn to Inanna/Venus is here made explicit: It is in the singular context of the *hieros gamos* that the sun-god "raised his head in the land," presumably for the first time. The phraseology employed here is significant, for the very same language is routinely used to describe the epiphany of the sun. Witness the following hymn to Utu: "He has raised his head over the mountains; he is indeed their king!"[291]

It is doubtless no coincidence that this very same formulaic expression is regularly employed to describe the Sumerian king as he enters into sexual union with Inanna/Venus. Witness line 187 from Iddin-Dagan's marriage hymn: "The king goes to her holy thighs with head held high." The very same phrase appears in "A song of Inana and Dumuzi (D1)" during an account of the sacred marriage: "With head high he goes into the holy embrace of Inana."[292] The fundamental import of such passages, in our view, is that Dumuzi was conceptualized as transfigured into a "sun" as a result of his sexual union with the planet Venus. This, in essence, is the central mystery encoded in the Sumerian sacred marriage rite: By impersonating Dumuzi in a simulated marriage with Inanna/Venus, the Sumerian king aspired to secure his status as the sun-like "god" or "king" of his people.

This archaic symbolism is most clearly expressed in the third-millennium text *Enmerkar and the Lord of Aratta*, called "probably the finest piece of poetic storytelling ever produced by Old Babylonian authors."[293] There we learn of the early king Enmerkar who, as the beloved of Inanna, engages in a sacred marriage with the planet-goddess, although much of the language and imagery is allusive and cryptic in nature.[294] Shortly thereafter we find Enmerkar described as follows: "The Sun-god of the Land raised his head."[295] In the final lines of the epic Enmerkar credits the planet-goddess with investing him with kingship: "The ever-sparkling lady gives me my kingship."[296]

The word translated as "ever-sparkling" here is mul-mul-e, "to shine, or radiate," a verb formed from the Sumerian word for star (mul) and hence referring to the luminous splendor of Venus itself. The clear import of this passage, beyond any shadow of a doubt, is that kingship was a gift of the planet Venus.[297] Far from

---

translated in Y. Sefati, *Love Songs in Sumerian Literature* (Jerusalem, 1998), p. 34.
[291] Line 21 from "A Hymn to Utu (Utu B)," *ETCSL*.
[292] Line 66 from "A song of Inana and Dumuzi (D1)," *ETCSL*.
[293] H. Vanstsiphout, *Epics of Sumerian Kings* (Leiden, 2004), p. 49.
[294] C. Woods, "Sons of the Sun: The Mythological Foundations of the First Dynasty of Uruk," *JANER* 12 (2012), p. 33 notes: "Enmerkar, of course, represents Dumuzi in the sacred marriage ritual."
[295] Line 309 as translated in H. Vanstiphout, *op. cit.*, p. 86.
[296] Line 632 from "Enmerkar and the lord of Aratta," *ETCSL*.
[297] E. Cochrane, *On Fossil Gods and Forgotten Worlds* (Ames, 2021), pp. 162-176. See also the

being figurative in nature, the language of *Enmerkar and the lord of Aratta* is best understood in literal fashion: It is the planet Venus who "makes" the king by enveloping him with a starry mantle or crown of "glory." Otherwise stated: The Sumerian king gains universal sovereignty solely as a result of his *hieros gamos* with Venus, after which he shines forth as a "sun."

To return to the kenning quoted at the outset of this chapter: In Mesopotamia, much as in Egypt, Creation was remembered as the "day when the 'first' blossom came forth" precisely because, at the Time of Beginning, the nascent sun first rose to brilliance while in conjunction with a flower-like star (see appendix five). The union in question, associated as it was with a spectacular greening of the cosmos, was remembered as producing universal joy, abundance, and prosperity—all connotations of the word $giri_{17}$-zal. It was this momentous event that the Sumerian king was trying to reenact by simulating sexual intercourse with Inanna/Venus, for it was only through sexual union with Venus that universal sovereignty and prosperity was achieved.

---

discussion in J. Westenholz, "King by Love of Inanna," in *NIN* 1 (2000), pp. 75-82.

09 The Thundergod and Creation

Lightning was depicted as the heavenly fire.[298]

The source of the lightning is the sun, the heavenly fire: the Thunder-god gets fire from the solar wheel by rotating his lightning-club in the nave of the solar wheel.[299]

Cosmogonic myths from around the globe report that Creation was sparked by the Thundergod inseminating or "marrying" the earth, as a result of which all living things were produced. The archaeologist Marija Gimbutas documented the stubborn persistence of these archaic ideas among Baltic peoples well into modern times:

> Such beliefs among the Balts and Slavs are universal and certainly stem from very early times. The earth is barren until the Thunder strikes her in the springtime—until in his epiphany of thunder Perkunas weds the Mother Earth, Zemyna.[300]

Sacred traditions from ancient India preserve remnants of analogous conceptions. Thus it is that the *Rig Veda* includes scattered allusions to Parjanya, an archaic Indo-European Thundergod whose name is cognate with that of the Lithuanian Perkunas.[301] In addition to hurling fertilizing thunderbolts, Parjanya is

---

[298] C. Blinkenberg, *The Thunderbolt in Religion and Folklore* (Cambridge, 1911), p. 42.
[299] M. Gimbutas, "Perkunas/Perun: The Thunder God of the Balts and Slavs," *Journal of Indo-European Studies* 1 (1973), p. 475.
[300] *Ibid.*, p. 471.
[301] R. Jacobson, "Linguistic Evidence in Comparative Mythology," in S. Rudy ed., *Selected*

credited with depositing the *garbha*, translated alternately as "embryo" or "germ of the Beginning":

> The winds blow forth; the lightning bolts fly. The plants shoot up; the sun swells. Refreshment arises for all creation, when Parjanya aids the earth with his semen…. (Parjanya), come nearby with this thundering, pouring down the waters as the lord, our father. Roar! Thunder! Set an embryo![302]

Parjanya, like Perkunas, was celebrated for his marriage with the earth. This idea is alluded to in the following passage from the *Atharva Veda*, the second oldest collection of Sanskrit texts: "To the earth, the wife of Parjanya."[303]

It is significant that the Vedic Thundergod was believed to reside within the center of the earth (*nabha prthivyah*). The *Rig Veda* attests to this idea: "In the navel of the earth, on the mountains he has established his dwelling place."[304]

While such traditions will never find a satisfactory explanation by reference to the natural world as we know it, wherein the atmospheric Thundergod (or lightning) has no conceivable relationship to the center of the earth, they mirror ancient traditions surrounding the Fire-god, who was likewise represented as residing at the center or "navel" of the earth (see the discussion in Chapter X).[305]

Looking beyond the Old World, it is possible to discern analogous conceptions among the indigenous cultures of the New World as well. According to Skidi Pawnee tradition, the Thundergod was known by the name of Paruxti and it was he who enlivened the earth with his semen:

> The first thunder in the spring was thought to be the voice of Paruxti, a deity who was the messenger of Tirawa…He passed over the land in a storm, and as he spoke, the earth awakened, and life was kindled anew.[306]

Writings, Vol. VII (Berlin, 1985), p. 20. See also T. Gamkrelidze & V. Ivanov, *Indo-European and the Indo-Europeans* (Berlin, 1995), p. 694.
[302] *RV* 5:83:4-7.
[303] *AV* 12:1:42 as translated in M. Bloomfield, *Hymns of the Atharva-Veda* (Oxford, 1897), p. 204.
[304] *RV* 9:82:3.
[305] See *RV* 3:5:9, wherein Agni is invoked: "Praised, the young one has flared up through his kindling, upon the summit of heaven and the navel of the earth."
[306] R. Linton, "The Thunder Ceremony of the Pawnee," *Field Museum of Natural History* 5 (Chicago, 1922), pp. 9-10.

During the annual Thunder ritual Skidi priests joined in dance and chanted songs that celebrated the Thundergod's propensity for fertilizing the earth. In one such song Paruxti is credited with having penetrated into Mother Earth:

> They have put new life into the earth. Paruxti speaks through the clouds, And the power has entered Mother Earth. The earth has received the powers from above.[307]

Much the same idea is evident in the following song:

> The power is now hidden in the earth. The earth now possesses the power. Paruxti's power is the power in the earth.[308]

The indigenous cultures of Mesoamerica likewise preserved a wealth of traditions about the Thundergod's seminal role in Creation.[309] In the K'iche' Maya text *Popol Vuh* the Thundergod Huracan is depicted as the supreme procreative force generating fertility and abundance: "[Huracan] you who give abundance and new life, and you who give daughters and sons."[310] Elsewhere in the same sacred document the god is reported to have sparked Creation:

> Then they arranged for the germination and creation of the trees and bushes, the germination of all life and creation, in the darkness and in the night, by Heart of the Sky, who is called Huracan.[311]

In the passage quoted above, Huracan is assigned the epithet $U_4ux\ cah$, "Heart of the Sky."[312] A celestial power is evidently being described. Yet the same god was also known by the epithet "Heart of the earth"—$u_4ux\ uleu$—thereby recalling the residence of Vedic Agni at the navel of the earth and the summit of heaven.[313]

The highest deity in the K'iche' pantheon, Huracan was credited with being the "source of all energy and life in the universe."[314] Indeed, it was the Thunder-

---

[307] *Ibid.*, p. 10.
[308] *Ibid.*, p. 11.
[309] O. Mazeriegos, *Art and Myth of the Ancient Maya* (New Haven, 2017), p. 79 observes of K'awiil/lightning: "A phenomenon that is often associated with the fertilization of the earth in Mesoamerica."
[310] A. Christenson, *Popol Vuh* (New York, 2003), p. 289.
[311] *Ibid.*, p. 70.
[312] D. Tedlock, *op. cit.*, p. 341.
[313] *RV* 3:5:9.
[314] M. Preuss, "A Study of Jurakán of the *Popol Vuh*," in E. Magana & P. Mason eds., *Myth*

god's union with the earth that set Creation in motion: "The sky [i.e., Huracan as the Heart of the Sky] represents the male component of the fecundating act, and the earth symbolizes the womb."[315] Such traditions mirror the Vedic hymns celebrating Parjanya's demiurgic feats from within the navel of the earth, the latter region being conceptualized as "womb of everything" and "the source of life, energy, or reality."[316]

The name Huracan is thought to denote "One Leg" (*jun raqan*).[317] Although scholars have been hard-pressed to offer a coherent explanation for this peculiar moniker, it has been observed that it seemingly marks the K'iche' god as being a close cognate of such Mesoamerican gods as Tezcatlipoca and K'awiil, each of whom was represented as one-legged:

> In its simplest interpretation, *Juraqan* means 'One Leg.' Belief in a one-legged god was widespread throughout Precolumbian Mesoamerica. An important example was the Maya god K'awiil (God GII of the Palenque Triad, who is often depicted with one anthropomorphic foot and the other a serpent), associated with kingship and the sky.[318]

We will return to the intriguing subject of the one-legged god in a chapter to follow.

Tohil

Another name for Huracan was Tohil, a one-legged god whom Karl Taube identifies as "the Quichean god of lightning and storms."[319] The god's name is thought to derive from the Mixe-Zoque word for thunder: *toh-mel*.[320]

In addition to his role as Thundergod, Tohil was also remembered as the prototypical driller of fire. According to the *Popol Vuh*, the god generated fire by twirling about on his leg:

---

and the Imaginary in the New World (Amsterdam, 1986), p. 360.
[315] *Ibid.*, pp. 362-363.
[316] *AV* 12:1:43. See also J. Gonda, *Aspects of Early Visnuism* (Utrecht, 1954), p. 85.
[317] K. Bassie-Sweet, *Maya Sacred Geography and the Creator Deities* (Norman, 2008), p. 103. See also N. Henne, *Reading Popol Wuj* (Tucson, 2020), pp. 91-92.
[318] A. Christenson, *Popol Vuh* (New York, 2003), p. 70.
[319] K. Taube, *The Major Gods of Ancient Yucatan* (Washington D.C., 1992), p. 76. See also D. Tedlock, *op. cit.*, p. 300.
[320] A. Christenson, *op. cit.*, p. 211. See also D. Tedlock, *op. cit.*, p. 343.

Then he brought forth fire. He twist drilled inside his shoe.[321]

It is to be noted that the indigenous authors of the *Popol Vuh* elsewhere identify Tohil with Quetzalcoatl. The following passage is representative in this regard: "Tohil is the god of the Yaqui people, who they call Yolcuat Quitzalcuat."[322]

Tohil is elsewhere identified with the Morning Star *Junajpu*, or Hun Hunahpu, much as we might expect given his identification with Quetzalcoatl.[323] How, then, are we to square this particular identification with the traditions identifying Tohil as a thundergod?

In Mesoamerica there is a notable tendency for Morning Star avatars to assume the attributes of the archetypal Thundergod. A striking example of this phenomenon is offered by the Tz'utujil (Maya) thundergod Santiago, who was known as *nima chu'mil*, "the Great Star"—i.e., the very epithet commonly ascribed to the Maya Morning Star.[324] Yet the same star-god was elsewhere conceptualized as an agent of lightning and storm:

> [Santiago] is the principal deity that brings fertility to the earth…
> In Tz'utujil cosmology, the sword of Santiago also represents lightning that clefts the earth to allow germinating seeds to grow…
> Santiago is also analogous to the lowland Maya god Chak who wields an axe-like lightning bolt associated with both war and cracking open the primordial earth to allow maize to germinate and grow.[325]

As a lightning-wielding god that cracks open the primordial earth to bring forth maize, the Tz'utujil Morning Star recalls the Nahuat Nanahuatl, who was widely celebrated for his role in splitting open Sustenance Mountain and thereby releasing the first foodstuffs.[326] Most significant, perhaps, is the fact that Nanahuatl—invoked as "Old Thunderbolt"—was explicitly remembered as the penetra-

---

[321] A. Christenson, *op. cit.*, p. 214.
[322] *Ibid.*, p. 231.
[323] B. Tedlock, "The Road of Light," in A. Aveni ed., *The Sky in Mayan Literature* (Oxford, 1992), p. 28. Dennis Tedlock, interestingly, pointed to a possible relationship with Mars: "Tahil's closest apparent relationships are to Hun Hunahpu, with whom he shares a 1 Ahau birth date marked by a heliacal rise of Mars."
[324] G. Cook & T. Offit, *Indigenous Religion and Cultural Performance in the New Maya World* (Albuquerque, 2013), p. 7 quote a native informant as follows: "The old ones said that the great star [*nima chu'mil*] that appears in the morning before the sunrise is Santiago."
[325] A. Christenson, *Art and Society in a Highland Maya Community* (2010), p. 134.
[326] J. Taggart, *Nahuat Myth and Social Structure* (Austin, 1997), p. 109.

tor of earth: "They [modern Nahuat traditions] describe how Nanawatzin and the other lightning-bolts break open Sustenance Mountain much as a man penetrates a woman in the act of love."[327] Nanahuatl's role as the lightning-like penetrator of the Earth during Creation marks him as a prototypical masculine force, analogous to the Vedic Parjanya and Baltic Perkunas. Recall again the passage quoted earlier: "The earth is barren until the Thunder strikes her in the springtime—until in his epiphany of thunder Perkunas weds the Mother Earth, Zemyna."[328]

Tezcatlipoca

The Aztec god Tezcatlipoca offers a paradigmatic example of the Thundergod and, as such, perhaps the closest New World parallel to the Greek god Zeus. Like Zeus, Tezcatlipoca was conceptualized as the King of the Gods and archetypal sovereign. And much like the Greek god, Tezcatlipoca was intimately associated with lightning, thunder, and other meteorological phenomena.

As noted earlier, scholars have long recognized that Tezcatlipoca offers a close parallel to the K'iche' Huracan (the Aztec god was commonly depicted with one leg, for example).[329] The epithet *Tepeyollotl*, "heart of the mountain," recalls Huracan's name "Heart of the earth" and encodes the god's connection with the innermost regions of the earth or Underworld.[330] And as a denizen of the earth's interior, Tezcatlipoca would appear to be functionally analogous to, if not ultimately identical with, the fire-god Xiuhtecuhtli (more than one scholar, in fact, has drawn this very conclusion).

Tezcatlipoca's intimate connection with the earth's interior is also attested in religious iconography. Thus, a popular scene on Mesoamerican artworks shows the god springing forth from the body of the earth mother (see figure one). Henry Nicholson called attention to the cosmogonical significance of this iconography many years ago:

> Since the god on our carving appears springing or emerging naked from the *chalchihuitl* symbol on the abdomen of the earth monster, the most obvious interpretation of this scene would seem to be one of birth or genesis from out of the heart of the earth on the date 2. Acatl.[331]

---

[327] *Ibid.*, p. 92.
[328] M. Gimbutas, "Perkunas/Perun: The Thunder God of the Balts and Slavs," *Journal of Indo-European Studies* 1 (1973), p. 471.
[329] See figure five in *Codex Fejérváry-Mayer*, for example.
[330] G. Olivier, *Mockeries and Metamorphoses of an Aztec God* (Boulder, 2003), p. 97 writes: "Tepeyollotl means 'heart of the mountain,' namely the interior of the earth."
[331] H. Nicholson, "The Birth of the Smoking Mirror," *Archaeology* 7:3 (1955), p. 170.

Figure one

The popularity of this image across Mesoamerica belies its importance in Aztec cosmogony. This, in turn, prompts the question: What specific episode in Creation were the Aztec artists trying to convey by depicting Tezcatlipoca springing forth from the heart of the earth? According to the *Codex Chimalpopoca,* the date 2 *Acatl,* or 2 Reed, is the date traditionally associated with the prototypical drilling of the New Fire:

> Now, it was in a year 2 Reed that the skies were [again] smoked. This is how we ourselves exist, how the fire drill ignited…[Yes,] this is how the fire drill ignited, when the fire appeared [for the new-fire ceremony]. Now, it was dark for twenty-five years. Well, it was in the year 1 Rabbit that the sky was established…And after the fire drill had ignited—after Tezcatlipoca had drilled fire—he smoked the skies once more, and this was in a year 2 Reed.[332]

Tezcatlipoca's explicit connection with the inaugural drilling of fire, coupled with his one-leggedness, parallels the traditions associated with Tohil, the prototypical fire-driller in the *Popol Vuh.* How interesting, then, to find that the *Codex Borbonicus* (folio 34) depicts the New Fire being drilled in a *chalchihuitl*-like structure exactly like that associated with the pioruetting Tezcatlipoca in figure one (see figure two).

---

[332] J. Bierhorst, translator. *History and Mythology of the Aztecs: The Codex Chimalpopoca* (Tucson, 1992), p. 144.

Figure two

Recalling the fundamental affinity between the drilled fire and the origin of the "sun" in the Aztec traditions surrounding Nanahuatl, we are led to deduce that the sacred traditions attached to Tezcatlipoca's prototypical "drilling" likely shared a similar cosmogonical significance and natural history. Certainly it is of interest to find that Tezcatlipoca is said to have been transformed into a sun *in illo tempore*:

> In the beginning, the world was in almost total darkness, and a sun was needed to illuminate it. According to the *Historia de los mexicanos por sus pinturas*, Tezcatlipoca turned himself into a sun, and that was the real beginning of an era.[333]

---

[333] M. Graulich, *Myths of Ancient Mexico* (Norman, 1997), p. 63.

It will be noted that Tezcatlipoca's metamorphosis into a sun was said to have occurred at the Time of Beginning, when the world was in near total darkness, thereby recalling the circumstances prevailing when Nanahuatl was transformed into the prototypical sun. The same cosmogonic history evidently informs Aztec artworks depicting the drilling of fire: Witness the scene illustrated in figure two, wherein the temple is known as *Tlillan*, literally "House of Darkness."[334]

In lieu of Tezcatlipoca's identification as the primordial "sun" and prototypical fire-driller, it is important to remember that the two mythological themes were fundamentally analogous (recall that the New Fire ceremony commemorated the "birth" or creation of the new sun Nanahuatl=Tonatiuh). In this sense, then, the testimony of the Aztec traditions surrounding Tezcatlipoca, like the traditions attached to Nanahuatl, leads one to deduce that the drilling of the first fire was functionally analogous to the creation of the "sun."

To summarize our findings in this chapter: According to the express testimony of the Amerindian mythmakers, Creation was conceptualized as the insemination of Mother Earth by the Thundergod or by analogous gods such as Huracan, Tohil, and Nanahuatl (see appendix six). Thus it is possible to posit a fundamental affinity between the Thundergod and Fire-god: As the Thundergod penetrated into and inseminated Mother Earth, thereby implanting an embryo and creating all life so, too, did the Fire-god generate all life from within the navel of the earth-goddess.[335] Likewise, the drilling of fire by the "twirling" of the Thundergod Tohil's single leg offers a precise functional parallel to the drilling of fire in the hearth.[336]

---

[334] D. Carrasco, *City of Sacrifice* (Boston, 1999), p. 100. See also the discussion in M. Jansen & G. Jimenez, *Time and the Ancestors* (Leiden, 2017), pp. 407-408.

[335] Agni appears as the *garbham* of prototypical fire-drilling at the time of Creation. See *RV* X:184:3.

[336] D. Tedlock, *Breath on the Mirror* (Albuquerque, 1993), p. 17: "So there he was, standing on one leg, and his foot was the point of a fire drill and his sandal held the socket."

10 The Coupling of Heaven and Earth

He who has read the writings of the ancients and has lived much in books, he knows that Zeus once loved the lovely Semele.[337]

The classic example of the ἱερος γαμος [*hieros gamos*] is the alliance between the sky-god and the earth-goddess, in which cosmic life finds its origin. This conception is universal and is found among numerous peoples…The fruit of this marriage is always new life.[338]

Zeus as sky-father is in essential relation to an earth-mother. Her name varies from place to place and from time to time…everywhere and always either patent or latent, the earth-mother is there as the necessary correlative and consort of the sky-father.[339]

The idea that Heaven and Earth engaged in a *hieros gamos in illo tempore* is one of the world's oldest and most widespread cosmogonic themes.[340] An early Sumerian hymn states simply: "Heaven impregnated, Earth gave birth."[341] *The Debate Between Tree and Bird* describes the coupling as fol-

---

[337] Lines 452-453 of Euripides, *Hippolytus* as translated by D. Grene in D. Grene & R. Lattimore, *Greek Tragedies, Vol. 1* (Chicago, 1960), p. 252.
[338] C. J. Bleeker, *Hathor and Thoth* (Leiden, 1973), p. 95.
[339] A. B. Cook, *Zeus, Vol. 1* (New York, 1964), p. 779.
[340] M. West, *Theogony* (Oxford, 1966), p. 199 observes: "The marriage of Earth and Sky is a very common mythological motif." See also J. Lisman, *At the Beginning: Cosmogony, Theogony and Anthropogeny in Sumerian texts of the Third and Second Millennium BCE* (Leiden, 2013), p. 10: "The cosmic marriage between heaven and earth, which can be found in the oldest Sumerian literature."
[341] J. Black, "The Sumerians and Their Landscape," in T. Abusch ed., *Riches Hidden in Secret Places* (Winona Lake, 2002), p. 56, citing the Šumunda grass poem translated by Samuel Kramer.

lows: "An, the exalted heaven, had intercourse with the vast earth."[342] Yet another hymn reports: "As the heaven inseminated the earth, (so that) vegetation became abundant."[343] Leo Oppenheim, surveying the relevant Mesopotamian traditions, offered the following general summary:

> The opposition heaven-earth is basic in Mesopotamian cosmography, although Sumerian theogonic speculations posit an original sexual union between the two, whereupon earth gave birth to gods, mankind, and animals.[344]

Heaven and Earth are commonly paired in Indo-European tradition as well. The idea of the sovereign sky-god entering into a sexual union with Mother Earth is a familiar motif in ancient Greek lore. According to the cosmogony preserved in Hesiod's *Theogony*, a sexual union between Ouranos and Gaia produced the gods:

> Celebrate the holy race of deathless gods who are for ever, those that were born of Earth and starry Heaven.[345]

The *Rig Veda* includes a number of hymns wherein Heaven and Earth are invoked as a couplet. The following hymn is representative in this regard: "O Heaven (our) father, Earth (our) guileless mother."[346] Stephanie Jamison and Joel Brereton, the translators of the *Rig Veda*, offered the following commentary on this state of affairs:

> In the Rgveda, Heaven as a divinity is generally paired with the female Earth, who is frequently referred to as 'mother,' with the two a complementary parental pair. They are normally grammatically joined in a dual *dvandva* compound (*dyava-prthivi*), and several hymns are dedicated to this couple.[347]

According to the *Aitareya Brahmana*, the two primordial gods were involved in a *hieros gamos*. Witness the following passage: "The gods then brought the two

---

[342] Line 6 as translated in J. Lisman, *op. cit.*, p. 38.
[343] *Lugale* 26 as translated in Å. Sjöberg, "In the Beginning," in T. Abusch ed., *Riches Hidden in Secret Places* (Winona Lake, 2002), p. 245.
[344] A. L. Oppenheim, "Man and Nature in Mesopotamian Civilization," in C. Gillispie ed., *Dictionary of Scientific Biography, Vol. 15* (New York, 1981), p. 639.
[345] Lines 105-106 as translated in H. Evelyn-White, *Hesiod* (Cambridge 2002), p. 87.
[346] *RV* 6.51.5 as translated in M. West, *Indo-European Poetry and Myth* (Oxford, 2007), p. 181.
[347] S. Jamison & J. Brereton, *The Rigveda* (Austin, 2014), p. 50.

(Heaven and Earth) together, and when they came together, they performed a wedding of the gods."[348]

Father Sky and Mother Earth are also attested in the New World. John Bierhorst offered the following observation with regard to Amerindian religious practices:

> American Indian religion in one of its many phases has tended to conceptualize the universe in terms of its halves—the familiar Mother Earth and Father Sky.[349]

Mircea Eliade, in common with many of the best minds in modern scholarship, considered the thematic pattern to be well-nigh universal in nature:

> The cosmic hierogamy, the marriage between Heaven and Earth, is a cosmogonic myth of the widest distribution. It is found above all in Oceania, from Indonesia to Micronesia; but also in Asia, Africa and the two Americas. This myth is more or less similar to that of which Hesiod tells us in the *Theogony* (126, etc.). Ouranos, Heaven, unites with Gaia, the Earth, and the divine pair engender the gods…All that exists—the Cosmos, the Gods and Life—takes birth from this marriage.[350]

How, then, are we to understand or visualize Heaven's coupling with the Mother Earth from the vantage point of an ancient mythmaker? According to a widespread tradition, it occurred in the midst of a raging storm and was marked by prodigious lightning. A representative example of this motif is attested in an early Mesopotamian text known as the Barton cylinder, wherein An (Heaven) has intercourse with Ki (Earth):

> That day…the storm raged, lightning flashed. (Over) the shrine of Nippur the storm raged, lightning flashed: (it was) heaven (An) who spoke with earth (Ki).[351]

---

[348] As translated in J. Murdoch, *Vedic Hinduism and the Arya Samaj* (London, 1902), p. 22.
[349] *Four Masterworks of American Indian Literature* (New York, 1974), p. 3.
[350] M. Eliade, *Myths, Dreams, and Mysteries* (New York, 1960), p. 172.
[351] Lines 7-12 of the Barton Cylinder as translated in R. Clifford, *Creation Accounts in the Ancient Near East* (Washington, D.C., 1974), p. 25.

Figure one

Perhaps the most lurid example of this mythological theme finds Zeus taking the form of a fiery thunderbolt and coupling with Semele (see figure one).[352] This myth is alluded to in the opening lines of Euripides' *Bacchae*: "Semele brought to bed by the lightning-fire."[353] According to Greek tradition, the thunderbolt not only impregnated the maiden—thereby producing Dionysus—it killed her instantly. Apollodorus provides a much embellished and humanized account of this macabre tale:

> As for Semele, Zeus fell in love with her, and slept with her in secret from Hera...Zeus came to her in her bedchamber in a chariot to the accompaniment of lightning and thunder, and [he] hurled a thunderbolt. Semele died of fright, but Zeus snatched her aborted six-month child from fire, and sewed it into his thigh.[354]

Evident here is the widespread idea that the sky-god descended as lightning or "divine fire" in effecting his sexual union with the primeval Earth.

The name Semele denotes "earth" and is cognate with the names of analogous goddesses from Old Europe.[355] It is patently obvious, therefore, that the

---

[352] Adapted from figure 11 in A. B. Cook, *Zeus, Vol. II* (New York, 1965), p. 25.
[353] Line 3 as translated in A. B. Cook, *op. cit.*, p. 28.
[354] *The Library of Greek Mythology* (Oxford, 1997), p. 101, citing III.3.
[355] M. Dexter, "Earth Goddess," in J. Mallory & D. Adams eds., *Encyclopedia of Indo-European Culture* (Chicago, 1997), p. 174 "The existence of an IE [Indo-European] 'Earth goddess', who is juxtaposed with a 'Father Sky', is underwritten by cognate names confined to the Baltic, Slavic, Thracian and Phrygian (Greek) traditions. The Slavic Earth(-mother) goddess, *Mati Syra Zemlja* ('mother moist earth') is linguistically related with Latvian *Zemes Mate*, Lithuanian *zemyna*, Phrygian and Thracian (Attic Grk) Σεμέλη (cf. Indo-European terms for earth)...The name of the Greek heroine Semele is etymologically related to the other IE earth

Greek myth of Zeus's coupling with Semele in the form of a fiery thunderbolt forms a close parallel to the Baltic tradition recounting Perkunas's "marriage" with Zemyna. In each case we are met with an archaic conception of the sky-god or Thundergod entering into a sexual union with Mother Earth.[356]

Hesiod also describes Zeus in the role of husband to Mother Earth. Thus the Boeotian bard makes passing reference to an old prayer of magic chanted during ploughing season: "Pray to Zeus of the Earth and pure Demeter for Demeter's holy grain to ripen heavy."[357] As Martin West pointed out, this prayer is best understood as reflecting the idea that Zeus had entered into an *hieros gamos* with the Mother Earth: "Here again the earth-goddess is coupled with the sky-god, even if he is now understood as a Zeus of the earth (*Chthonios*), that is, Zeus operating in the earth."[358]

Yet how is it possible to conceptualize a sky-god like Zeus as "operating in the earth"? A Zeus *Chthonios* is an oxymoron by any normal definition of terms.

A likely clue to understanding Hesiod's prayer to Zeus is provided by the Vedic traditions attached to the Thundergod Parjanya, a recognized analogue to the Baltic Perkunas. Recall again the passage from the *Rig Veda*, quoted above, wherein Parjanya is said to have made his dwelling in the center of the earth: "In the navel of the earth, on the mountains he has established his dwelling place."[359] If we take our cue from this report that Parjanya somehow *entered into the navel of the earth*, it is plausible to assume that Hesiod's prayer regarding Zeus operating "in the earth" has its origin in the very same cosmogonic tradition. The same scenario will also explain the widespread belief that the Thundergod, the sovereign God of Heaven, formerly entered into the navel of the earth in order to consummate the divine union with Mother Earth. In entering into, or *penetrating*, Mother Earth, the Vedic Thundergod was conceptualized as inseminating her:

> The winds blow forth; the lightning bolts fly. The plants shoot up;
> the sun swells. Refreshment arises for all creation, when Parjanya

---

goddesses (though borrowed from some other IE source than inherited in Greek)." See also A. Willi, "Demeter, Gê, and the Indo-Europeans word(s) for 'earth'," *Historische Sprachforschung* 120 (208), p. 171.

[356] J. Puhvel, *Comparative Mythology* (Berkeley, 1987), pp. 226-227 quipped: "The Thracian myth of Semele 'dead from the thunderstroke'…or 'midwived by [Zeus's] lightning-born fire'…was a fulgural hierogamy that 'got out of hand'." The same scholar adds: "In Greece the entire primal Heaven:Earth mating has been shunted to the ancestral track of Ouranos:Gaia, but the hierogamy of Zeus and Hera still replicates it to a point."
[357] *Op.* 465-466 as quoted in M. West, *Indo-European Poetry and Myth* (Oxford, 2007), p. 183.
[358] *Ibid.*, p. 183.
[359] *RV* 9:82:3.

aids the earth with his semen.... (Parjanya), come nearby with this thundering, pouring down the waters as the lord, our father. Roar! Thunder! Set an embryo![360]

As the "heavenly Lord and Father," the Vedic Parjanya forms a striking parallel to the Greek Zeus.

Such age-old conceptions, reverberating down through the ages, left an indelible mark on early religious ritual and literature. As a case in point, consider the testimony provided by the Greek dramatist Aeschylus, who had Aphrodite utter the following words in his *Danaids* (ca. 463 BCE):

> The sacred Heaven yearns to penetrate Earth, and Earth herself is yearning for the wedding too; desire makes showers of love fall down from Heaven, impregnate Earth...Of all these things I am the cause.[361]

Particularly significant here is Aeschylus's statement that Heaven longs to "penetrate" or enter into the body of the Earth. As a dramatist with a notable flair for incorporating archaic mythological traditions, albeit in often allusive or riddling language, it can be assumed that Aeschylus had ample basis in Greek cosmogonical lore for this particular turn of phrase.

This deduction receives a measure of support from the fact that Euripides later offered a very similar sentiment in one of his lost tragedies. Witness the following fragment preserved by Athenaeus:

> Holy heaven, filled with rain, loves to fall on to earth, through Aphrodite. And when the two are mingled into one they make all things grow for us...[362]

It will be noted that Aeschylus and Euripides both identify Aphrodite as the divine power responsible for uniting Heaven and Earth in sexual intercourse. The idea that all things spring from this union, in turn, echoes the Skidi Pawnee tradition that "all life" sprang forth as a result of the primeval sexual union of Mars and Venus.[363]

---

[360] *RV* 5:83:4-7.
[361] Nauck fragment 44 as translated in T. Papadopoulou, *Aeschylus: Suppliants* (London, 2011), p. 20.
[362] Fragment 898 (Athenaeus XIII 599F) as translated in P. Dronke, *Fabula* (Leiden, 1985), p. 91.
[363] G. Weltfish, *The Lost Universe* (New York, 1965), p. 112 observes: "The pit symbolized the Garden of the Evening Star from which all life originates."

The archaic tradition that Zeus married Mother Earth ultimately came to inform early Greek cosmology. According to the history of the cosmos preserved in Pherecydes (6th century BCE), the marriage of Zas and Chthoniê [=Gê=Mother Earth] not only sparked Creation, it served as the divine prototype for all human marriages.[364]

It is instructive at this point to pause and take stock of our findings. In a previous chapter we documented that the archetypal Fire-god was described as residing in the navel of the earth. Thus it is that the Vedic Agni and Aztec Xiuhtecuhtli were each represented as dwelling at the navel of the earth, in the center of the cosmos. As is evident from the Vedic traditions surrounding Parjanya—not to mention the Greek traditions attached to Zeus—the very same dwelling place was assigned to the archaic Thundergod (=Heaven). This is but one of countless clues indicating that the Fire-god and Thundergod are fundamentally identical in nature and share a common natural history. Herakleitos's otherwise cryptic epigram identifying Zeus as the elemental Fire (=*Keraunós*) can thus be understood as preserving the same basic idea.[365]

It is possible to develop this argument even further: If, as we have argued here, the fire-god, Thundergod, and Heaven were early on considered to be analogous masculine agents whose fundamental role in Creation involved the penetration and insemination of Mother Earth, it stands to reason that Heaven itself should have been conceptualized as residing *within* the navel of the earth—this despite what we think possible from the standpoint of modern cosmology. It is this unique situation, in our opinion, that is reflected in the curious tradition surrounding Zeus *Chthonios*, referenced above, wherein the Greek sky-god is described as "operating in the earth." The archaic epithet Zeus *Katachthonios* points to the same conclusion, describing the sky-god as residing within the earth as the lord of the Underworld.[366] Hence the otherwise puzzling identification of Zeus with Hades, the latter described as living deep within the earth (see appendix seven).[367]

---

[364] Pherecydes DK 7 B 2, col. 1 as cited in L. Reitzammer, *The Athenian Adonia in Context* (Madison, 2016), p. 18. See the discussion in M. Munn, *The Mother of the Gods, Athens, and the Tyranny of Asia* (Berkeley, 2006), p. 49.

[365] B64. See the discussion in A. B. Cook, *Zeus, Vol. 2* (Cambridge, 1925), pp. 11-12: "For Zeus in his early zoïstic stage was the burning sky. Hence Herakleitos had common opinion behind him, when he called his elemental Fire both Zeus and Keraunos."

[366] *Iliad* 9:457. On this point, Robert Parker, *On Greek Religion* (Ithaca, 2011), p. 81 observed: "Zeus Chthonios, the farmer's friend, can scarcely be dissociated from that Zeus Katachthonios whom Homer presents as ruling alongside Persephone."

[367] *Iliad* 20:61: "And beneath the earth, Hades, the king of those below…". See also D. Evans, "Dodona, Dodola, and Daedala," in G. Larson ed., *Myth in Indo-European Antiquity* (Berkeley, 1974), p. 116: "The name Hades, although undoubtedly old, does not appear in the very earliest times as the exclusive name for a distinct god of the underworld. Instead, as

11 In the Beginning: Heaven and Earth Were One

> Heaven and earth were once a single form, but when they were separated from each other into two, they bore and delivered into the light all things…[368]

> The Sumerian credo that in most ancient primeval days heaven and earth were united, and had to be separated…was current to some extent through all the millennia of Mesopotamian history.[369]

An archaic and widespread cosmogonic tradition reports that Heaven and Earth were formerly united as one, only to be separated during the tumultuous natural events remembered as Creation. Such traditions are attested in ancient Greece, Vedic India[370], China[371], Egypt, and North America.[372] Yet it is in early Sumerian texts where the idea receives its fullest treatment and thus this testimony is decisive in reconstructing this important thematic pattern.

---

early as Homer we find this god called Zeus Katachthonios, Zeus Eubouleus, Zeus Bouleus, Zeus Chthonios, and Zeus Trophonios."

[368] Fragment 484 as translated in C. López-Ruiz, *When the Gods Were Born: Greek Cosmogonies and the Near East* (Cambridge, 2010), p. 36.

[369] S. Kramer, *From the Poetry of Sumer* (Berkeley, 1979), p. 26.

[370] See R. Dandekar, "Universe in Vedic Thought," in J. Ensink & P. Gaeffke ed., *India Maior* (Leiden, 1972), p. 98: "It was believed that the heaven and the earth were originally joined together."

[371] See the creation tradition in M. Bender & A. Wuwu, *The Nuosu Book of Origins* (Seattle, 2019), p. 9: "In the ancient past, before the separation of the sky and earth."

[372] Of the Skidi Pawnee creation myth, George Dorsey, *Traditions of the Skidi Pawnee* (Boston, 1904), p. 3 stated: "In the beginning heaven and earth are unseparated."

A literary hymn from Lagash thought to have been composed during the Early Dynastic period (circa 2700-2350 BCE), is the so-called Sollberger Corpus Ukg. 15 (AO 4153). It includes the following statement about Heaven (An):

> An, the En, was standing (there) as a youthful man. An-Heaven and Ki-Earth were 'resounding' together…The sunlight was not (yet) shining forth. The moonlight was not (yet) coming forth.[373]

Evident here is the idea that, at the time of the primordial union of Heaven and Earth, the Sun did not yet shine forth in the sky.

A text from the Ur III period known as NBC 11108 offers corroborating testimony. There, too, Heaven is described as originally conjoined with Earth: "An-heaven lived together with Ki-earth."[374]

How exactly we are to conceptualize the union of Heaven and Earth—an Ur-Conjunction, as it were—remains a matter of ongoing debate among scholars. For Joan Westenholz and Géza Komoróczy, analogical thinking was responsible: "An analogical explanation of the belief in this unity [of Heaven and Earth] is that it was predicated on the visual experience of the sky merging at the horizon with the land."[375]

It is our opinion that this so-called analogical explanation involving an amorphous "sky" and terrestrial horizon would never occur to any prehistoric sky-watcher whose very life and livelihood depended on a hypersensitive, rational approach to the heavens, much less to sky-watchers around the globe (the idea that Heaven was formerly united with the Earth during the Time of Beginning is seemingly universal in scope). Rather, in order to explain the manifold and richly detailed traditions speaking of a primordial conjunction between Heaven and Earth, it seems necessary to envision two clearly distinguishable cosmic entities—perhaps two different celestial bodies—orbiting in close proximity to each other. Such a conjunction, moreover, must needs be sustained in duration and readily visible to the vast majority of terrestrial sky-watchers.

---

[373] Translation according to Å. Sjöberg, "In the Beginning," in T. Abusch ed., *Riches Hidden in Secret Places* (Winona Lake, 2002), p. 231.

[374] Line 5 as translated in J. Lisman, *At the Beginning: Cosmogony, Theogony and Anthropogeny in Sumerian texts of the Third and Second Millennium BCE* (Leiden, 2013), p. 222.

[375] J. Westenholz, "Heaven and Earth," in J. Stackert & T. Abusch eds., *Gazing on the Deep* (Bethesda, 2010), pp. 295-296. In this view Westenholz endorses the hypothesis defended by G. Komoróczy, "The Separation of Heaven and Earth," *Acta Antiqua Academiae Scientiarum Hungaricae* 21 (1973), p. 38: "It [Heaven and Earth] was brought about by a visual experience, viz. the sight of the sky merging in the horizon with the level land."

In light of our previous discussion documenting the striking parallels between Heaven (=the Sky-god) and the Thundergod—both gods participated in an *hieros gamos* with Mother Earth and were said to reside in the navel of the Earth—it stands to reason that the Ur-Conjunction between Heaven and Earth reflects the very same state of affairs and, in the final analysis, describes the placement of Heaven within the interior of Earth. The evidence in favor of this hypothesis, while largely circumstantial in nature and preliminary at this stage, will be summarized below.

The first point to be made is that the primordial union of Heaven and Earth bears all the earmarks of a *hieros gamos*, as various scholars have recognized. Jan Lisman, for example, observed with reference to the aforementioned Ukg. 15 (AO 4153): "This text may refer to the primal '*hierós gámos*', viz. that of an and ki."[376]

Equally telling is the fact that the union between Heaven and Earth results in a luxuriant garden much as the *hieros gamos* between Dumuzi and Inanna produced a burgeoning garden and verdant greenery.[377] This much is implied in another passage from Ukg. 15: "He has lowered the inlets of the irrigation channels in it, in order to make earth appear in luxuriance: a garden, moist and cool; water has filled the holes in the earth."[378] According to Lisman, the translator of this text: "In other words: ki [=earth] has been transformed into a garden."[379]

Complementary testimony is hinted at in other early Sumerian literature. A slightly later text known as *The Debate between Tree and Reed* includes the following statement: "An, the exalted heaven, had intercourse with the vast earth."[380] Reading between the lines of this archaic text, it is possible to discern a likely allusion to the planet Venus:

> Then she [Earth] has embellished herself as with a *bardul*-garment…The earth, the fragrant vegetation, covered herself with attractiveness, covered herself with attractiveness. The pure earth, the virgin earth, has beautified herself for the holy An. An, the exalted heaven, had intercourse with the vast earth…The earth, full of joy, bore abundance.[381]

---

[376] J. Lisman, *At the Beginning: Cosmogony, Theogony and Anthropogeny in Sumerian texts of the Third and Second Millennium BCE* (Leiden, 2013), p. 212.

[377] See also the discussion in J. Bremer, "The Meadow of Love," *Mnemosyne* 28 (1975), p. 269: "The [primeval *hieros gamos* in Greek tradition] between Earth and Heaven is consummated in a meadow, or, to put it more precisely, creates the meadow."

[378] Column 1 lines 2-5 as translated in J. Lisman, *op. cit.*, p. 210.

[379] *Ibid.*, p. 29.

[380] Line 6 as translated in J. Lisman, *op. cit.*, p. 229.

[381] Lines 1-5 from *The Debate between Tree and Reed* as translated in J. Lisman, *op. cit.*, p. 229.

The phraseology of the last line—ki-kiri₃-zal-e ḫe-gal—preserves the very term denoting the luxuriant "joy" or prosperity (kiri₃-zal) which burgeoned forth in the wake of the *hieros gamos* between Dumuzi and Inanna.³⁸² So, too, it is this same word that is used to describe Venus in a passage from *Enmerkar and the Lord of Aratta*, quoted in a previous chapter, wherein Inanna/Venus was expressly called the giri₁₇-zal "splendor, joy, prosperity" of An: "Thereupon the splendor of holy An, the lady of the mountains, the wise, the goddess whose kohl is for Ama-usumgal-ana, Inana, the lady of all the lands, called to Enmerkar…"³⁸³ Note also that Inanna/Venus is here said to "embellish" herself for Dumuzi much as Earth embellished herself for An in the passage above.³⁸⁴ Such language hints at a close relationship as formerly existing between Inanna/Venus and An/Heaven. Is there any evidence, then, pointing to a possible *hieros gamos* between these two celestial entities?

Historically, Inanna's cult is first attested at Uruk in the fourth millennium BCE, where she is regularly associated with An, the head of the pantheon. Indeed, there is some reason to believe that Inanna/Venus was formerly the consort of An/Heaven: Thus, in an early hymn Inanna was invoked as "Consort of Heaven."³⁸⁵ So, too, Inanna was described as the "beloved lady of An" in another early hymn.³⁸⁶ A subsequent line from the same hymn implies that she and An shared the same dwelling-place:

> Great An feared your precinct and was frightened of your dwelling-place. He let you take a seat in the dwelling-place of great An and then feared you no more, saying: 'I will hand over to you the august royal rites and the great divine rites.³⁸⁷

To return to the primordial conjunction between Heaven and Earth: Another early text describing the coupling of Heaven and Earth is the Barton cylinder, conventionally dated to circa 2400 BCE. There the occasion is marked by prodigious bouts of thunder and lightning:

---

³⁸² Kirzal is identical with girizal. See M. Cohen, *op. cit.*, p. 783.
³⁸³ Lines 65-68 from "Enmerkar and the lord of Aratta," *ETCSL*.
³⁸⁴ J. Lisman, *op. cit.*, p. 231 noted the same point.
³⁸⁵ B. Foster, *The Age of Agade* (London, 2016), p. 331. See also W. Hallo & J. van Dijk, *The Exaltation of Inanna* (New Haven, 1968), p. 97: "In the Sargonic theology, Inanna-Ishtar did in fact become the wife of An, replacing Ki (mother earth), or becoming identified with her."
³⁸⁶ Line 93 in "A Hymn to Inana (Inana C)," *ETCSL*. Witness also Inanna's epithet: nu-gig-an-na, "the hierodule of An."
³⁸⁷ Lines 106-108 in "A Hymn to Inana (Inana C)," *ETCSL*.

> Those days were indeed faraway days. Those nights were indeed faraway nights. Those years were indeed faraway years. The storm roared, the lights flashed. In the sacred area of Nibru, the storm roared, the lights flashed. Heaven talked with Earth, Earth talked with Heaven.[388]

The word translated as "talked with" here is Sumerian $šeg_{12}...gi_{4}$, denoting a roaring akin to thunder.[389]

It is doubtless no coincidence that a prodigious roaring also attended the *hieros gamos* between the Thundergod Enlil and Mother Earth.[390] Witness the following passage from *The Debate between Winter and Summer*: "As Enlil copulated with the earth, there was a roar like a bull's."[391] Enlil's *hieros gamos* with the Earth, in turn, resulted in burgeoning abundance and fertility.

Ancient India preserved analogous traditions. Recall again the Vedic hymn to the Thundergod Parjanya:

> The winds blow forth; the lightning bolts fly. The plants shoot up; the sun swells. Refreshment arises for all creation, when Parjanya aids the earth with his semen....(Parjanya), come nearby with this thundering, pouring down the waters as the lord, our father. Roar! Thunder![392]

Here it is the roaring, thundering Parjanya who inseminates Earth and brings fertility and abundance to the world, much as An does in Ukg. 15 and the Barton cylinder. Such converging traditions and terminology not only underscore the fundamental affinity of the Thundergod and Heaven, they encode the turbulent nature and *fundamentally catastrophic* context of the *hieros gamos* at the time of Creation.[393]

---

[388] Lines 1-14 as translated in J. Black, "The Sumerians in Their Landscape," in T. Abusch ed., *Riches Hidden in Secret Places* (Winona Lake, 2002), p. 45.

[389] J. Lisman, *op. cit.*, p. 30, translates this passage as follows: "An-heaven is shouting together with Ki-earth." A. George, "Die Kosmogonie des alten Mesopotamien," in M. Gindhart & T. Pommerening eds., *Anfang & Ende: vormoderne Szenarien von Weltentstehung und Weltuntergang* (Darmstadt, 2016), p. 6 translates: "Sky and Earth made noise together."

[390] E. Håland, *Greek Festivals, Modern and Ancient, Vol. 2* (Cambridge, 2017), p. 121: "The marriage of the Sky Father with the Earth Mother also takes place in the thunderstorm."

[391] Line 14 from "The Debate between Winter and Summer," *ETCSL*.

[392] V:83:4-7 as translated in S. Jamison & J. Brereton, *The Rigveda* (Austin, 2014), p. 766.

[393] See especially Y.S. Chen, *The Primeval Flood Catastrophe* (Oxford, 2014), p. 113: "In Sumerian mythological prologues, stormy weather is used metaphorically to depict the cosmic union or reproduction (cosmogony), as seen in mythological compositions from the Early

To return to Ukg. 15: It is notable that An is described as a youth—Sumerian šul—at the time of the primordial conjunction of Heaven and Earth. What exactly this means has thus far been passed over in virtual silence by Sumerologists. Why would the "King of the Gods" be described as a youth?[394]

It will be remembered that this is exactly how Zeus was described in the Dictaean Hymn—as a *Kouros*, indeed as the greatest (*Megistos*) *Kouros*. And it is in this capacity that Zeus is implored to leap forth from the earth and bring verdant fertility to the world: "What the god is being asked to do, however, is to spring up from the lower world into the upper."[395]

For us the epithets šul and *Kouros* likely reference Heaven's diminutive form while ensconsed—i.e., hidden—in the navel of the earth. At the time of the primordial union of Heaven and Earth, according to the hypothesis defended here, Heaven (=Mars) was positioned in close proximity to, and directly in front of, the much larger Venus. From the vantage point of the terrestrial sky-watchers, Heaven/Mars appeared to be positioned in the innermost center of Earth/Venus.

The same history will also explain the otherwise inexplicable anomaly in which so many Thundergods reside in the earth, whereupon they are deemed responsible for underground thunder or "earthquakes." So, too, we understand at once why Thundergods around the globe are described as dwarves or diminutive in stature. The Nahuat Nanahuatl, as documented previously, was conceptualized as a dwarf.[396] Of him it was said: "When there was not yet a sun, it is said there was little Nanauatl."[397] So, too, the dwarf-god resided in the Underworld before becoming the sun: "And before it was the sun, its name was Nanahuatl, whose home was yonder in Tamoanchan."[398]

Analogous traditions are attached to the Quiché Tohil: "Tahil was small, a mere boy or even a baby in size, but his ax was a lightning-striking ax with a

---

Dynastic III period such as the *Barton Cylinder*...and AO 4153 (NFT 180=Sollberger Corpus Ukg. 15), ii 2. As pointed out by van Dijk, this primeval event was conceived as both 'le prototype de toute violence destructive' and 'naissance de la vie'."

[394] An is identified as the King of the Gods in line 11 of "A praise poem of Shulgi (Shulgi P)," *ETCSL*, among other Sumerian sources.

[395] M. West, "The Dictaean Hymn to the Kouros," *Journal of Hellenic Studies* 85 (1965), p. 158.

[396] B. Brundage, *The Fifth Sun* (Austin, 1979), pp. 224-225: "His name also appears as Nanahuatzin or Nanahuaton, both translated as Little Nanahuatl, the implication being that he was a dwarf or was thought to be strikingly small in stature. He appears among the Quichés as Nanahuac and is one of their early creator gods, along with Gukumatz (Quetzalcoatl), and he is called by them 'dwarf,' or 'green,' that is, young."

[397] B. Sahagún, *Florentine Codex: Book 1* (Sante Fe, 1953), p. 83.

[398] J. Bierhorst, *History and Mythology of the Aztecs: The Codex Chimalpopoca* (Tucson, 1992), p. 147, citing 77:27 through 77:30.

flaming blade."³⁹⁹ The Latvian Thundergod Perkons, likewise, was remembered as a "little man" and credited with generating the first fire ever.⁴⁰⁰ Perhaps the most relevant parallel to Zeus and An occurs in the career of the Vedic Indra who, at the time of the separation of heaven and earth and the ordering of the cosmos, is described as *kanina,* "little one," as well as *kumaraka,* "boy/youth," and *yuvan* "youth."⁴⁰¹ Remarkably, the King of the Gods is invoked as follows in one Vedic hymn: "Like a teeny-tiny wee little boy, he mounted his new chariot."⁴⁰²

According to a wealth of evidence, it was from *within* the Earth/Venus that the Thundergod first launched his lightning, thereby shattering the Primeval Hill and setting in motion the unfolding of Creation, remembered alternately as the separation of heaven and earth; the release of the imprisoned waters or light; the deliverance of foodstuffs; and countless other mythical variations. In a classic example of this mytheme, Nanahuatl cast forth his lightning and thereby released the maize at the time of Creation: "Nanahuatl, personifying lightning, splits open the fabulous cache (i.e., the 'mountain' of food that is the earth) in order to make its contents available to man."⁴⁰³ Indigenous accounts of this archaic myth frequently emphasize that Nanahuatl broke open the Mountain "much as a man penetrates a woman in the act of love." James Taggart, in his analysis of the modern stories surrounding the god, observes:

> The analogy between creation and procreation developed by all Nahuat narrators of the story has lightning-bolts standing to Sustenance Mountain as the penis stands to the vagina and womb. It is based on the masculine identity of Nanawatzin and the feminine identity of the earth…⁴⁰⁴

In summary, the archaic myth of the primordial conjunction between Heaven and Earth is best understood as a variation upon the *hieros gamos* theme. In this sense the *hieros gamos* between Heaven and Earth is functionally analogous to the *hieros gamos* between the Thundergod and Mother Earth and that between Dumuzi (Mars) and Inanna/Venus.

---

³⁹⁹ D. Tedlock, *Breath on the Mirror* (Albuquerque, 1997), p. 17.
⁴⁰⁰ G. Nagy, "Perkunas and Perun," *Innsbrucker Beiträge zur Sprachwissenschaft* 12 (1974), p. 113.
⁴⁰¹ *RV* 3:48:1.
⁴⁰² *RV* 8:69:15.
⁴⁰³ J. Bierhorst, *Four Masterworks of American Indian Literature* (Tucson, 1974), p. 8.
⁴⁰⁴ J. Taggart, *Nahuat Myth and Social Structure* (Austin, 1983), p. 92.

12 Zeus: Thundergod Extraordinaire

> Come then, celebrate too his earth-shattering thunder and the fiery lightnings of Zeus and the awesome fulgerent thunderbolt.[405]

> As the mountain of data grows, it becomes harder and harder to get a clear idea of Zeus, particularly if one must now abandon Victorian ideas like nature and evolution as a means of patterning the information.[406]

For the ancient Greeks there was no more formidable or awe-inspiring natural force than Zeus, the King of the Gods. According to the earliest literary testimony, Zeus was a capricious agent of heaven-sent destruction, whose invincible thunderbolt was capable of incinerating its intended target in an instant. Hesiod's account of the god's combat with the Typhon dragon in the *Theogony* offers a panoramic view of the Thundergod in all his fulgural glory, one well worthy of a Cecil B. DeMille Hollywood blockbuster:

> The whole earth seethed, and sky and sea: ...and there arose an endless shaking...So when Zeus had raised up his might and seized his arms, thunder and lightning and lurid thunderbolt, he leaped from Olympus and struck him, and burned all the marvelous heads of the monster about him.[407]

---

[405] Lines 1744-1747 from *Birds* as translated in J. Henderson, *Aristophanes* (Cambridge, 2000), p. 249.
[406] K. Dowden, *Zeus* (London, 2006), p. 14.
[407] Lines 850-856 as translated in H. Evelyn-White, *Hesiod, Homeric Hymns, Epic Cycle, Homerica* (Cambridge, 2002), p. 141.

As several scholars have noted, Hesiod's description of the dragon combat is impossible to square with the natural world as we know it. Thunderstorms, after all, are not agents of cosmic upheaval and disaster. Nor, for that matter, are terrestrial thunderstorms characterized by the presence of fire-breathing dragons. William Guthrie, who argued this point most forcefully, opined that the God's signature battles, such as his smiting of the Titans, belonged to a completely different order than at present:

> Take a passage from the *Theogony*, say the battle of Zeus and his allies with the Titans. Great rocks hurled, the earth and its forests are set on fire, they crash and cry aloud, the surface of the land heaves and boils as does the sea. Heaven rocks and groans and Olympus is shaken to its base. Lightning and thunder, flame and thunderbolt, are the weapons of Zeus, and all nature is convulsed…Events of those days, or the days when Prometheus stole fire, were events of a different order, they were different in kind, from what went on in the Boeotia of Hesiod himself or the world of those who came after him.[408]

This is exactly right. The world-convulsing events alluded to in Hesiod's account of Zeus's combat with the Titans or Typhon properly describe apocalyptic catastrophes at the dawn of time and, as such, have no natural counterpart in the modern world.[409]

Inherent in the Greek traditions attached to Zeus's heaven-hurled thunderbolt is the idea that it manifested as "fire" (*paltòn pûr*). For Pindar (ca. 518-438 BCE) and other Greek poets, Zeus's thunderbolt was "fire-thrown" and intimately associated with the concept of Victory: "Following previous beginnings, now too we shall sing loudly the so-named joy of proud victory, the thunderbolt, the fire-thrown weapon of thunder-raising Zeus, the blazing bolt that fits every success."[410] So, too, Euripides' *Bacchae* describes the bolt which destroyed Semele as "lightning-borne fire" (ἀστραπηφόρῳ πυρί).[411]

In composing these lines, the Greek poets were not simply waxing eloquent with regards to the familiar flash or crackling boom that occasionally accompa-

---

[408] W. Guthrie, *A History of Greek Philosophy, Vol. 1* (Cambridge, 1962), p. 141.
[409] R. Woodard, "Hesiod and Greek Myth," in R. Woodard ed., *The Cambridge Companion to Greek Mythology* (Cambridge, 2007), p. 89 observes: "In near apocalyptic language, Hesiod describes how the attack of the Olympians, the counterattack of the Titans, and, most conspicuously, Zeus's unrestrained lightning-bolt bombardment shake creation to its core."
[410] *Olympian Ode* 10:78-83 as translated in K. Dowden, *op. cit.*, p. 64.
[411] Line 3 as translated in R. Seaford, *The Bacchae* (Warminster, 1996), p. 69.

nies the local thunderstorm. Nothing could be further from the truth. Rather, they were struggling to describe the ineffable: Specifically, the *extraordinary* and *extraterrestrial* pyrotechnics associated with Zeus's epiphany as a terrifying lightning-hurling agent. Walter Burkert is one of the few modern scholars to fully grasp this point:

> The thunderbolt…is the weapon of Zeus which he alone commands; it is irresistible, even gods tremble before it, and enemies of the gods are utterly destroyed when it strikes; in the face of such a manifestation of divine energy, man stands powerless, terrified and yet marveling.[412]

A better description of the religious experience of *mysterium tremendum et fascinosum* would be hard to imagine.[413]

Especially telling are traditions reporting that Zeus launched the lightning-borne fire from his "eye," where it had been fashioned by the Cyclopes. Aeschylus described the Greek Thundergod as follows: "The jealous eye of God hurls the lightning down."[414] The same conception is evident in Euripides' *Bacchae*: "Unveil the Lightning's eye."[415] With apparent reference to these archaic idioms preserved by the great dramatists, the grammarian Hesychius observed that the phrase "eye of Zeus" meant "a flash of lightning."[416] A. B. Cook, reviewing such testimony, concluded: "These passages certainly seem to imply that lightning is a glance shot from the jealous eye of Zeus."[417]

Yet where in all the sky is an eye capable of launching lightning? Confronted with the testimony linking Zeus's eye to lightning, modern scholars have virtually nothing to offer by way of a scientific explanation for its natural historical origin or specific meteorological context. Witness the facile analysis offered by the esteemed Classicist Jean-Pierre Vernant:

> That the Cyclopes should each have just a single eye is understandable: The eye itself is like fire. For the ancients—for the people

---

[412] W. Burkert, *Greek Religion* (Cambridge, 1985), p. 126.
[413] With reference to Otto's famous formulation, M. Eliade, *The Sacred and Profane* (New York, 1959), p. 9 remarked of Zeus-like deities that "It was a terrible power, manifested in divine wrath."
[414] Line 470 from *Agamemnon* as translated in L. Farnell, *The Cults of Greek States*, Vol. 1 (Oxford, 2005), p. 76.
[415] Line 594 as translated in G. Murray, *The Collected Plays of Euripides* (London, 1954), p. 35.
[416] *Frag. trag. adesp.* 278 as translated in A. Cook, *Zeus, Vol. 1* (Cambridge, 1914), p. 502.
[417] *Ibid.*, pp. 503-504.

who thought up these stories—a gaze is a person's essential light beaming from the eye. But the light that springs from Zeus's eye is actually lightning.[418]

"The eye itself is like fire"? A gaze is a person's "essential light." Really? Is this the best analysis modern scholarship has to offer? Not even the most naïve sky-watcher would visualize a Cyclops or an "angry gaze" in a thunderstorm, much less in the flash of lightning or the strike of a thunderbolt.

Vernant is seemingly unaware that the idea of an angry Sky god hurling lightning from his eye is a globally attested thematic pattern.[419] An Old Babylonian hymn provides an archaic example of this idea:

> May Utu, at his rising from (his) chamber, Gaze with his favorable eye toward it (the throne dais). My king, raised his head toward heaven there. May everyone praise him together when he raises his eyes flashing like lightning.[420]

Analogous ideas are attested in the New World. The Iroquois Thundergod, for example, was renowned for the lightning emanating from his eye.[421] For the indigenous Indians of the Canadian Subartic, it was said of the Thunderbird: "When the Thunderbird blinks its eyes, lightning bolts shoot out."[422] Such testimony, which could be amplified *ad nauseam*, is enough to dispel Vernant's suggestion that the tradition in question is a made-up story and reflects a figurative interpretation of light/vision peculiar to ancient Greece. In the case of Zeus's lightning-hurling Eye we have to do with an extremely widespread belief-system, one inextricably interlinked with archaic conceptions of the Thundergod. Such ideas do not arise from speculation or metaphorical processes. Rather, they *always* encode a lived reality and specific natural-historical context—in this case, the awe-inspiring spectacle of a massive planetary "god" brandishing thunderbolts in the northern circumpolar heaven, a god distinguished by a Cyclopean "eye."

---

[418] Jean-Pierre Vernant, *The Universe, the Gods, and Men* (New York, 2001), p. 21.
[419] See here the extensive discussion in W. Roscher, *Die Gorgonen und Verwandtes* (Leipzig, 1879), pp. 63-71. See also E. Cochrane, "Thundergods and Thunderbolts," *Aeon* 6:1 (2001), pp. 102-103 for numerous examples from the New World.
[420] YOS 11, 54, 13-16 as translated in J. Polonsky, *The Rise of the Sun-God and the Determination of Destiny in Ancient Mesopotamia*. Ph.D. dissertation, University of Philadelphia (2002), p. 191.
[421] H. Alexander, "North American," in L. Grey ed., *The Mythology of All Races, Vol. 10* (Boston, 1917), p. 24.
[422] S. Kallen, *Native Peoples of the Subartic* (Minneapolis, 2017), p. 24.

In order to understand the imagery in question, it is first necessary to identify an obvious celestial prototype for Zeus's lightning-hurling eye—obvious, that is, for prehistoric sky-watchers around the globe. Consider the image depicted in figure one, analogues of which are ubiquitous in rock art everywhere.[423] Can it be doubted that, were such an astronomical apparition to present itself in the northern circumpolar heaven, traditions of a Sky-god's Cyclopean "Eye" would be virtually certain to follow?

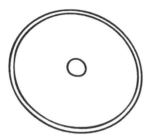

Figure one

Now consider the image depicted in figure two, a close variation on the previous image, representing a slightly later phase in the evolutionary history of the polar configuration, in which fiery lightning-like filaments radiate across the disc of the sun.[424] In our view the global traditions of a lightning-discharging "Eye" likely find their origin here (here the central "eye" is composed of the conjoined orbs of Mars and Venus).

Figure two

---

[423] Adapted from figure 19 in M. Green, *The Sun-Gods of Ancient Europe* (London, 1991), p. 37.
[424] Figure 113 from B. Teissier, *Egyptian Iconography on Syro-Palestinian Cylinder Seals of the Middle Bronze Age* (Fribourg, 1996), p. 73. For analogous images from the Old Babylonian period, see L. Werr, S*tudies in the Chronology and Regional Style of Old Babylonian Cylinder Seals* (Malibu, 1988).

Note further that the Greek word for lightning—*asterope*—preserves the inherent link to a material celestial body, inasmuch as *aster* denotes "star."[425] This etymology alone offers compelling circumstantial evidence for the conclusion that the Greek concept of lightning was quite literally a star-based phenomenon. The archaic phrase "star-flung thunderbolt" (*asterobletos keraunón*) preserved in an Orphic hymn points to the same conclusion, needless to say.[426]

Postscript

For the past century or so, the dominant trend in Classical circles has been to deny any and all reality to the ancient gods. Richard Seaford, a world-renowned expert on ancient Greek religion, argued the point most forcefully: "Greek deities are human constructions."[427] Ken Dowden, the author of a recent biography of Zeus, offered a similar opinion: "Zeus is a projection in heaven of kings on earth."[428] It follows, according to this currently prevailing orthodoxy, that the millennia-old myths telling of Zeus's dragonslaying and lightning-hurling eye are the stuff of fiction, projections of human affairs onto an imaginary Olympus, as it were. It is our opinion that such learned opinions are wholly misguided and stand in blatant contradiction to the express testimony of ancient sky-watchers around the globe. The Greek gods were indisputably real and of material form, of that we can be absolutely certain. The myths attached to the gods, likewise, are empirically based in origin and encode catastrophic natural events during the recent prehistoric period. A final point will suffice to underscore the need for a radical revaluation of all scholarship on ancient myth and religion.

One of the most familiar tropes in Greek mythology is that the sun-god Helios sees everything—hence the epithet *panoptes*, "all-seeing."[429] In the *Iliad*, for example, Helios is invoked as "You who see all things."[430] The very same claim appears in the *Odyssey* and in various plays of the great dramatists.[431] This idea is employed for comedic effect in the famous scene in the *Iliad* wherein Zeus assures Hera

---

[425] H. Lloyd-Jones, *Aeschylus: The Oresteia* (London, 2014), p. 42: "The bolt of the stars: the thunderbolt; *aster ope* or *astrape* (lightning) was derived from *aster* or *astron* (star)." See also R. Janko, *The Iliad: A Commentary, Vol. IV* (Cambridge, 1994), p. 230.

[426] H. G. Liddell & R. Scott, *A Greek-English Lexicon* (Oxford, 1996), p. 261. See also the discussion in E. Csapo, "Star Choruses: Eleusis, Orphism, and the New Musical Imagery and Dance," in M. Revermann & P. Wilson, *Performance, Iconography, Reception* (Oxford, 2008), p. 271.

[427] R. Seaford, *Dionysos* (London, 2006), p. 95.

[428] K. Dowden, *Zeus* (London, 2006), p. 73.

[429] *Iliad* 3.277; *Works and Days* 267-268.

[430] *Iliad* 3:277.

[431] *Odyssey* 11.109.

that their furtive lovemaking will be invisible even to Helios thanks to the golden cloud he has created: "Not even Helios can look at us through it although beyond all others his light has the sharpest vision."[432]

Why exactly Helios was ascribed sharp vision has never been answered. The conventional explanation, wholly ad hoc in nature, maintains that inasmuch as the solar orb travels across the entirety of the sky with each passing day he must perforce be capable of seeing anything and everything. Martin West's opinion is representative in this regard: "The Sun's capacity for seeing everything that people do qualifies him as a supervisor of justice, or at least gives him a valuable role as the god of justice's eye and as a trusty witness."[433]

Interestingly enough, Zeus was described in analogous terms. In *Works and Days* Hesiod states that "The eye of Zeus sees all things."[434] Far from being an error on the part of the Boeotian bard, the same idea is evident among the early poets. Thus, Sophocles makes reference to the ever-vigilant eye of Zeus *Morios*: "For the sleepless eye of the Morian Zeus beholds it."[435] Here we find an unequivocal reference to the "round eye" or *kuklos* of Zeus. Yet *kuklos* is the very phrase employed by Aeschylus to describe Helios' all-seeing eye: "the all-seeing orb of the sun."[436]

It is significant that a cognate term is employed to denote the eye of the sun (Surya) in Indic lore—namely, *cakra*, commonly translated "wheel": "With his eye on men, he sits in the middle of heaven."[437] So, too, the Indic sun-god is described as "all-seeing" (*visvacaksas-*) and "wide of vision" (*urucaksas-*) just like the Greek Zeus (*euryopa*).[438]

How or why the ancient sun-god should be equipped with an all-seeing wheel-like eye remains unexplained. Certainly there is nothing about the present appearance of the solar orb that would suggest a wheel-like eye. Yet one glance at the image depicted in figure three reveals a possible celestial referent. Prehistoric in nature, the image in question resembles nothing so much as a wheel centered on the solar disk—a wheel-like "eye" in the middle of heaven, as it were. Hence we would understand the wheel-like eyes of Zeus, Helios, and Surya.

---

[432] *Iliad* 14: 343-345.
[433] M. West, *op. cit.*, p. 199.
[434] *Works and Days* 267.
[435] Line 704 as translated in R. Jebb, "Oedipus at Colonus," in W. Oates & E. O'Neill, *The Complete Greek Drama, Vol. One* (New York, 1938), p. 638.
[436] *Prometheus Bound* 91.
[437] *RV* 10:139:2.
[438] *RV* 7.35.8, 63.4 and 1.40.2, 7.63.1. See also *Works and Days* 229 and 239.

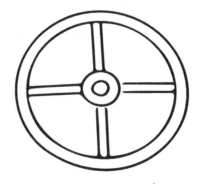

Figure three

If the sun-god's Cyclopean eye was conceptualized as a "wheel"-like object, it follows that the sending forth or emission of fiery "rays" might well be conceptualized as the act of "seeing." In fact, it is possible to document an indissoluble connection between solar radiation and the act of seeing in various ancient languages—witness Indo-European *leuk-, denoting both "to see" and "to shine."[439] Much the same idea is evident in an Aztec name for the sun-god: *Techtlatlatztinemi* "he (the sun) goes along seeing us by means of fire."[440]

Yet Zeus's eye also flashed lightning and thus we must expect to find an equally anomalous connection between the act of seeing and lightning-like pyrotechnics. Such is the case in ancient Greek, where *dérkomai* denotes "to see/look" but also "flashing fire [or lightning] from his eyes."[441] Ruth Bielfeldt, surveying the Greek evidence, drew a direct connection between the act of seeing and fire:

> In both the *Iliad* and the *Odyssey*, we find the idea that fire, light and vision form an inseparable unity: not only is fire endowed with sight, but the eyes are in turn also conceived as fire-like, their glance figured as spraying sparks. Homer considers eyes and glances as themselves emissive of fire.[442]

The concrete nature of this meteorological imagery is most explicit in the

---

[439] J. Mallory & D. Adams, *The Oxford Introduction to Proto-Indo-European and the Proto-Indo-European World* (Oxford, 2006), p. 326.
[440] J. Bierhorst, *A Nahuatl-English Dictionary and Concordance to the Cantares Mexicanos* (Stanford, 1985), p. 351.
[441] *Odyssey* 16:439. See also H. G. Liddell & R. Scott, *A Greek-English Lexicon* (Oxford, 1996), p. 379.
[442] R. Bielfeldt, "Sight and light: reified gazes and looking artefacts in the Greek cultural imagination," in M. Squire ed., *Sight and the Ancient Senses* (London, 2016), p. 124.

Egyptian language, where *m33* denotes the act of "seeing" while *m3wt* signifies the rays of the sun or "rays of light" (The latter word is written with the hieroglyph for an eye—the sign representing *m3*.)[443] Yet *m3wt* also denotes "lightning" and the "spokes of a wheel," a startling extension of meaning apart from the historical reconstruction defended here.[444]

Such conceptions have no conceivable basis in human biology. Nor for that matter do they reflect the projection of human ideas onto the celestial landscape, rather the exact opposite: These ocular idioms were directly inspired by astronomical phenomena—namely, the mesmerizing spectacle presented by a lightning-discharging "eye" in the northern circumpolar sky. If figure one above was conceptualized as a Cyclopean-eyed sun, the second figure illustrates the sending forth of fiery lightning-like radiation from the god's central eye, universally conceptualized as a lightning-like glance, fiery emission, or the act of "seeing" (Witness the universal mythological motif whereby lightning is conceptualized as the "glance" or winking of a solar eye).[445] Insofar as the radiant filamentary structures in question pervaded the entire cosmos—defined in ancient times as the unified heaven and earth[446]—it follows that the old sun-god saw everything that transpired in the cosmos.

---

[443] R. van der Molen, *A Hieroglyphic Dictionary of Egyptian Coffin Texts* (Leiden, 2000), p. 157.
[444] Gabor Takács, *Etymological Dictionary of Egyptian*, Vol. 3 (Leiden, 2008), p. 66.
[445] G. Reichel-Dolmatoff, *Amazonian Cosmos* (Chicago, 1971), p. 78: "Lightning (*miari*)…is also interpreted as a 'glance from the Sun,' a rapid twinkle (*ku-miari*)."
[446] D. Ragavan, "Entering Other Worlds," in *Ibid., Heaven and Earth* (Chicago, 2013), p. 202. See also R. Dandekar, "Universe in Vedic Thought," in J. Ensink & P. Gaeffke ed., *India Maior* (Leiden, 1972), p. 98: "The universe is said to be constituted of *dyaus* (heaven) and *prthivi* (earth)."

13 The Primordial Earth

From the center of the earth (*tlalxico*, the 'navel') four quadrants extended out to the four directions (*nauhcampan*).[447]

He has founded the earth on its pedestals, so that it will never totter.[448]

Archaic conceptions of the earth are remarkably uniform across cultures. The earth was commonly conceptualized as feminine in nature—hence the widespread moniker Mother Earth. So, too, the idea that Mother Earth was responsible for the origin of all living things is found around the globe and at all times. In ancient Greece, for example, the *Homeric Hymn to Gaia* celebrates the great goddess as follows: "I will sing of well-founded Earth, mother of all, eldest of all beings."[449] What is true of Gaia is also true of the Vedic earth-goddess, invoked as the mother of all living things in the *Atharva Veda*: "The earth, womb of everything."[450] The same idea is found in the New World, where the Aztec (Huastec) earth goddess Tlazolteotl is recalled as *Teteoinnan*, "Mother of the Gods" and "the genetrix of all living things."[451]

---

[447] H. B. Nicholson, "Religion in Pre-Hispanic Central Mexico," in *Handbook of Middle American Indians, Vol. 10* (Austin, 1971), p. 403.
[448] *Psalms* 104:5-7.
[449] Lines 1-2 of *Homeric Hymn to Gaia* as translated in H. Evelyn-White, *Hesiod, Homeric Hymns, Epic Cycle, Homerica* (Cambridge, 1936), p. 457.
[450] *AV* XII:1:43 as translated in W. Whitney & C. Lanman, *Atharva-Veda Samhita, Part 2* (Cambridge, 1905), p. 668.
[451] T. Sullivan, "Tlazolteotl-Ixcuina: The Great Spinner and Weaver," in E. Boone ed., *The Art and Iconography of Late Post-Classic Central Mexico* (Austin, 1990), p. 14. See also H. B. Alexander, "Latin American Mythology," in L. Gray ed., *The Mythology of All Races* (New York,

In addition to being conceptualized as the archetypal "mother," the primordial earth is everywhere described in analogous terminology, common epithets including "wide," "broad," and "fixed." Such epithets encode the widespread idea that the earth was spread out or otherwise "extended" during the extraordinary events attending the ordering of the cosmos at the time of Creation.[452] We will return to this important mytheme later in the chapter.

Among the most puzzling epithets of the primordial earth is one that has received virtually no discussion at the hands of comparativists—namely, the idea that it is four-cornered in structure.[453] Such was the case in ancient Mesopotamia: "The earth was viewed as a rectangular field with four corners, an image which persisted, at least as a formulaic expression, until much later times."[454]

The same idea is attested in pre-Columbian Mesoamerica. Thus it is that the preamble to the *Popol Vuh* alludes to the primeval occasion on which "the measuring cord was brought and …stretched in the sky and over the earth, on the four angles, on the four corners."[455] A four-cornered earth oriented to the four cardinal directions was central to Yucatek Maya cosmology, as various scholars have documented: "One of the more important parts of the Chilam Balam accounts is the discussion of the creation of the world with four pillars holding up the four corners of the world."[456]

It is Indic tradition, perhaps, which has preserved the clearest articulation of this archaic belief-system. Already in the *Rig Veda* the earth was described as *catur-bhrsti*, "four-cornered." The wording of the hymn leaves no doubt that the "earth" in question is to be found in the distant sky, not on this planet:

1964), p. 74: "Universally Earth is the mythic Mother of Gods and Men, and Giver of Life; nor does the Mexican pantheon offer an exception to this rule."

[452] See the discussion in A. Macdonell, *Vedic Mythology* (Strassburg, 1897), p. 88 who notes that the *Taittiriya Samhita* and *Taittiriya Brahmana* derive the earth's name (*Prthivi*) from the root *prath*, to extend, because she is extended.

[453] For a notable exception, see M. van der Sluijs, *Traditional Cosmology, Vol. 3* (London, 2011), pp. 97-103.

[454] J. Black & A. Green, *Gods, Demons and Symbols of Ancient Mesopotamia* (London, 1992), p. 52. See also H. Hunger, "Kosmologie," in J. Hazenbos & A. Zgoll eds., *Das geistige Erfassen der Welt im Alten Orient* (Wiesbaden, 2007), p. 222: "Der Ausdruck 'die vier Weltecken' (an-ub-da-limmu, akk. *kibratum arba'um* 'die vier Ufer') scheint die Vorstellung von der Erde als einem viereckigen Feld zu zeigen."

[455] Per the translation offered by Adrián Recinos in D. Goetz & S. Morley, *Popol Vuh* (Norman, 1950), p. 80. See also the discussion in D. Tedlock, *Popol Vuh* (New York, 1985), pp. 243-244.

[456] H. McKillop, *The Ancient Maya* (Santa Barbara, 2004), p. 206. See also K. Bassie-Sweet, *Maya Sacred Geography and the Creator Deities* (Norman, 2008), p. 316: "The Maya replicated the quadrilateral world order, or parts of it, whenever they made a cornfield, built a house or town, or constructed a ritual space."

> If your mind has gone to heaven, if to earth far away…If your mind has gone to the four-cornered land far away…If your mind has gone to the four quarters far away, we will make it turn hither to you, here to live and dwell.[457]

Evident here is the idea that the earth's four corners are inextricably related to the four quarters of heaven (*cátasraḥ pradisas*). The same idea is expressed elsewhere in the *Rig Veda*: "The earth has four quarters."[458]

In the *Atharva Veda*, Mother Earth (*Prithivi*) is credited with generating the four quarters. Witness the following passage: "O goddess, when, spreading (*prathamânâ*) forth, named (*prithivi* 'broad') by the gods, thou did extend to greatness, then prosperity did enter thee, (and) thou didst fashion the four regions."[459] The "four regions," in turn, are to be identified with the four quarters or cardinal directions.[460]

The *Brahmanas* expand upon this theme: "Now this earth is four-cornered, for the quarters are her corners."[461] Elsewhere in the same text the earth's epithet is explained as referencing the primordial ordering of the cosmos:

> The earth is round. The Brahmanas repeatedly say that the whole earth, once floating and mobile remained in this condition until the cardinal points, becoming fixed themselves, also fixed the earth. In its fixed position it is spoken of as four-cornered (*catur-bhrsti*; RV X.58.3) or pointed (*catussvakti*, S. B. VI. 1.2.29).[462]

Now here is a curious tradition, not easily explained by reference to the present natural world. In what sense is it possible to imagine the invisible and incorporeal four cardinal directions playing a decisive role in the earth's fixing? And how, for that matter, are we to understand the four corners of the primordial earth?

---

[457] *RV* 10:58:1-4.
[458] *RV* 10:19.8.
[459] *AV* XII:1:55 as translated in M. Bloomfield, *Hymns of the Atharva-Veda* (Oxford, 1897), p. 206.
[460] W. Whitney, *Atharva-Veda Samhita, Part 2* (Cambridge, 1905), p. 670 translates this last clause as follows: "thou didst make fit the four directions." See also W. Kirfel, *Die Kosmographie der Inder* (Bonn, 1920), p. 9: "Mag hier auch auf die so oft genannten vier Weltgegenden angespielt werden, so zeigt die Stelle doch, dass Erde als eine nach den Himmelsrichtungen orientierte einheitliche Fläche vorgestellt wurde."
[461] *SB* VI.1.1.29 as translated in J. Eggeling, *The Satapatha Brahmana* (New Delhi, 1990), p. 155.
[462] S. Kramrisch, *The Hindu Temple, Vol. 1* (New Delhi, 1976), p. 29.

Analogous traditions are attested in the New World. The Sioux, according to the anthropologist Alice Fletcher, held that the four cardinal directions supported the primordial earth: "These four quarters are spoken of as upholding the earth."[463] According to the Cheyenne, the four directions were conceptualized as four posts.[464] A similar belief-system is evident among the Chorti of Mesoamerica, who hold that the earth is supported by "four corner posts."[465] The four stabilizing posts, in turn, were intimately associated with the four cardinal directions throughout Mesoamerica: "The erection of the corner posts and world trees relates to both the creation and delineation of ordered space and the raising of the sky."[466]

The untold antiquity of such cosmogonic traditions is confirmed by the fact that similar conceptions are evident in Egyptian literature from the third millennium BCE. In one hymn the Egyptian sun-god is implored to establish the earth upon its "beams" and place Heaven and Earth upon their supports: "Lasset dieses Land auf seinen Balken bleiben, und Himmel und Erde auf ihren Stützen."[467] Another early text attributes the genesis of the four cardinal directions to the primordial earth—"[The ear]th gave birth [to...] the four corners"—thereby echoing the tradition from the *Atharva Veda*.[468]

How is it possible to explain such widespread beliefs? Certainly not by reference to the terrestrial "earth," where four projecting "corners" or sky-props are nowhere to be found. Yet the mere fact that cosmogonic traditions around the globe recount the sudden appearance of four columnar structures that serve to "fix" the earth and uphold the sky strongly suggests that some readily visible celestial phenomenon was being described.

Here, too, prehistoric artworks and pictographs offer a wealth of insight into the principal themes of cosmogonic myth. Recall the image depicted

---

[463] J. Dorsey, "Indian Names for the Winds and Quarters," *The Archaeologist* 2 (1894), p. 41.

[464] G. Grinnell, *The Cheyenne Indians, Vol. 1* (New Haven, 1923), p. 233: "In offering to the cardinal directions, certain poles of the lodge represented them."

[465] K. Taube, "The Jade Hearth: Centrality, Rulership, and the Classic Maya Temple," in S. Houston ed., *Function and Meaning in Classic Maya Architecture* (Cambridge, 1998), p. 429.

[466] K. Taube, "Creation and Cosmology: Gods and Mythic Origins in Ancient Mesoamerica," in D. Nichols & C. Pool eds., *The Oxford Handbook of Mesoamerican Archaeology* (Oxford, 2012), p. 744.

[467] Leiden I 347 9-11 as translated in J. Zandee, *Der Amunshymnus des Papyrus Leiden I 344 verso, Vol. 2* (Leiden, 1992), p. 445.

[468] The Astarte Papyrus as translated by R. Faulkner, "Astarte and the Insatiable Sea," in W. Simpson, ed., *The Literature of Ancient Egypt* (New Haven, 2003), p. 109. See also N. Ayali-Darshan, "The Other Version of the Story of the Storm-god's Combat with the Sea in the Light of Egyptian, Ugaritic, and Hurro-Hittite Texts," *Journal of Ancient Near Eastern Religions* 15 (2015), p. 36.

in figure one, one of dozens of similar artworks from prehistoric Iran (Susa) (circa 4000-3000 BCE).[469]

Figure one

For Mircea Eliade and other scholars, these images depict the "navel of the earth" and the four cardinal directions.[470] Yet Eliade and virtually everyone else overlooked the celestial context of the artworks in question. As is evident from our discussion in chapters one and two, such images depict the primal "sun." The cylinder seal illustrated in figure two offers a striking parallel and serves to corroborate this deduction. To be more precise: The archaic image in question depicts a particularly memorable phase in the evolving history of the polar configuration, one in which the primordial earth's four corners had already been "spread" out to the four directions (i.e., the four radiating streamers comprising the cruciform structure). In this sense, the image is best understood as a cosmogram—as a snapshot of a particularly memorable historical phase in the ordering of the celestial landscape.

---

[469] J. de Morgan, *Memoires, Vol. 12* (Paris, 1912), figures 11:3, 12:2, 4, 6, 7; 13:1-4, 6-7; 14:2, 4; 15:1-7; 16:1, 3, 4-7; 17:4, 5, 7; 18:1-6; 41:3; and 42:1, 2, 4, 5.

[470] M. Eliade, *History of Religious Ideas, Vol. 1* (Chicago, 1978), p. 26: "As early as 1914, W. Gaerte had collected a large number of prehistoric signs and images that could be interpreted as cosmic mountains, navels of the earth, and paradigmatic rivers dividing the 'world' in four directions." See also W. Gaerte, "Kosmische Vorstellungen im Bilde prähistorischer Zeit," *Anthropos* 9 (1914), pp. 956-979.

Figure two

Reimagining Creation

A cornerstone of the present historical reconstruction is the claim that cosmogonical myths have their origin in witnessed celestial events of a catastrophic nature.[471] This hypothesis derives from the finding that creation accounts around the globe describe a catastrophic ordering of the cosmos in virtually identical terminology—a logical impossibility if analogical reasoning, nature-allegory, and speculation were the primary factors in the genesis of cosmogonic traditions as per the conventional opinion.[472]

A corollary of this hypothesis is that traditions describing a (re)ordering of the cosmos after a period of turbulent chaos and darkness point to a radically different solar system than presently configured. As a case in point, consider the classic

---

[471] So far as I know, David Talbott was the first scholar to offer the hypothesis defended here. See now the authoritative analysis provided by Marinus Anthony van der Sluijs in the multivolume series *On the Origin of Myths in Catastrophic Experience* (Vancouver, 2019).

[472] G. Komoróczy, "The Separation of Heaven and Earth," *Acta Antigua Academiae Scientiarum Hungaricae* 21 (1973), p. 36 would explain the primeval separation as analogical in origin: "In the final conclusion Mesopotamian cosmogonic mythology is of speculative origin." A. Seidenberg, "The Separation of Sky and Earth at Creation (II)," *Folklore* 80 (1969), p. 194 sought to explain the universal myth as a "reflection of the dual organization of the social group." According to A. Bernabé, "The question of the Origin: Cosmogony—Introduction," in S. Fink & R. Rollinger eds., *Conceptualizing Past, Present and Future* (Münster, 2018), p. 366: "every cosmogony is invented."

account of Creation in the *Rig Veda* in which the Thundergod Indra is said to have ordered the cosmos by forcibly propping up heaven and spreading out the earth: "You propped up the heaven with a prop; you spread out the earth."[473] Much the same scenario is described in the following hymn:

> He propped up lofty heaven on (the midspace) that has no pole.
> He filled the two world-halves and the midspace. He held the
> earth fast and spread it out.[474]

It will be noted that Indra's spreading out of the earth during the ordering of the cosmos is regularly coupled with his propping up of heaven. Although this could be interpreted as simply describing two temporally related but fundamentally distinct phases in the unfolding of Creation, it is probable that the Vedic scribes are implying that Indra's spreading out of the earth and propping up of heaven were coterminous events and functionally analogous in nature. On this understanding the sudden and spectacular appearance of the four radiating streamers in figure one not only represented the "spreading out" or "extension" of the primordial earth but also the erection of four "supports" upholding heaven (see appendix eight).[475]

This deduction receives a measure of support from the fact that ancient Egyptian accounts of Creation offer complementary testimony. The following solar hymn is representative in this regard:

> Hail to you, Re...who came forth in the beginning without his
> equal who raised high the heaven and established the earth.[476]

The word translated as "established" here is *smn*, literally "fixed."

The elevation of heaven and the spreading out of earth is described in other Egyptian texts as well. The following hymn is representative in this regard:

---

[473] *RV* 6:72:2.
[474] *RV* 2:15:2.
[475] Hence we would understand the otherwise anomalous fact that ancient Indian texts speak of heaven *and* earth both being supported by posts: "Heaven and earth are very often described as having been supported (*skabh* or *stabh*) with posts (*skambha* or *skambhana*)." See A. Macdonell, *Vedic Mythology* (Strassburg, 1897), p. 11. Compare the Chinese creation myth in M. Bender & A. Wuwu, *The Nuosu Book of Origins* (Seattle, 2019), p. lxii: "Four pillars that supported the sky and earth stood in the four directions, supporting them."
[476] Tomb 84 as translated in J. Assmann, *Egyptian Solar Religion in the New Kingdom* (London, 1995), p. 111. See also J. Zandee, *Der Amunshymnus des Papyrus Leiden I 344 verso, Vol. 2* (Leiden, 1992), p. 484: "Der den Himmel erhob und die Erde festigte (*šwj pt smn tꜣ*)."

You have raised up heaven high…Who spreads out the earth in her length. You have made it broad.[477]

The "spreading out" of the earth is elsewhere linked with the initial movements of the primal sun, alternately described as a "striding" or "walking around."[478] Thus it is that Egyptian accounts of Creation credit the sun's "striding" (*njm, nmtt, ḥpt*) with effecting a spreading out of the earth (the words *njm* and *nmtt* are written with the ⋀ determinative, implying a striding forward on legs).[479] This idea is evident in the following passage: "You have raised heaven as far as your arms reach, you have extended the earth as far as your footsteps reach."[480]

The sun's striding (*nmtt*), in turn, is inextricably linked with solar rays as evinced by the recurring phrase *nmtt iʒḥw*, conventionally translated "sunshine-stride" or "movements of sunlight."[481] Note further that the sun's demiurgic movements are frequently described in the Egyptian Texts as *wsḫ nmtt* or *pd ḥpt*, phrases which translate literally as "wide of stride" or wide-striding.[482] Yet *wsḫ* and *pd* are the very terms Egyptian scribes employed to describe the "spreading out" or "extension" of the primordial earth! Recall again the aforementioned passage: "You have spread out the earth with your striding."[483] How this "sunshine-striding" and/or spreading out of the earth is to be conceptualized from the standpoint of natural history or modern science is never explained by Egyptologists.

As bizarre as the Egyptian testimony linking the sun's "striding" to the spreading out of the earth is to the modern mind, very similar conceptions are attested in the *Rig Veda*. Famously, Vishnu appears as a sun-like celestial body whose "striding" orders creation: "Viṣnu, who measured out the earthly realms, who propped

---

[477] J. Zandee, *op. cit*. p. 482: "Du hast den Himmel hochheben…Der die Erde hinbreitet in ihrer ganzen Länge. Du hast [sie] breit gemacht." Translation by author.

[478] *Ibid.*, p. 448 describes it as Fusswanderung. Of the sun's striding in the *Rig Veda* S. Jamison & J. Brereton, *op. cit.*, p. 331 observe: "These strides are also conceived as footsteps."

[479] J. Zandee, *op. cit.*, p. 444: "Die Tagesfahrt wird mit der üblichen Formel *njm.k pt* beschreiben."

[480] P. Berlin 3050 VIII 1-3 as translated in J. Assmann, *op. cit.*, p. 176. See also J. Zandee, *op. cit.*, p. 367: "Du hast den Himmel erhoben soweit deine Arme reichen (*sqʒ.n.k pt r ʒw ꜥwj.kj*), du hast die Erde ausgebreitet mit deinem Lauf (*swsḫ.n.k tʒ m ḥpt.k*)."

[481] *PT* 1680 as translated by R. Faulkner, *op. cit.*, p. 249. J. Zandee, *op. cit.*, p. 374 translates *nmtt iʒḥw* as "Schreiten des Lichtes." See also J. Serrano, "Origin and Basic Meaning of the Word *ḥnmmt* (The So-Called 'Sun-Folk')," *Studien zur Altägyptischen Kultur* 27 (1999), pp. 366-367.

[482] R. Hannig, *Ägyptisches Wörterbuch I* (Mainz, 2003), p. 633.

[483] "Du hast die Erde ausgebreitet mit deinem Lauf (*swsḫ.n.k tʒ m ḥpt.k*)."

up the higher seat, having stridden out three times, the wide-ranging one."[484] Evident here is the idea that Vishnu's extensive striding (*vicakramanás*) "measures" out the earthly realms (*rájamsi*) at the same time as the heavens are propped up, thereby implying that there is no fundamental difference between the "measuring" out of the earthly realms and the "spreading out" of the primordial earth.[485]

The Vedic texts confirm that the "measuring" out in question is to be understood as the ordering of the cosmos at Creation.[486] Hence it is that the one-footed Aja Ekapâda (=Rohita, the ruddy one), alternately identified with the sun or with Agni, was also credited with measuring out the cosmos.[487] The following passage from the *Atharva Veda* is telling in this regard:

> The ruddy one made firm heaven-and-earth; by him was established the sky (*svàr*), by him the firmament (*naka*); by him the atmosphere, the spaces (*rájas*) were measured out.[488]

It will be noted that Aja Ekapâda measured out the *rájas* at the same time as he propped up heaven, much as Vishnu measured out the *rájamsi* when propping up heaven at the Time of Beginning. In each case we appear to be met with a measuring or "spreading out" of the *rájas*, commonly translated as "earthly realms."

Yet how on earth is it possible to understand such cosmogonic traditions? In what sense does the sun's "striding" about the sky cause the earth to "spread" out or extend to the four corners of the cosmos?[489] A Vedic account of Creation offers

---

[484] *RV* 1:154:1.

[485] A. Macdonell, *Vedic Mythology* (Strassburg, 1897), p. 11 offered a similar opinion well over a century ago: "Connected with this idea [the measuring out of the cosmos/creation] is that of spreading out the earth, an action attributed to Agni, Indra, the Maruts, and others."

[486] See P. Horsch, "From Creation Myth to World Law: The Early History of 'Dharma'," *Journal of Indian Philosophy* 32 (2004), p. 431: "Interestingly maya also is connected with cosmogonic myth: *ma-* = 'to measure', 'to determine by measuring', 'to construct', 'to create', 'to form', applies to the world-creating activity of the gods and indicates an architectonic basic philosophy, as do 'to bear', 'to hold' and 'to support' (*dhr-*)." Recall that a "measuring" is also mentioned in conjunction with the prototypical appearance of the four directions/corners in the *Popol Vuh*'s account of Creation.

[487] On the identification with Agni, see *RV* 1:67:5: "Like Aja (Ekapad) he [Agni] supports the broad earth; he props up heaven."

[488] *AV* 13:1:7 as translated by W. Whitney & C. Lanman, *Atharva-Veda Samhita*, Part 2 (Cambridge, 1905), p. 711. See also D. Srinivasan, *Many Heads, Arms and Eyes* (Leiden, 1997), p. 37.

[489] For a comparable tradition from the New World, compare the following Kato account from California reported in E. Gifford & G. Block, *Californian Indian Nights* (Lincoln, 1930), p. 79: "Before this world was formed there was another world. The sky of that world was made of sandstone rock. Two gods, Thunder and Nagaicho, looked at the old sky because it

a possible clue: It reports that, at the time of his birth, Agni "stretched" forth his limbs (*angai*) throughout the *rájas*:

> Stretching through the airy realm [*rája*] with his blazing limbs… clothing himself all around in flame, and being the life of the waters, he measures out his splendors.[490]

Here the "measuring" out of the fire-god's splendors (*sriyo*=radiance, light) is seemingly connected to the stretching forth of his blazing limbs throughout the *raja*. But what does it mean that Agni's limbs stretched forth across the sky? An epithet describing Agni as "four limbed"— *caturanga*—is relevant here. According to Doris Srinivasan, the epithet encodes the god's intimate relation to the four directions: "In RV 10.92.11, the term *caturanga*, 'four-limbed', is used as an epithet of Agni Narasamsa, naming him after his capacity to fill out, as fire, in the four directions."[491] While this epithet is difficult to explain by reference to the ritual fire, it makes perfect sense if the original referent was the primal sun at the center of the cosmogram depicted in figure one, in which case Agni's four radiant "limbs" would correspond to the four pillar-like beams extending outwards to the four directions (it will be remembered that cultures as disparate as the Balts and Navaho depicted fire as a cruciform structure). With this image in mind, it is telling that the *Rig Veda* describes Agni as extending in all directions: "When the beams of powerful Agni go forth in all directions."[492]

Other evidence points to the same conclusion. The most familiar Sanskrit word for "limb/leg/foot" is *pada*, cognate with Latin *pes* and Greek *poús*. Especially interesting here is an archaic kenning describing the primal sun as "footed." Thus it is that, in the *Rig Veda*, Heaven and Earth—themselves "footless"—are said to have given birth to the sun: "The two unmoving and footless, conceive an ample embryo, moving and footed."[493] The footed sun is elsewhere remembered as a great strider: "The one-footed [=sun?] has stridden farther than the two-footed."[494] Here, too, it is probable that an underlying connection to the four quarters exists: Thus *pada* also denotes "quarter," "column," and "pillar," a strong hint that the celestial "leg(s)" in question originally functioned as a sky-prop(s) serving to

---

was being shaken by thunder…Then they stretched the sandstone rock of the sky, walking on the sky as they did so. Under each of the four corners of the sky they set up a great rock to hold it."

[490] *RV* 3:1:5.
[491] D. Srinivasan, *op. cit.*, p. 31.
[492] *RV* 1:97:5.
[493] *RV* 1:185:2.
[494] *RV* 10:117:8.

demarcate the four directions.[495] The fact that *pada* also denotes a "ray of light" is consistent with this interpretation, needless to say.

Analogous conceptions are attested in ancient Egypt. In an obscure passage from the *Coffin Texts* the sun-god's "legs" (*rdwy*) are expressly linked with the supports of the sky (*shnwt*): "May you extend your legs over the supports of the sky."[496] Absent an obvious celestial referent for the sun's legs, Egyptologists have nothing constructive to offer on this symbolism. Yet if we approach the Egyptian testimony from the cosmogram depicted in figure one a ready solution is at hand: The "supports of the sky" are simply the four radial "beams" that issue from the central earth/sun, alternately conceptualized as four columnar "sky-props," "four cardinal directions," and "four legs" among a myriad of other symbols.[497]

Granted that the polar configuration appeared to revolve about the sky as the Earth turned on its axis—a central tenet of Talbott's original theory—it follows that the four "legs" (=sky-props) would turn or "stride" around the northern circumpolar region with the daily cycle. The sun-god's striding (*nmtt*), in this sense, is nothing but the rotary movement of the four sky-props (=legs) as they circled about the sky with the axial rotation of the Earth. In this understanding of a singular event during the unfolding of creation, it follows that as the primal sun "stretched" forth its legs and circumambulated about the sky it "spread" the earth to the four directions. Inasmuch as the legs in question were quite literally "sunbeams" on high, we are able to make sense of the Egyptian texts alluding to the "striding sunshine."

---

[495] M. Williams, *A Sanskrit-English Dictionary* (Oxford, 1872), p. 617. Comparable is the Latin cognate *pedamentum*, denoting at once "leg" and a pillar-like prop or post. See M. de Vaan, *Etymological Dictionary of Latin and the other Italic Languages* (Leiden, 2008), p. 462.
[496] *CT* 1:264.
[497] D. Kurth, *Den Himmel Stützen* (Brussels, 1975), pp. 74-75 notes the symbolic equivalence of the four Shu-supports with the legs of the heavenly cow and the four roots/branches of the World Tree. See especially the groundbreaking analysis in D. Talbott, *The Saturn Myth* (New York, 1980), pp. 120-144. See also A. Jeremias, *Handbuch der altorientalischen Geisteskultur* (Berlin, 1929), p. 142: "Den vier Weltecken entspricht die Teilung des Kosmos in vier Weltquadranten und die Teilung des Horizontes nach vier Windrosen, aus denen vier Winde wehen."

14 The King of the Four Quarters

> The cosmogonic myth occurs at the beginning, according to which one of the Vedic gods separated, pressed apart and 'supported' (*dhr-*) sky and earth. Through this support and provision of a prop [*Haltverleihen*] a 'cosmos', an order, was first produced out of the dark, chaotic uniformity.[498]
>
> The myths were clearly too well known to require straight narrative retelling. In veda text, stories are only alluded to, often as elliptically and enigmatically as possible for artistic effect.[499]
>
> Those religions which hold that human order was brought into being at the creation of the world tend to dramatize the cosmogony by reproducing on earth a reduced version of the cosmos. Sacrality (which is synonymous with reality) is achieved through the imitation of a celestial archetype…Throughout the continent of Asia…there was thus a tendency for kingdoms, capitals, temples, shrines, and so forth, to be constructed as replicas of the cosmos…[500]

In Vedic India, as in other cultures around the globe, Creation is characterized by the separation of heaven and earth. In traditional accounts describing these singular catastrophic events it is reported that the Sun-god or Thundergod propped up the heavens and spread out the earth, thereby ordering the cosmos.

---

[498] P. Horsch, "From Creation to World Law: The Early History of *Dharma*," in P. Olivelle, *Dharma* (Delhi, 2004), p. 12.
[499] S. Jamison, *The Ravenous Hyenas and the Wounded Sun* (Ithaca, 1991).
[500] P. Wheatley, *The Pivot of the Four Quarters* (Chicago, 1971), p. 417.

The question is how to understand these millennia-old traditions from the vantage point of the ancient sky-watcher cum mythmaker? In the previous chapter we proposed that the cosmogonic theme of the earth's extension or spreading out had reference to the explosive appearance of four heaven-spanning "rays" or columnar structures, the latter everywhere conceptualized as four cardinal directions (=sky-props). According to the Hymn to Mother Earth preserved in the *Atharva Veda*, the primordial earth suddenly produced four regions: "O goddess, when, spreading (*prathamânâ*) forth, named (*prithivi* 'broad') by the gods, thou did extend to greatness, then prosperity did enter thee, (and) thou didst fashion the four regions."[501] The four regions, as noted in a previous chapter, are to be identified with the four cardinal directions.[502]

In a number of passages in the *Rig Veda* and *Atharva Veda*, the extended "regions" are denoted by the term *rájas*.[503] In what amounts to little more than guesswork, commentators on the Vedic texts typically translate *rájas* as "earthly realms" or "regions of space" or by some equally nebulous phrase. Such is the case in Jamison and Brereton's rendition of Vishnu's cosmogonic striding, quoted in the previous chapter: "Viṣnu, who measured out the earthly realms, who propped up the higher seat, having stridden out three times, the wide-ranging one."[504]

Insofar as Vishnu himself is evidently identified with the primal sun in this particular hymn it stands to reason that *rájas* references a celestial region or structure. A survey of the relevant Vedic passages will readily confirm this deduction. Thus the sun-god Savitar is elsewhere described as he "who measured out the earthly (spaces)…(also) measured out the (heavenly) spaces [*rájamsi devá*]."[505]

The fire-god Agni is also said to have "measured out the regions of space" (*vi yó rájamsi*).[506] The same god is elsewhere described as follows: "He measured across the airy realm along the paths that lead straight to the goal," wherein "airy realm" is *rájo*.[507]

---

[501] *AV* XII:1:55 as translated in M. Bloomfield, *Hymns of the Atharva-Veda* (Oxford, 1897), p. 206.
[502] W. Whitney & C. Lanman, *Atharva-Veda Samhita, Part 2* (Cambridge, 1905), p. 670 translates the last phrase as "thou didst make fit the four directions."
[503] T. Burrow, "Sanskrit *rájas*," *Bulletin of the School of Oriental and African Studies* 12 (1948), p. 648: "The plural *rájamsi* is common in the Rig Veda in the sense of 'regions of space' or 'the regions of the world'."
[504] *RV* 1:154:1.
[505] *RV* 5:81:3.
[506] *RV* 6:7:7 as translated in T. Burrow, *op. cit.*, p. 646. S. Jamison & J. Brereton, *The Rigveda* (Austin, 2014), p. 781 translate this passage as "He, the very resolute one, who measured out the dusky spaces."
[507] *RV* 1:58:1.

The ordering of the *rájas* is elsewhere attributed to Indra, the god most commonly credited with separating heaven from earth and ordering the cosmos. Witness the following passage: "You extended the surface of the earth, O Indra, and you supported on high the expanse [*rája*] of the sky."[508] Here, too, the extension (*aprathaya*) of the primordial earth is coterminous with the supporting (*astabhayah*) of the sky on the *rája*.

Indra is repeatedly celebrated for his role in ordering the cosmos at the time of Creation. A telling passage, quoted previously, describes these events as follows: "When you spread out the immovable foundation [=earth], you set the airy realm on the doorposts of heaven with your lofty power."[509] Here "airy realm" is *rájo* and "doorposts of heaven" is *diva atasu*, a probable reference to the four sky-props (Karl Geldner's translation appears to be more faithful to the original myth: "When you extended the foundation, you confidently placed the immovable air space on the pillars of heaven.")[510] Properly understood, this passage implies that the *rájas* and pillars of heaven were inextricably related if not actually one and the same.[511]

Granted the central role of *rájas* in Vedic cosmogonic myth it is imperative that we delve deeper into the word's etymology and fundamental meaning. According to Jan Gonda and other authorities, the primary sense of *rájas* is "to stretch out" or "to extend."[512] Indeed, the word is commonly traced to the Sanskrit root *raj-* "to stretch out, make straight."[513] At the same time *rájas* is a recognized cognate of Latin *regio*, signifying "region" but also "direction": "Latin *regio* from the same root can be compared

---

[508] *RV* 1:62:5 as translated in T. Burrow, *op. cit.*, p. 645.

[509] *RV* 1:56:5. P. Horsch, "From Creation to World Law: The Early History of *Dharma*," in P. Olivelle, *Dharma* (Delhi, 2004), p. 11 translated the passage as follows: "When you (Indra) expanded the unshakeable prop [*Halt*], with power you set the atmosphere within the framework of Heaven." There he notes that "the 'unshakeable prop' refers probably to the earth as the 'foundation' of the cosmos."

[510] *RV* 1:56:5 as translated in K. Geldner, *Der Rig-Veda* (Cambridge, 2003), p. 73: "Als du die Grundfeste ausdehntest, da hast du den unverrückten Luftraum zuversichtlich auf die Pfeiler des Himmels gestellt." Translation courtesy of Birgit Liesching.

[511] The possibility must also be considered that, in the previous passage, the second clause is in apposition to the first, thereby implying that the "spreading out of the earth" is fundamentally equivalent with the establishment of the *rájo* on the doorposts/pillars of heaven. If so, it follows that the *rájo/rájas* are likely structurally analogous with the four regions or cardinal directions (=four sky-props) associated with the spreading out of the primordial earth.

[512] J. Gonda, *Ancient Indian Kingship from the Religious Point of View* (Leiden, 1969), p. 122. See also T. Burrow, *op. cit.*, pp. 647-648: "From this survey it emerges that the meaning of *rájas* in the Rgveda is simple and straightforward...Any etymology must be based on the meaning 'space, extent, expanse, etc.'"

[513] T. Burrow, *op. cit.*, p. 648.

('region' will often translate *rájas*); in form it corresponds more directly to Sanskrit *rājí-* direction."[514]

The same root *raj-* is believed to be cognate with the Sanskrit word for king, *raj-* or *rajan-*. How or why the Vedic king came to be associated with the root idea of "stretching out," "extension," or "direction," remains unexplained. Gonda speculated that the archetypal king was he who stretched out his arms: "The king being the one who 'stretched himself out and protected (other men) under his powerful arms'."[515] In their comprehensive survey of Proto-Indo-European ideology Mallory and Adams offered a similar interpretation:

> The deeper etymology of this word [IE *h_3regs-, whence Sanskrit *raj-*] has been frequently discussed; it is usually explained as an agent noun of *h_3reg- 'stretch out the arm, direct' with some arguing that the word derives from the concept of a king who stretches out his arms in rituals, especially those laying out a precinct, or perhaps a more direct semantic development from 'direct' to 'rule'.[516]

Such interpretations not only strain credulity, they offer little insight with regard to the word's primary function in archaic Vedic cosmogonical traditions, wherein *rájas* evidently denotes a visible celestial structure that was "extended" or measured out during the primordial ordering of the cosmos (the *Rig Veda* speaks of a time when no *rájas* existed).[517] The historical reconstruction advanced here offers a perfectly coherent and evidence-based solution to the problem: Granted the inherent link between the root *raj-* and *rájī-*, "direction," it stands to reason that *rájas* might have some reference to the four cardinal directions that were extended or spread outwards from the primordial earth, thereby "fixing" it in place and propping up heaven. So far as I'm aware, however, no other researcher has ever entertained this possibility.

Central to our argument is the deduction that *rájas* itself is almost certainly cognate with *raj*, "ray."[518] One of the earliest extant commentaries on the *Rig Veda*, Yaska's *Narukta*, made this claim well over two thousand years ago:

---

[514] *Ibid.*, p. 648.
[515] J. Gonda, *op. cit.*, p. 122.
[516] J. Mallory & D. Adams, *The Oxford Introduction to Proto-Indo-European and the Proto-Indo-European World* (Oxford, 2006), p. 268.
[517] *RV* 10:129:1. See also the discussion in R. Dandekar, "Universe in Vedic Thought," in J. Ensink & P. Gaeffke eds., *India Maior* (Leiden, 1972), p. 108.
[518] See J. Gonda, *op. cit.*, p. 48, citing *The Nirukta* 2, 3.

> *Rajas* is derived from the root *raj*. Light is called *rajas*…The worlds are called *rajamsi*.[519]

Here, in our view, is the likely common semantic denominator that provides the key to the mystery surrounding *rájas's* role in Vedic cosmogonic myth. If we take our cue from the cosmogram depicted in figure one, the manifold senses of the word *raj-* will become evident at once. By *rájas* the Vedic scribes had reference to the four ray-like arms of the solar cross, conceptualized as the four directions or regions (among other things). It was these "rays" or radii-like directions (*ráji-*="directions") that were "spread out" or "extended" during the extraordinary natural events remembered as the ordering of the cosmos at the time of Creation, thereby separating the divine world into four regions or quadrants.[520]

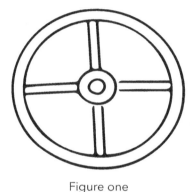

Figure one

Yet if *rájas* is to be identified with the radiant structures or "directions" extending outwards from the primordial earth/sun, how does this finding contribute to our understanding of ancient conceptions associated with the king (*rajan*) or universal sovereign? A probable clue comes from the sacred rituals attending the coronation of a new king. In ancient India, as around the globe, coronation rituals reenacted the central events of cosmogony.[521] Thus it is significant to find that, in the enthronement ritual known as the Rajasuya *(king-engendering)*, the king was required to mount "the quarters of space (*digvyastha-panam*)."[522] The apparent

---

[519] J. Muir, *Original Sanskrit Texts, Vol. 2* (London, 1874), p. 71.
[520] J. Gonda, *Ancient Indian Kingship from the Religious Point of View* (Leiden, 1969), p. 123 notes that the verb *tan-*, "to spread, extend" is "occasionally used with *rájas*."
[521] M. Eliade, *Myth and Reality* (New York, 1963), p. 39: "On the accession of a sovereign the cosmogony was symbolically repeated." With specific reference to the *Rajasuya*, J. Hani, *Sacred Royalty* (Paris, 2011), p. 26 wrote: "In accordance with all ancient rites, the *Rajasuya* consisted in a reiteration of the creation."
[522] M. Wiltshire, *Ascetic Figures Before and in Early Buddhism* (Berlin, 1990), p. 229. See also A.

purpose behind this ceremony, according to modern scholars, was to establish the king's rule or sovereignty over the four directions (Indic kings, like their royal counterparts in Mesopotamia, ruled the four directions).[523]

It was in the Rajasuya that the king stretched forth his arms in a patent attempt to simulate or reenact the erection of the World Pillar (see appendix nine). Jan Heesterman summarized the ritual as follows:

> The cosmic implications of the unction ceremony [=investiture at the time of the king's coronation] are clearly brought out by its setting; the scene of the unction is a replica of the universe: the king standing in the centre and stretching his arms to the sky impersonates, as has been seen, the cosmic pillar; round him the officiants are standing and confer on him his new body from the four points of the compass.[524]

Such symbolism, as Heesterman and Eliade have documented, is cosmogonic in tenor and origin.[525] Hence it is that sun-gods around the globe are said to stretch out their arms and/or legs while ordering the cosmos at the time of Creation—this despite the fact that the present sun does not betray any indication of having either arms or legs.[526] Thus the *Rig Veda* describes the sun as stretching out its arms: "Savitar has stretched forth his two arms, at his impulsion causing the moving world to settle down."[527] Evident here is the archaic conception that the stretching forth of the sun's arms signals the stabilization or "ordering" of the cosmos.

Parpola, *The Roots of Hinduism* (Oxford, 2015), pp. 191-193.

[523] J. Heesterman, *The Ancient Indian Royal Consecration* (Leiden, 1957), p. 104: "He wins the quarters of space or the seasons, thus mastering the whole of the universe." See also F. Wiggermann, "Scenes From the Shadow Side," in M. Vogelzang & H. Vanstiphout eds., *Mesopotamian Poetic Language: Sumerian and Akkadian* (Groningen, 1996), p. 209: "From the Akkad period onwards the world as ruled by Mesopotamian kings on behalf of Enlil is called in Sumerian an-ub-da-limmu$_2$-ba, the 'four-corners-and-sides'."

[524] *Ibid.*, p. 120.

[525] M. Eliade, *Myth and Reality* (New York, 1963), pp. 39-40: "The third phase of the *rajasuya* comprises a series of rites whose cosmogonic symbolism is sufficiently emphasized by the texts. The king raises his arms; he is symbolizing the raising of the *axis mundi*. When he is anointed, he stands on the throne, arms lifted; he is incarnating the cosmic axis fixed in the navel of the Earth (that is the throne, the Center of the World)."

[526] For a striking parallel from the New World, see the account in R. Bunzel, "Introduction to Zuni Ceremonialism," *Annual Report of the Bureau of American Ethnology* 47 (1929-1930), p. 514: "This altar is the center of the world, the spot beneath the heart of *känastep'a* [=the Sun-father] when he stretched forth his arms."

[527] *RV* 4:53:3.

The same basic symbolism can be discerned in ancient Egypt. Thus a *Coffin Text* speaks of the sun-god's extended arms: "I have extended my arms as Rēꜥ."[528] So, too, the Egyptian king, as an incarnation of the primal sun, announces: "I have extended my arms, I have ruled the sky, I have taken possession of the earth."[529] Here, as in the Indic passage quoted above, the stretching out of the sun-god's arms is explicitly associated with rulership. This is not a coincidence, as we will document in the section to follow.

To return to the Indic traditions attached to kingship: In addition to being identified with the sun, the ruler is elsewhere celebrated for his fiery *tejas*, the latter conceptualized as a radiant energy or vital power extending to the four directions (Indologists have observed that the word *tejas* itself is virtually interchangeable with *rajas*).[530] Witness the following observation offered by Gonda:

> The Earthly ruler is formed or constituted of the supranormal principle of fiery energy (*tejas*)…In a late text like the *Kathasaritsagara* kings are still described as illuminating the quarters of the sky by their *tejas*.[531]

Such traditions are difficult to understand apart from the king's identification with the primal sun and the latter's propensity for sending forth rays (=fiery energy) to the four quarters of the cosmos, as in the cosmogram depicted in figure one.[532] And so it is that the Indic king was elsewhere implored to "Shine thou like the sun unto the four quarters."[533] In short, if the macrocosmos featured the primal sun as universal sovereign securely ensconced at the nexus of the four directions so, too, did the Indic king endeavor to organize his microcosmos by reference to the same cruciform configuration.

---

[528] *CT* VI:90.
[529] *CT* II:164.
[530] M. Williams, *A Sanskrit-English Dictionary* (Oxford, 1872), p. 454.
[531] J. Gonda, *Some Observations on the Relations Between "Gods" and "Powers" in the Veda* ('S-Gravengage, 1957), p. 61.
[532] A close parallel is evident in Mesopotamia: See B. Foster, *Before the Muses* (Bethesda, 2005), p. 637: "O Shamash, when you rise, the four quarters brighten."
[533] *AV* 19:33:5 as translated in W. Whitney & C. Lanman, *Atharva-Veda Samhita, Part 2* (Cambridge, 1905), p. 950. In another passage from the same text, the sun's "rays" are explicitly associated with the four quarters: "[Him], shining (*svar*) with the brightness (*arcis*) of the foreknowing quarters…who with his rays shines unto all the quarters."

The Maintenance of Cosmic Order

Arguably the ruler's most important responsibility was to maintain order throughout the kingdom.[534] To be more precise: The king was charged with preserving the order of the cosmos as it had been established at the time of Creation.[535] In ancient India, for example, it was commonly believed that the ruler was the living incarnation of *dharma*, a term conventionally translated as "order" and generally considered one of the most important concepts in Indic tradition.[536] Jan Gonda summarizes the symbolism as follows: "A true king is *dharmatman-*, an embodiment of *dharma*, of order, truth, norm, and justice."[537]

Dharma(n), according to Indic tradition, was established at the time of Creation. Indeed, it is *dharman* that was responsible for the primordial separation of heaven and earth: "Heaven and earth were propped apart according to the foundation of Varuna," wherein *dhármana* is translated as "foundation."[538]

The verb *dhr*, the root of *dharma*, was commonly employed to denote the act of supporting, holding apart, or "fixing" heaven and earth during the primeval ordering of the cosmos.[539] Thus in a famous passage in the *Rig Veda* it is reported that Indra "fixed" (*dharayad*) the earth in the Beginning: "He held the earth fast and spread it out."[540] The same idea is evident in another hymn extolling Indra's demiurgic activities: "Who made firm [*adrmhad*] the wavering earth, who settled the quaking mountains, who gave the midspace wider measure, who propped up heaven."[541]

In the Hymn to Earth in the *Atharva Veda* we read of the "fixed earth (*bhumi*), the earth maintained by ordinance" wherein "fixed" is *dhruvam* and ordinance

---

[534] A. Lloyd, "Expeditions to the Wadi Hammamat," in J. Hill et al eds., *Experiencing Power, Generating Authority* (Philadelphia, 2013), p. 374: "The most important function of the Egyptian king was his priestly role as guarantor of the entire cosmic order."

[535] See here the classic study of H. Frankfort, *Kingship and the Gods* (Chicago, 1948), p. 149. See also S. Maul, "Der assyrische König—Hüter der Weltordnung," in K. Watanabe eds., *Priests and Officials in the Ancient Near East* (Heidelberg, 1999), pp. 201-214.

[536] J. Gonda, "Ancient Indian Kingship from the Religious Point of View (Continued)," *Numen* 3 (1956), p. 153: "Der König ist der verkörperte dharma und der verkörperte Staatsgedanke." P. Olivelle, "Preface," in P. Olivelle ed., *Dharma* (Delhi, 2009), p. vii wrote of *dharma*: "This term and the notions underlying it clearly constitute the most central feature of Indian civilization down the centuries…" See also J. Brereton, "Dharman in the Rgveda," *Journal of Indian Philosophy* 32 (2004), pp. 449-489.

[537] J. Gonda, *op. cit.*, p. 53.

[538] *RV* 6:70:1. See here the discussion in W. Halbfass, *India and Europe* (Delhi, 1990), p. 371.

[539] A. Bowles, *Dharma, Disorder and the Political in Ancient India* (Leiden, 2007), p. 84: "In vedic cosmogony, the verb plays a similar role to other synonymous verbs, principally referring to the supporting (/*dhr*) of the sky, the holding apart (*vi-/dhr*) of the earth and sky, and the strengthening of the unstable, just-created cosmos."

[540] *RV* 2:15:2.

[541] *RV* 2:12:2.

is *dharmana*.⁵⁴² Apparent here is the archaic idea that the earth's "fixing" formed a pivotal phase in the ordering of the inchoate primordial cosmos. Prior to that time the primordial earth was "wavering" or floating about as in the Vedic passage above and in Pindar's *Hymn to Zeus* (see appendix eight).⁵⁴³

Analogous conceptions were associated with the Sanskrit term *dis-*: In addition to denoting "order" the same word also signifies "direction, quarter, and region."⁵⁴⁴ *Dis-* also carries the meaning "fixed."⁵⁴⁵ It was the four cardinal directions, as we saw in the previous chapter, that "fixed" the primordial earth during Creation.⁵⁴⁶

Sanskrit *dis-* finds a close cognate in the Greek term *dike*, denoting cosmic order and justice but also *cardinal direction*.⁵⁴⁷ Zeus himself, as the ideal king, was responsible for maintaining *dike* by means of his thunderbolt.⁵⁴⁸ Integral to the Greek concept of *dike* is the idea of "straightness."⁵⁴⁹ True or honest speech, accordingly, is "straight *dike*."⁵⁵⁰ Thus it is that Hesiod praises kings who offer straight judgments (*itheieisi dikeis*).⁵⁵¹ The same poet elsewhere credits Zeus with having the straightest *dike*: "Let us decide this quarrel through straight judgments which come from Zeus and are the best."⁵⁵²

The idea of "straightness" or making straight—hence the related meanings of "to put in order" or "make right"—is also inherent in the Sanskrit *raj-/rájas*, "to make straight."⁵⁵³ The same meaning is discernible in the Latin cognate *regio-*: witness *corrigere*, "to make straight."⁵⁵⁴ So, too, the explicit connection with ancient

---

⁵⁴² *AV* 12:1:17 as translated in W. Whitney & C. Lanman, *Atharva-Veda Samhita, Part 2* (Cambridge, 1905), p. 664. P. Horsch, "From Creation Myth to World Law: The Early History of 'Dharma'," *Journal of Indian Philosophy* 32 (2004), p. 427 translates this passage as follows: "The firm, wide earth, which is borne up by the supporting power."

⁵⁴³ R. Dandekar, "Universe in Vedic Thought," in J. Ensink & P. Gaeffke eds., *India Maior* (Leiden, 1972), p. 107 states: "Shaky as it had been in the primordial condition, subsequently it came to be firmly fixed by means of pegs."

⁵⁴⁴ A. Macdonell, *A Practical Sanskrit Dictionary* (Delhi, 2004), p. 120.

⁵⁴⁵ A. Volpe, *op. cit.*, p. 42.

⁵⁴⁶ S. Kramrisch, *The Hindu Temple, Vol. 1* (New Delhi, 1976), p. 29.

⁵⁴⁷ J. Puhvel, *Comparative Mythology* (Berkeley, 1985), p. 131.

⁵⁴⁸ D. Burton, "Nike, Dike and Zeus at Olympia," in J. McWilliam et al eds., *The Statue of Zeus at Olympia* (Cambridge, 2011), p. 52.

⁵⁴⁹ G. Nagy, *The Ancient Greek Hero* (Cambridge, 2013), p. 349: "*Dike* or 'justice' is *straight*, and *direct* and *unidirectional*." So, too, M. Gagarin, "Dike in Archaic Greek Thought," *Classical Philology* 69 (1974), p. 193 references "the original idea of a straight *dike*."

⁵⁵⁰ M. Gagarin, *op. cit.*, p. 193.

⁵⁵¹ *Theogony* 85-86.

⁵⁵² *Works and Days* 9, 36.

⁵⁵³ T. Burrow, *op. cit.*, p. 648.

⁵⁵⁴ M. de Vaan, *Etymological Dictionary of Latin and the Other Italic Languages* (Leiden, 2008), p. 517.

conceptions of "justice" is preserved in the Old Persian cognate *rasta-*, "straight, right, and true" but also, in the nominal case, "justice."⁵⁵⁵

At this point an all-important question presents itself: Given the intimate relationship between Vedic *rájas* and cosmic "regions" or structures ordered during Creation—not to mention the term's inherent connection with ancient conceptions of direction (*rájí*) and straightness—where is a straight structure to be found in the present sky? Certainly it is difficult to point to any familiar celestial structures that would be readily perceived as straight by ancient Indic sky-watchers. Yet one glance at the cosmogram depicted in figure two suffices to reveal the probable natural-historical prototype for such widespread traditions: The straight structures in question are to be identified with the four "rays" or columnar forms extending outwards from the primal sun/earth—i.e., the very same four rays/columns that were conceptualized as the four cardinal directions said to uphold (*dhárman*) or "fix" (*dhr*) the order of the cosmos established at Creation.⁵⁵⁶

Figure two⁵⁵⁷

A decisive key to understanding the vast and multivalent symbolism preserved in cosmogonic mythology is that ancient conceptions of world order and kingly rule are inherently connected to the "rays" of the primal sun. This idea is attested in a hymn from the *Rig Veda* wherein the sun-god (Surya) is invoked as follows:

---

⁵⁵⁵ *Ibid.*, p. 517.

⁵⁵⁶ Hence we find it reported that the primordial earth is fixed by "beams" of light: "Thou proppest asunder these two worlds, O Vishnu; with beams of light didst thou hold fast the earth on all sides." R. Griffith, *The Texts of the White Yajurveda* (Benares, 1899), p. 37. See also J. Eggeling, *The Satapatha Brahmana* (New Delhi, 1990), p. 130.

⁵⁵⁷ Adapted from figure 226 in W. Ward, *The Seal Cylinders of Western Asia* (Washington D.C., 1910).

He rules [/shines] widely in many places. The lofty (light) blazing forth, well supported…is fitted into the foundation, the buttress of heaven.[558]

The concrete basis of the formulaic language in question is encoded in the very first line, wherein to rule widely is inseparable from to shine widely: "*vi rajasi* means both 'shine in every direction' and 'rule in every direction.'"[559] Evident here is the archaic idea that the universal sovereign's "rule" stems from his ability to shine forth to the four cardinal directions. Note also that the sun is explicitly described as "fitted into" the buttress of heaven (=*divo dharúna*=World Pillar), which, in turn, provides it with support.[560] The inescapable conclusion is that the sun god was indissolubly connected to the World Pillar, the latter essential to world order (*dhárman*).

The same astronomical imagery informs the rich symbolism attached to the Vedic rituals surrounding the generation of fire. Thus it is said of Agni that he was "kindled according to his first foundations," wherein the word for foundations is *dhárma*.[561] The underlying message, as Paul Horsch pointed out, is that the ritual drilling of Agni was believed to reenact the central events of Creation and encode his fundamental relation to world order: "Hence it is said that the fire god Agni is set aflame in accordance with the first *dhármani*, that is to say the primordial, world-supporting, cosmo-preserving powers."[562] This can only be the case if Agni's "flames" (=rays) literally generated the *dhármani* (=sky-props) upholding—and separating—the sky and earth.

In attempting to deconstruct cosmogonic myths such as those preserved in the *Rig Veda* it is absolutely essential to ferret out the natural history behind the formulaic language employed by the ancient poets. In each and every case, one should seek to find a concrete basis behind the imagery in question. Consider the following hymn:

You, o Agni, the sovereign king over the peoples…Shine as a herdsman of truth in your house…You rule in every direction.[563]

---

[558] *RV* 10:170:1-2.
[559] S. Jamison & J. Brereton, *The Rigveda* (Austin, 2014), p. 482 with respect to *RV* 3:10:7.
[560] See especially the illuminating discussion in P. Horsch, "From Creation Myth to World Law: The Early History of Dharma," in P. Olivelle, *Dharma* (Delhi, 2004), p. 11.
[561] *RV* 3:17:1.
[562] P. Horsch, "From Creation Myth to World Law: The Early History of 'Dharma'," *Journal of Indian Philosophy* 32 (2004), p. 429.
[563] *RV* 3:10:1-7.

The word translated as "truth" here is *rtá*, an early Sanskrit term for "order." Encoded in this formulaic language is the archaic—and universal—conception that the world order established at Creation is inherently connected to solar radiation and the celestial structures generated by it.[564] Note also that the fire-god's status as universal sovereign is expressly linked to his capacity for ruling (=shining) in every direction.

Elsewhere in the *Rig Veda* it is said that Agni was "born in truth": "The head of heaven, the spoked wheel of the earth, Agni Vaisvanara, born in truth."[565] While it is tempting to see metaphor at work here, it is Agni's identification with the sun—the central theme of this particular hymn—that points the way to a successful interpretation: It is the inaugural appearance or flaring up of the nascent sun's straight "rays" that announced his "birth" and constituted the "order, truth" in question.[566] Note also the reference to Agni as a "spoked wheel"—a stock epithet of the god is "spoked wheel of heaven."[567] Now I ask: How better to describe the celestial power depicted in figure two than as a "spoked wheel"?

The historical reconstruction advanced here receives additional corroboration from the fact that ancient Egyptian lore offers complementary testimony on this score. The Egyptian word for cosmic order is *Maat* (*m3't*). A recurring theme in Egyptian cosmogonic traditions is that *Maat* was first established or "fixed" at the time of Creation and remained normative for all time.[568] To be more precise: It is reported that *Maat* originated in conjunction with the prototypical sunrise: "Maat was established at the creation, when the sun rose into the world for the first time."[569]

Why exactly the sun was conceptualized as the paragon of Maat has never been explained. Ken Kitchen's conjecture does not exactly inspire confidence: "As the sun blazing with light in the sky was deemed to see everything on earth, the Egyptians vested justice in their preeminent sun-god, Re (or Ra)."[570] Really? Is

---

[564] See the discussion in J. Jurewicz, "The Concept of *rtá* in the *Rgveda*," in R. Seaford ed., *Universe and Inner Self in Early Indian and Early Greek Thought* (Cambridge, 2010), p. 34, who observes: "*Rtá* is the first sunrise."

[565] *RV* 6:7:1.

[566] The same symbolism is evident in Iranian (Zoroastrian) religion, wherein Asha—the exact cognate of Vedic *rtá* denoting "order, law"—"manifests itself in fire." So, too, the fire is said to be "strong through Asha." See *Yasna* 34:4.

[567] *RV* 2:2:2, 3; 7:5:1; 10:3:2.

[568] J. Allen, *Genesis in Egypt* (New Haven, 1988), p. 27: "The order [Maat] of the world…was written in the beginning and remains fixed."

[569] J. Allen, *Middle Egyptian* (Cambridge, 2014), p. 147.

[570] K. Kitchen, "Maat," in T. Longman & P. Enns, *Dictionary of the Old Testament* (Downer's Grove, 2008), p. 448. Likewise S. Maul, "Der assyrische König—Hüter der Weltordnung," in K. Watanabe eds., *Priests and Officials in the Ancient Near East* (Heidelberg, 1999), p. 201.

this the best answer modern scholarship has to offer? The explicit link between Re and the order established at the time of Creation is completely ignored by Kitchen and yet it is obvious that this correlation is the key to a proper interpretation of the symbolism. Whatever Maat is it is certain that it was established *in illo tempore* at the time of the ordering of the cosmos and by means of solar radiance (see appendix ten).

Maat itself derives from the root *mꜣꜥ* "to direct," "straight," "true," or "just."[571] Yet the same word is cognate with *mꜣwt*, denoting the sun's "rays" or radiance and thus there can be no denying the fact that the Egyptian concept of cosmic order was indissolubly connected to the primal sun and its radiant structures.[572] An early hymn testifies to such conceptions: "When you shine forth in the *akhet* you appear in justice."[573] Richard Wilkinson summarized the evidence as follows:

> Another symbol of *maat* is found in the narrow hieroglyphic sign which resembles a straight rule or measure. The concept of 'straightness' which this represents is seen literally in the word *maut* which can signify the shaft of a spear, a staff, stalk, or rays of light, and figuratively in *maa*: true, just, and right.[574]

In short, the Egyptian word *mꜣꜥ*—whence derives Maat—signifies "straight" or "to direct" and is inherently related to solar radiation. In this sense it forms a remarkable parallel to the Indo-European root *$*h_3reg$-*, "straight" or "to direct" but also "to rule, radiate."[575] One finds much the same semantic range in German *strahlen*, which signifies "ray, beam" but also "straight line."[576] As we have argued here, the most logical way to explain this semantic development is by reference to the straight rays of the primal sun *in illo tempore*.

---

[571] G. Takács, *Etymological Dictionary of Egyptian, Vol. 3* (Leiden, 2008), p. 47: "The original idea of Egyptian *mꜣꜥ* seems to have been 'to (be) direct(ed) in the right direction.'" There he cites a number of associated meanings including to "stretch out the arms" and direct the "limbs/winds"—i.e., the very meanings we would expect from our analysis in the previous chapter.

[572] J. Assmann, "Solar Discourse," *Deutsche Vierteljahrsschrift für Literaturwissenschaft und Geistesgeschichte* 4 (1994), p. 119 acknowledges the point but provides little insight into the origin of the association: "Maat ('truth, justice, order') is believed to emanate from the sun god through his radiation and motion and to fill the world with order and meaning."

[573] J. Zandee, *Der Amunshymnus des Papyrus Leiden I 344 verso, Vol. 1* (Leiden, 1992), p. 401: "Wenn du strahlst im Lichtland (*psd.k m ꜣḫt*), erscheinst in Gerechtigkeit (*hꜥ.k m mꜣꜥt*)." Translation by author.

[574] R. Wilkinson, *Reading Egyptian Art* (London, 1992), p. 37.

[575] A. Byrd, *The Indo-European Syllable* (Leiden, 2010), pp. 5-6.

[576] J. Horne, *A Basic Vocabulary of Scientific and Technological German* (Oxford, 1969), p. 265.

As a general rule of thumb—one is tempted to deem it a *natural law* of human cognition—the primary structures referenced in cosmogonic myth *never* trace to metaphorical or analogical processes. Rather, cosmogonic traditions *always* encode witnessed natural events and concrete structures and, as such, reflect experiential learning. Until now, however, the natural history of the epochal catastrophic events remembered as Creation has remained all but unknown to modern science and thus it is not surprising that the root meanings of such fundamental concepts as Maat continue to elude even the best scholars.

In order to understand the multiform symbolism associated with the manifestation of order at the Time of the Beginning, it is helpful to have a rough outline of cosmogonic history before us. The natural events remembered as Creation, as we have documented in a number of publications, occurred during a historical context in which darkness and chaos prevailed. During the pre-Creation period in question, the nascent "sun" or "fire" was "hidden" in the primordial earth, during which time a prodigious storm whirled about the circumpolar heavens, darkening the sky and buffeting the earth. The catastrophic conditions in question were interpreted in countless different ways—as an apocalyptic eclipse of the sun, as the imprisonment of a solar hero within the earth (=Underworld, a hole in the earth, Venusberg), as the swallowing of the warrior-hero by a dragon, as the withholding or hoarding of riches or food within a mountain, etc. With the flaring up of the nascent sun (=the kindling of the fire), the solar "rays" extending to the four directions first came into view, thereby partitioning and "ordering" the cosmos while dispelling the darkness. Hence we would understand the Egyptian tradition that Maat originated at the very time of the prototypical sun's appearance *in illo tempore*, not to mention the meaning "ray/radiance" inherent in the cognate term *mꜣwt*.[577] The essence of the symbolism is captured by an inscription of King Tut which speaks of the establishment of *maat* instead of *jsft* (chaos and disorder): "His Majesty drove out disorder (*jsft*) from the Two Lands so that order (*mꜣꜥt*) was again established in its place;… the land was as at 'the first time' [=the creation]."[578]

Maat's association with direction and straightness, likewise, has its origin in the inherent connection between the solar rays and cardinal directions, both of which were straight in appearance. It was the dramatic appearance of "straight" rays at the time of the prototypical sunrise that was conceptualized as the ordering of the cosmos and, accordingly, as the establishment of moral order and justice

---

[577] See the brilliant analysis in R. Finnestad, *Image of the World and Symbol of the Creator* (Wiesbaden, 1985), p. 30: "Making the darkness *mꜣꜥ* means, dispelling the darkness and thus turning chaos into cosmos."
[578] K. Kitchen, *op. cit.*, p. 534.

(hence the root meaning of "straight" in Maat, *dike*, and *rájas*). If, from the standpoint of cosmic geography, the sun's rays were conceptualized as four straight pillars or cardinal directions "fixing" or supporting the hitherto floating earth, from the vantage point of religious morality the rays were conceptualized as straight "judgments," "directives," "rules," or "ordinances."[579]

Such language is firmly rooted in natural history and human memory. Essential to understanding the attendant symbolism is the fact that the "straightening out" in question followed a period of apocalyptic darkness and turbulence in which Venus's disheveled "hair" whirled about the circumpolar heavens, unleashing prodigious lightning storms and blood-curdling sound effects (witness the Sumerian traditions describing Inanna/Venus as a raging whirlwind, closely paralleled by the Egyptian myth of the raging Eye of Horus, deconstructed by us elsewhere).[580] With the stabilization of the nascent cosmos, the whirling hair or cyclonic "wind" eventually became ordered or "straightened," thereby inspiring traditions of a reordering of the cosmos. Hence, we find that the term *mꜣꜥ* was employed to describe the ordering of hair or wind.[581]

It must be remembered, moreover, that the solar rays presented a luxuriant turquoise color during the explosive events associated with the prototypical sunrise. Hence, we would understand the ancient Egyptian testimony to the effect that Maat resided in a turquoise-colored field in the sky.[582] Much the same symbolism is evident in Greek tradition, where we find an otherwise baffling association between *dike* and a verdant garden.[583] So far as I know, it was Gregory Nagy who first documented this thematic pattern:

> In ancient Greek poetics, a primary metaphor for *dike* is a flourishing *field* or *garden* or *vineyard* or any other place where vegetation is cultivated.[584]

---

[579] Chinese cosmogonic myth likewise alludes to four straight pillars upholding the world. See M. Loewe, *Faith, Myth and Reason in Han China* (Cambridge, 2005), p. 65.
[580] E. Cochrane, *On Fossil Gods and Forgotten Worlds* (Ames, 2021), pp. 61-78.
[581] R. van der Molen, *A Hieroglyphic Dictionary of Egyptian Coffin Texts* (Leiden, 2000), p. 153. See also D. Kurth, "Wind," *LÄ* VI (1990), col. 1269.
[582] J. Zandee, *Der Amunshymnus des Papyrus Leiden I 344 verso*, Vol. 1 (Leiden, 1992), p. 363.
[583] A. Della Volpe, "Problems of Semantic Reconstruction: PIE *deik-* 'to show'," in D. Disterheft, M. Huld & J. Greppin et al eds., *Studies in Honor of Jaan Puhvel* (Washington, D.C., 1997), observes of the connection between *dike* and gardens that "The semantics of the terms listed above are extremely difficult to account for."
[584] G. Nagy, *The Ancient Greek Hero* (Cambridge, 2013), p. 345.

Yet why should this be? What possible connection could there be between ancient conceptions of justice and flourishing gardens?[585]

The answer, as we have documented here, traces to the luxuriant garden-like structure that burgeoned forth in the immediate aftermath of the *hieros gamos* involving the planet Venus *in illo tempore*. The celestial garden in question was explicitly associated with the four cardinal directions, as evinced by the third millennium BCE Sumerian Temple Hymns: "The four corners of heaven became green for Enlil like a garden."[586] If one mythical interpretation saw the sudden appearance of the four cardinal directions as four straight pillar-like structures "fixing" the primordial earth *in illo tempore* (*dike*=fixed), another interpretation conceptualized the cardinal directions (*dike*) as four "straight" judgments or ordinances associated with a garden-like structure.[587]

---

[585] Nagy, *op. cit.*, p. 386 provides part of the answer: "[He, the King or leader] will give the city a sense of *direction, directness, directedness*. He will become the ultimate Director. He will be the exponent of *dike*, which is seen metaphorically both as a straight line and as a flourishing *field* or *garden* or *orchard* or *grove* or *vineyard* or any other such place where vegetation is cultivated."

[586] Line 6 from "The Keš temple hymn," *ETCSL*.

[587] A. Volpe, *op. cit.*, p. 41 observed of *dike*: "In Homer, its primary meaning was that of 'something fixed, a set way, or manner'."

15 The King's Fire

A perpetual fire shall be burning upon the altar, it shall not go out.[588]

For the fire to go out was the greatest of catastrophes.[589]

In October of 334 BC, Alexander the Great was on the verge of conquering the then known world when his beloved comrade Hephaistion suddenly became ill and died in quick succession during a major public festival and drinking bout at Ecbatana in western Iran. In what must rank as one of the most extravagant displays of public mourning in all recorded history, the Macedonian general ordered that sacred fires be extinguished throughout the entire Near East. The Greek historian Diodorus Siculus chronicled the occasion as follows:

> He proclaimed to all the peoples of Asia that they should sedulously quench what the Persians call the sacred fire, until such time as the funeral should be ended. This was the custom of the Persians when their kings died....[590]

Modern scholars have confirmed Diodorus's account of these traditional Persian rituals. Mary Boyce offered the following commentary:

> Until very recently the age-old custom was still observed in traditionalist Zoroastrian villages in Iran of extinguishing a hearth fire

---
[588] *Leviticus* 6:6.
[589] S. Pyne, *Vestal Fire* (New York, 2011), p. 76.
[590] *Diodorus*, 17:114:4.

at the death of the master of the house; and that of extinguishing hearth fires generally when a chief or king died probably goes back likewise to a remote past, far older than the Achaemenian era.[591]

What was true of the ancient Persians was also true of cultures around the globe, civilized and indigenous alike. In the event of the king's death—or that of a chief or beloved tribal leader—the sacred fire was ordered extinguished for a period of mourning after which it would be reignited by ritual means—i.e., by drilling a fire with two wooden sticks conceptualized as male and female. Tor Irstam documented such practices across a wide swath of Central Africa:

> The fire was not permitted to go out as long as the king lived (Ganda, Nyoro, Shilluk, Dar Fur, the Congo, Loango, Kuba, Tonga, Monomotapa, Rundi, Nkole and other places). The sacred flame of the fire was a symbol for the king's life, and thus also for the prosperity of the country. When the king died his sacrificial death, all the fires in the land must be extinguished.[592]

The customs prevailing among the Bantu Buganda from Uganda are representative here. There, too, the sacred fire was extinguished upon the death of the local king.[593] The death of a king was "announced to the people by the words, 'The fire has gone out.'"[594]

Similar conceptions are evident in the New World. Among the Natchez Indians of the Mississippi Valley region, for example, a perpetual fire was kept near the hut of the chief, the latter known as "Great Sun." According to James Frazer, "the greatest care was taken to prevent its extinction; for such an event would have been thought to put the whole nation in jeopardy."[595] With the chief's death, his fire was extinguished and "this was the signal for putting out all the other fires in the country."[596]

A related idea found the hearth fire being extinguished upon the death of the household-head. This practice is well attested from one end of the Indo-European

---

[591] M. Boyce & F. Grenet, *A History of Zoroastrianism* (Leiden, 1991), p. 17.
[592] T. Irstam, *The King of Ganda* (Stockholm, 1990), p. 141.
[593] S. Kyeyune, *Shaping the Society, Vol. II* (Bloomington, 2012), p. 136: "The sacred fire was not extinguished unless the king died (*Tekizikira okuggyako ng'Omutanda akisizza omukono*). The customary phrase to announce the death of the Kabaka [i.e., the King] was: '*Omuliro gwe Buganda guzikide*,' meaning that the Buganda's fire has been extinguished.
[594] J. Frazer, *The Magic Art and the Evolution of Kings*, Vol. II (London, 1911), p. 261.
[595] *Ibid.*, p. 262.
[596] *Ibid.*, p. 263.

world to the other: "Among the ancient Germans, in Greece and India, at the death of the head of the household the fire was ceremonially extinguished."[597]

How are we to explain such widespread customs from the standpoint of natural science? Simply put, the ritual practices in question will never be explained apart from the extraordinary natural events outlined here. The ritual fire, as we have documented, was commonly considered to be a symbolic replica of the primal sun (recall here the traditions attached to Vedic Agni and Aztec Xiuhtecuhtli). In accordance with the age-old belief system that the microcosmos reflects the macrocosmos, the local king, chief, or household head was conceptualized as the "sun" of the land.[598] The death of the local king, in turn, was analogized to the death of the primal sun. And so it is that, upon the death of the Ur III king Urnammu (circa 2100 BCE), a commemorative inscription stated simply: "Utu does not rise in the sky."[599] The phrase "Utu does not rise in the sky" is tantamount to saying that the "king's fire has gone out."

Properly understood, the curious practice of extinguishing fires with the death of a king or the head of the household finds its historical origin and ideational foundation in the archaic conception that the primal "sun" was the archetypal sovereign—the exemplar or celestial prototype of kings—whose "death" or eclipse *in illo tempore* ushered in a Long Night and threatened to destroy the world. It was this prototypical "eclipse" of the primal sun and ensuing Long Night that was reactualized with every subsequent occlusion of the solar orb.[600] And inasmuch as the sun's eclipse or "death" portended cosmic disaster so, too, did the death of the local king elicit communal mourning and panic, requiring sundry apotropaic rituals to be performed in order to avert or alleviate the impending disaster. The Assyro-Babylonian practice of sacrificing a substitute king at the time of solar eclipse is merely the most obvious example of what was once, presumably, a widespread practice.[601]

---

[597] J. Mallory & D. Adams, *Encyclopedia of Indo-European Culture* (London, 1997), p. 263.

[598] C. Ambos, "Temporary Ritual Structures and Their Cosmological Symbolism," in D. Ragavan ed., *Heaven and Earth* (Chicago, 2013), observes: "According to Mesopotamian ideology, the king was the likeness of the sun on earth among the people." See also E. Frahm, "Rising Suns and Falling Stars," in J. Hill ed., *Experiencing Power, Generating Authority* (Philadelphia, 2013), p. 99: "Of all the heavenly bodies, it was, from early on, first and foremost the sun that provided the model for kingship in the pre-classical ancient world."

[599] J. Polonsky, *The Rise of the Sun-God and the Determination of Destiny in Ancient Mesopotamia*. Ph.D. dissertation, University of Philadelphia (2002), p. 266.

[600] E. Cochrane, *On Fossil Gods and Forgotten Worlds* (Ames, 2021), pp. 179-187.

[601] See the discussion in S. Parpola, "Excursus: The Substitute King Ritual," in S. Parpola, *Letters From Assyrian Scholars to the Kings Esarhaddon and Assurbanipal, Part II* (Winona Lake, 2007), pp. XXII-XXXII.

The historical reconstruction offered here will also shed light on countless other belief-systems or ritual practices associated with fire, hitherto considered baffling to the point of being incomprehensible. A peculiar idea, attested around the globe, found the local fire being conceptualized as the procreative masculine force. Witness the observation of Robert Forbes: "Fire was the male principle in life, a spark that could impregnate a virgin."[602] Indeed, numerous cultures preserve traditions that fire could inseminate a woman.

While the natural phenomenon of fire could never account for the origin of such ideas—fire itself, after all, is antithetical to living matter and never operates within a womb as a procreative or fertilizing agent—such is not the case with regards to *celestial* fire which, as the sun or lightning, is everywhere conceptualized as the impregnor par excellence.[603] The Indic god Agni, according to the *Rig Veda*, was remembered as the progenitor of all life: "I placed the embryo in the plants, I within all creatures, I generated progeny on earth, I (will generate) sons for wives in the future."[604]

What is true of the archetypal Fire-god is also true of the Thundergod. Zeus's impregnation of Semele in the form of a thunderbolt is a classic example of this widespread theme. Recall also the Vedic hymn invoking the Thundergod Parjanya: "Who creates the embryo of the plants, of the cows, of the steeds, or human women—Parjanya."[605] The same idea is evident in the following hymn:

> The bull is the inseminator of each and every (plant). In him is the life-breath of the moving (world) and of the still.[606]

To bring the argument fullcircle: A procreative function was also accorded to the celestial fire emitted by the planet Mars in Skidi lore. Witness the following summary by the anthropologist Gene Weltfish:

> As he [Morning Star Mars] rose every morning he sent his beam into the long entryway of the house and lit the fire in an act of cosmic procreation, symbolizing his first union with the Evening Star in the times of the great creation when he had to fight off the guardians of night with which the Evening Star had surrounded herself.[607]

---

[602] R. J. Forbes, *Studies in Ancient Technology* (Leiden, 1966), p. 2.
[603] S. Jamison & J. Brereton, *The Rigveda* (Oxford, 2014), p. 41 observe: "As a god he [Agni] is often identified with the sun, the celestial form of fire."
[604] *RV* 10:103:3.
[605] *RV* 7:102:1-2.
[606] *RV* 7:101:6.
[607] G. Weltfish, *The Lost Universe* (Lincoln, 1965), p. 64.

Here the radiant "beams" or arrow-like rays of the Morning Star (Mars) ignite the fire in the Venusian hearth, thereby generating all life.[608] Until that precise moment, Venus had been enshrouded in darkness.[609] As the same author observed: "In the creation story, fruitfulness and light had come into the world because Morning Star and his realm of light had conquered and mated with Evening Star in her realm of darkness."[610]

It is with such archaic conceptions in mind that the Skidi sky-watchers invoked the firesticks as follows: "You are to create new life even as Morning Star and Evening Star gave life to all things."[611] Hence the archetypal equation evinced in Skidi cosmogonic myth, wherein the drilling of fire symbolizes and somehow recreates the prototypical *hieros gamos* between Mars and Venus, the latter being the Big Bang that sparked Creation.

A related idea finds the hearth fire being conceptualized as a procreative force.[612] In ancient Rome, for example, a giant phallus was said to have suddenly emerged from Vesta's hearth and impregnated the mother of Servius Tullius.[613] Martin West offered the following commentary on this curious mytheme:

> A connection with the hearth fire is presupposed in the legends of Caeculus, the founder of Praeneste, and Servius Tullius: each of them was conceived as a result of his mother's contact with the hearth fire, and was said to be a son of Volcanus.[614]

Servius Tullius, of course, was a legendary king of ancient Rome. Caeculus was the founding king of Praeneste, an ancient city near Rome. Evident in such traditions is the archaic conception that the local king was literally *engendered* from the central hearth.[615] Once again we are met with a belief-system which makes absolutely no sense in terms of human biology or fire's familiar role in the

---

[608] The idea that solar rays or "arrows" could impregnate a woman is universal in nature.
[609] See J. Murie, "Ceremonies of the Pawnee," *Smithsonian Contributions to Anthropology* 27 (Cambridge, 1981), p. 34: "In the center of the earth in darkness he found the woman, conquered her, touched her with his war club, and turned her into the earth."
[610] G. Weltfish, *op. cit.*, p. 106.
[611] J. Murie, "Ceremonies of the Pawnee," *Smithsonian Contributions to Anthropology* 27 (Cambridge, 1981), p. 150.
[612] See the discussion in J. Frazer, *op. cit.*, pp. 195ff: "Such tales at least bear witness to an old belief that the early Roman kings were born of virgins and of the fire."
[613] Dionysus of Halicarnassus 4:2; Ovid, *Fasti* 6:627-635. See here the discussion in M. Beard, *Re-Reading (Vestal) Virginity* (London, 1995), p. 24.
[614] M. West, *Indo-European Poetry and Myth* (Oxford, 2007), p. 268.
[615] G. Nagy, *Greek Mythology and Poetics* (Ithaca, 1990), p. 143 observed: "The hestia 'hearth' as the generatrix of the authority that is kingship."

natural world.[616] Yet it makes perfect sense if the hearth fire represents the primal sun or central fire, the Impregnor par excellence and the celestial prototype for the universal sovereign.

It will be recalled that the prototypical fire or "sun" was generated within a cosmic hearth. Thus it is that the Aztec Nanahuatl was generated from the turquoise-colored hearth and conceptualized as the "King-star."[617] So, too, Agni was generated in the hearth and came to represent the universal sovereign. Granted that the local king was identified with the primal sun, it follows that his birth, together with his death, might have been analogized to that of his celestial counterpart. And much as the prototypical "sun" or "fire" was conceptualized as the primal masculine force and deemed responsible for sparking Creation and generating all life, it follows that analogous conceptions were associated with early kings.

---

[616] J. Frazer, *The Golden Bough: The Magic Art, Vol. II* (London, 1911), p. 233: "But why, it may be asked, should a procreative virtue be attributed to the fire, which at first sight appears to be a purely destructive agent?"

[617] F. Olquin, "Religion," in E. Moctezuma & H. Burden eds., *Aztecs* (London, 2002), p. 225.

16 An Obsession with Creation

> What happened in the brave days of old at the beginning of the present order is of practical importance because it has had a permanent effect on subsequent behaviour and the structure of society and its institutions.[618]

> The concern of the Mesopotamian culture with the past was, shall we say, omnipotent.[619]

The supremely awe-inspiring and transformative nature of the planetary cataclysms recounted here is best evidenced by the fact that ancient cultures around the globe were seemingly fixated on events that occurred at the Time of Beginning, organizing their religion and primary institutions in accordance with cosmogonic myth. While a number of scholars have called attention to this cultural phenomenon no one, to my knowledge, has sought to explain it. A few examples should suffice to illustrate the nature of the mystery to be explained.

In ancient Egypt the pharaoh was considered the earthly incarnation of Horus, the stellar god deemed responsible for initiating Creation and ordering the cosmos.[620] Egyptian kings, in accordance with this belief-system, were judged by how accurately their behavior emulated that attributed to Horus in cosmogonic myth. And thus it is that the pharaohs sought to commemorate Creation in everything

---

[618] E. O. James, *Creation and Cosmology* (Leiden, 1969), p. 3.
[619] S. Maul, "Walking Backwards into the Future," in T. Miller ed., *Given World and Time* (Budapest, 2008), p. 16.
[620] A late Edfu text describes Horus as follows: "He whose arm was strong from the first, when he established the sky upon its four supports." See A. Blackman & H. Fairman, "The Myth of Horus at Edfu—II," *Journal of Egyptian Archaeology* 29 (1943), p. 12.

they did, from the building of pyramids to the waging of wars. In their seemingly monomaniacal engineering programs, for example, they were duty-bound to duplicate the works of Creation. Any deviation from this Revealed Plan was considered an offense against the gods and to be avoided at all costs. Rundle Clark summarized the Egyptian worldview as follows:

> The creation of myths was founded on certain principles. These are strange and, as yet only partially understood. The most important elements seem to have been as follows:
> (a) The basic principles of life, nature and society were determined long ago, before the establishment of kingship. This epoch—'*Tep zepi*'—'the First Time'—stretched from the first stirring of the High God in the Primeval Waters to the settling of Horus upon the throne and the redemption of Osiris. All proper myths relate events or manifestations of this epoch.
> (b) Anything whose existence or authority had to be justified or explained must be referred to the 'First Time'. This was true for natural phenomena, rituals, royal insignia, the plans of temples, magical or medical formulae, the hieroglyphic system of writing, the calendar—the whole paraphernalia of the civilization.
> (c) All showings of force, whether natural or human, were re-enactments of some myth. The sun rose at the beginning of the world, but this great drama of creation is repeated every morning and every New Year's day…[621]

The same basic point was reiterated by Henri Frankfort. Frankfort's discussion of royal ideology aptly illustrates the profound hold cosmogonic myth had on the Egyptian civilization:

> The kingly occupant of that throne referred to the rule of the Creator with two stock phrases: he prided himself with having achieved 'what had not been done since the time of Re' (or 'since the beginning'), or, alternatively, he claimed to have restored conditions 'as they were in the beginning.' These two phrases are not in conflict with each other, for, in so far as the king had made innovations, he had merely made manifest what had been potentially present in the plan of creation. And both phrases illustrate the Egyptian tendency to view the world as static; the order estab-

---

[621] R. T. Clark, *Myth and Symbol in Ancient Egypt* (London, 1959), pp. 263-266.

lished at the beginning of the world was considered to be normative for all times.[622]

A similar ideology is evident in ancient Mesopotamia. There, too, the king's overriding concern in rebuilding temples was to "restore these temples to their original condition, without deviating an 'eyelash' from the ancient, original plan."[623] In this sense, strangely enough, Sumerian and Babylonian kings always had their eyes trained backward on the singular events *in illo tempore*. As Stefan Maul pointed out, an obsession with the ordering of the cosmos at the time of Creation governs early engineering programs:

> Our initial presumption regarding Akkadian temporal concepts—that the attention of Mesopotamian culture was directed towards the past and thus ultimately towards the origins of existence—is confirmed in royal architectural inscriptions, which often emphasized the intention of recreating conditions from the 'days of eternity.'… Implicit in this [ideology] is the Mesopotamian notion that all things in the cosmos—and this was by no means limited to natural objects—had a secure, inalterable place given to them by the gods during creation.[624]

What was true of ancient Egypt and Mesopotamia was true of all cultures around the globe.[625] The supremely dramatic and awe-inspiring events associated with Creation were considered to be paradigmatic in nature and normative for all times. Yet how are we to understand this single-minded obsession with Creation, a collective and seemingly species-wide psychological trait that has hitherto received virtually no analysis? The word fixation is evidently quite apropos here as there is a wealth of evidence that Earthlings everywhere were so *impressed* and traumatized by the catastrophic events in question that they felt compelled to re-enact them in a seemingly obsessive manner. Why this should be the case is a matter for

---

[622] H. Frankfort, *Kingship and the Gods* (Chicago, 1948), p. 149.
[623] S. Maul, "Die altorientalische Hauptstadt—Abbild und Nabel der Welt," in G. Wilhelm ed., *Die orientalische Stadt* (Saarbrücken, 1997), p. 112 (as translated by Thomas Lampert).
[624] *Ibid*. See also the same author's "Walking Backwards into the Future," in T. Miller ed., *Given World and Time* (Budapest, 2008), pp. 15-24.
[625] M. Eliade, *Rites and Symbols of Initiation* (New York, 1958), p. xi-xiii writes as follows: "For the man of traditional societies everything significant…that has ever happened took place *in the beginning*, in the Time of the myths…It is impossible to exaggerate the importance of this obsession with beginnings, which, in sum, is the obsession with the absolute beginning, the cosmogony. For a thing to be well done, it must be done as it was done *the first time*."

psychologists to determine. Certainly, there was a strong motivation to emulate the celestial gods' triumphant behavior and magnificent creations—to encode or instantiate the experience of *mysterium tremendum et fascinosum*, as it were. If the great gods above had created a wondrous dwelling with four pillars or life-giving pathways extending to the cardinal directions, terrestrial engineers designed their early cities according to an analogous pattern.[626]

How else but as an obsessive-compulsive attempt to appease the gods and/or reactualize *their* behavior are we to understand the apparently universal tendency for humans to sacrifice their loved ones, often in the most horrific manner? In the infamous rites of Moloch, for example, the Israelites and their neighbors (Phoenicians) offered up their children to fire. As bizarre as such practices must appear to the modern mind, very similar rites are found in Mesoamerica and elsewhere (see appendix eleven).[627] The purposeful sacrifice of children is so biologically costly and contrary to fundamental notions of self-interest that one is tempted to explain it as some sort of collective behavioral response to trauma.[628]

In addition to the seemingly all-consuming desire to replicate the behavior of the planetary gods, there is also a strong likelihood that the aforementioned ritual practices represented an attempt to temper or assuage the anxiety associated with the profoundly terrifying events in question. According to Sigmund Freud, especially traumatic events can produce compulsive behaviors that tend to repeat them.[629] Walter Burkert suggested that the repetition of traumatic events acted to assuage or mollify the fear: "It seems to be a psychological mechanism that anxiety, caused by some traumatic event, may be overcome by what is called trau-

---

[626] D. Carballo, *Collision of Worlds* (Oxford, 2020), p. 200 describes the Aztecan ideology as follows: "Like other Mesoamericans, the Aztecs viewed the universe as a quincunx, divided into four quadrants that converge on a central axis connecting the underworld to the heavens. For the Mexica of Tenochtitlan, this conceptualization was rendered in microcosm in the layout of their city, which was divided into four urban quarters (*naucampa*), with the sacred precinct serving as the hub or navel (*tlalxico*) around which the city and empire revolved."
[627] In the child sacrifices to Tlaloc, for example.
[628] The likely celestial prototype for such Molochian rites, as I have argued elsewhere, was Mars' fiery baptism in the boiling cauldron of Venus. Ancient sky-watchers who witnessed these dramatic events conceptualized it as the "boiling" or cremation of their local god, be he Heracles, Melqart, Horus, Mars, Quetzalcoatl, or Nanahuatl. Insofar as the god's "firing" was deemed to be efficacious in empowering him or ensuring his divinity so, too, would Earthlings everywhere seek to emulate this fiery transfiguration with their own children, thereby steeling them for the trials and tribulations of daily life. In this sense mothers around the globe purposefully imitated the behavior of Demeter in subjecting their children to fire. See appendix eleven.
[629] So, too, a recent study concluded "traumatic memories are not remembered, they are relived and re-experienced." See https://www.nytimes.com/2023/11/30/health/ptsd-memories-brain-trauma.html

matic repetition."[630] Aristotle's notion of catharsis is also relevant here: According to the celebrated Greek philosopher, a fundamental goal of Athenian dramatic performances was to elicit a catharsis among the audience members, by which he evidently meant a calming or relieving of terrifying emotions.[631]

Given humankind's evident fixation on imitating a celestial prototype, there is a sense in which such behavior resembles the imprinting behavior documented by Konrad Lorenz and other ethologists, whereupon certain birds (young ducklings and goslings, for example) will seek to imitate or blindly follow the first notable stimulus that presents itself after hatching. Confronted with the wide array of bizarre ritualistic behaviors celebrating Creation—the heart sacrifice to Xiuhtecuhtli in the Aztec New Fire ritual, the blistering of children in fire, the erection of the World Pillar amidst much revelry and shouting, the counterclockwise dancing that distinguishes so many ancient rituals, etc.—the possibility presents itself that, during supremely traumatic events, human beings become hypersensitive to suggestion.[632] It is also probable that memories formed under extraordinary and terrifying circumstances are more emotionally "charged" than memories formed under normalized conditions and thus more deeply ingrained and durable.[633] Indeed, I suspect that, during the catastrophic events attending Creation, the entire human race suffered a behavioral response akin to that known as the Stockholm syndrome, in which victims of a particularly traumatic experience come to identify with their assailants. In the almost unimaginably terrifying conditions like those envisioned here—wherein the respective planetary powers (gods) were threatening the very survival of all Earthlings through their seemingly capricious behavior and violent fulminations[634]—it is certainly conceivable that people might come

---

[630] W. Burkert, *Structure and History in Greek Mythology* (Berkeley, 1982), p. 49.

[631] See the discussion in R. Janko, *Aristotle: Poetics* (Cambridge, 1987), p. xx.

[632] G. Catlin, *O-kee-pa: A Religious Ceremony* (Lincoln, 1976). See also the account in B. Dippie, *Catlin* (Lincoln, 1990), pp. 325ff.

[633] This was certainly Nietzsche's position in *On the Genealogy of Morals* (New York, 1967), p. 61: "One can well believe that the answers and methods for solving this primeval problem were not precisely gentle; perhaps indeed there was nothing more fearful and uncanny in the whole prehistory of man than his *mnemotechnics*. 'If something is to stay in the memory it must be burned in: only that which never ceases to *hurt* stays in the memory'—this is a main clause of the oldest (unhappily also the most enduring) psychology on earth…Man could never do without blood, torture, and sacrifices when he felt the need to create a memory for himself; the most dreadful sacrifices and pledges (sacrifices of the first-born among them), the most repulsive mutilations (castration, for example), the cruelest of all the religious cults (and all religions are at the deepest level systems of cruelties)—all this has its origin in the instinct that realized that pain is the most powerful aid to mnemonics."

[634] The distinguished plasma physicist Anthony Peratt described the likely pyrotechnics associated with the polar configuration as follows in a private online discussion devoted to the

to identify with the planetary gods and thus seek to emulate their behavior. If so, one can perhaps begin to understand the apparent willingness of human beings to endure the extreme pain and suffering which must have accompanied numerous initiation rituals involving self-mutilation, whether through blood-letting, scourging, or mutilation through scarring or ordeal (think here of the tortures endured in the Mandan Indian ceremony of *O-kee-pa* immortalized in *A Man Called Horse* whereupon, in a ritual designed to reenact Creation, a warrior-initiate is suspended from the support beams of the lodge by rawhide ropes attached to hooks impaled in his pectoral muscles).[635] How else, but as an extreme form of imprinting or traumatically-induced associative conditioning on a mass scale, are we to understand man's terror in the face of eclipses? Humankind's apparent willingness to subject themselves to the sort of prodigious labors necessary to erect pyramids and ziggurats intended to honor and propitiate the gods likely belongs here as well. No sacrifice was too great, evidently, to appease the celestial gods.

In short, there can be no denying that the celestial catastrophes described herein had a profound effect on all those fortunate enough to survive. It is our opinion, in fact, that the ancient sky-watchers were so traumatized by the events in question that they were compelled to simulate them for many generations thereafter. In this sense, the "experiences"—if not the sins—of prehistoric Earthlings were passed on to their offspring since time immemorial.

---

subject: "Envision a tube of fluorescent jelly encompassing all the planets, 'constrained' by bars running lengthwise along it [the so-called toruses as discussed in his seminal paper from 2003]. The jelly is plasma and it displays life-like characteristics, morphing shapes as current pulses travel down it. It is more than florescent; it is very colorful like neon signs (a plasma) and quite bright, especially where the current pulse is located at any moment. Where it bends to direct the relativistic electrons towards you (synchrotron radiation) it is blinding. A Sun would be lackluster in comparison to this and the albedo of a 'solid' object insignificant. At times and places the jelly is a fusion burner, like the Sun, but much closer to Earth. Finally, imagine a red ball [the planet Mars] coming down the bars shooting enormous lightning bolts at you. At the very least you would be jumping." See also A. Peratt, "Characteristics for the Occurrence of a High-Current, Z-Pinch Aurora as Recorded in Antiquity," *IEEE Transactions on Plasma Science* 31:6 (2003), pp. 1192-2014.

[635] M. Eliade, *Rites and Symbols of Initiation* (New York, 1958), p. 99: "Among some tribes, the initiation also includes the novice's being 'roasted' in or at a fire."

17 Conclusion

> There are vague memories in our souls of those misty centuries when the world was in its childhood.[636]

Now that the case has been laid out, it is time to review our findings. We have documented that sacred traditions on both sides of the Atlantic told of a Turquoise Sun at the Time of Beginning. It was the explosive, utterly spellbinding appearance of this nascent or prototypical "sun" that formed the primary subject of creation myths around the globe. The riddle of Creation, for countless millennia the ever-elusive Holy Grail sought by wise men and philosophers alike, stands revealed as a collective memory of catastrophic natural events—specifically, as the awe-inspiring occasion when a former sun sent forth its straight rays to the four cardinal directions, thereby separating heaven from earth and ordering the visible cosmos.

Remembered as the "King of the Gods," the Turquise Sun ruled his quartered cosmos with a far-seeing "eye" and avenging thunderbolt, ultimately coming to serve as the exemplary role model for terrestrial kings, who themselves sought to reproduce his dazzling structures here on Earth. If the celestial "King" ruled from the nexus of the four cardinal directions so, too, did terrestrial kings describe themselves as the "King of the Four Corners." If the celestial "King" ruled from the navel of the earth so, too, did terrestrial kings describe themselves as ruling from the center of the world. If the celestial "King" was localized within a World Tree so, too, did terrestrial kings depict themselves in the guise of a World Tree (see appendix nine). And so it is with innumerable kingship practices from around the globe, all remarkably alike.

Truth be told, the testimony of comparative myth is not to be discounted when it speaks as if with one voice of catastrophic upheaval in the recent solar

---

[636] Sherlock Holmes, as quoted from *A Study in Scarlet*.

system. A cross-cultural comparative analysis of the sacred traditions surrounding the archaic fire-god showed that he is everywhere identified with the primal sun of cosmogonic myth. There is a perfectly logical reason for this circumstance: The archaic fire-god and primal sun were one and the same celestial entity. With the drilling of the first "fire," the primal sun was "born" and the cosmos was ordered.

A cross-cultural comparative analysis of the sacred traditions surrounding the archaic Thundergod, likewise, discovered a number of analogous characteristics shared with the fire-god. The Thundergod, like the fire-god, was described as residing at the navel of the earth wherefrom it generated all life. There is a simple reason for this overlap in functions and epithets: The Thundergod and fire-god were one and the same celestial entity—namely, the primal sun.

It follows from these several equations, accordingly, that the primal sun is indistinguishable from the Thundergod in the earliest sources. This is most obvious, perhaps, in the fact that the Sumerian logogram UD denotes both the primal sun and the archetypal Thundergod or storm.[637] Yet the same conclusion follows from a systematic analysis of the wheel-like eyes shared by the Greek Zeus and Vedic Surya, eyes which emitted lightning in a seemingly capricious manner. Properly understood, Zeus the Thundergod is not to be distinguished from Zeus the Sun-god (see appendix twelve). The ramifications of these findings, if valid, herald a revolution in our understanding of the recent history of the solar system: For if the primal sun was a central locus of prodigious lightning and apocalyptic storms it stands to reason that it must needs be distinguished from the present solar orb.

We began this book with a quote from Plato, who proclaimed that "marvelous" events in prehistory forever shaped humankind. A central purpose of the present work has been to proffer evidence in favor of this proposition. "The great event of history" alluded to by Plato was the fiery birth of the Turquoise Sun and the dramatic ordering of the cosmos—an event which left an indelible imprint on human beings at a cultural, linguistic, and likely a genetic level.[638]

---

[637] M. Cohen, *An Annotated Sumerian Dictionary* (University Park, 2023), p. 1409. See the discussion in E. Cochrane, "Written in the Stars," available online at https://www.maverick-science.com/wp-content/uploads/Written-in-the-Stars.pdf

[638] Recent experimental findings strongly suggest that the traumatic experiences of World War II left a heritable imprint on succeeding generations. See Y. Wang, H. Liu & Z. Sun, "Lamarck rises from his grave: parental environment-induced epigenetic inheritance in model organisms and humans," *Biological Reviews* 92:4 (2017), pp. 2084-2011. Insofar as the trauma induced by the war in question presumably pales alongside that evoked by the catastrophic events described here, we must expect that the latter were encoded at the genetic level and passed on to future generations.

History matters my friends, not only as a worthy intellectual endeavor in its own right but because it remains with us at all times, shaping us in countless ways seen and unseen. As William Faulkner once observed: "The past is never dead. It's not even past."[639] James Baldwin, likewise, maintained that history is deeply ingrained within each one of us:

> History, as nearly no one seems to know, is not merely something to be read. And it does not refer merely, or even principally, to the past. On the contrary, the great force of history comes from the fact that we carry it within us, are unconsciously controlled by it in many ways, and history is literally *present* in all that we do. It could scarcely be otherwise, since it is to history that we owe our frames of reference, our identities, and our aspirations.[640]

As we venture forth upon a voyage of discovery in an endeavor to recover and reconstruct the earliest remembered history of humankind—*the single most impactful historical events*, in fact—it is important to be mindful of Faulkner's dictum and George Santayana's dire warning: "Those who cannot remember the past are condemned to repeat it." The revolution's afoot.

---

[639] W. Faulkner, *Requiem for a Nun* (New York, 1950), p. 73.
[640] James Baldwin, "The White Man's Guilt," in *Ebony* 20:10 (August, 1965), p. 65.

Appendix One

A survey of the mythological traditions surrounding the Mesoamerican Fire-god has documented that Xiuhtecuhtli was regarded as the archetypal ruler residing within a turquoise enclosure. The turquoise enclosure, in turn, is specifically identified with the cosmic hearth. This naturally begs the following question: How are we to understand the archaic Fire-god and his hearth from the vantage point of modern astronomy?

According to the Skidi myth of Creation, the prototypical fire-driller was identified with the planet Mars, the latter conceptualized as the "Morning Star." The cosmic hearth, on the other hand, was identified with the planet Venus. Although the Skidi traditions have received precious little attention from scholars of comparative mythology, there is good reason to suspect that these identifications are fundamentally valid across numerous cultures.

Certainly there is a wealth of evidence supporting the Skidi identification of the archetypal fire-driller with the planet Mars. In ancient Babylonian astronomy, for example, the planet Mars was identified with the war-god Nergal. Yet Nergal was elsewhere known as the "Fire-Star."[641]

A common Babylonian name for the planet Mars was *Ṣalbatanu*, of uncertain etymology.[642] Yet according to Greek texts from the Hellenistic period, the planet in question was expressly identified as the "fire star" (*pyros aster*).[643] A Hellenistic name for the red planet—*Pyroeis*, "Fiery Star"—confirms that similar conceptions prevailed among the ancient Greeks.[644]

Analogous traditions are evident in Pahlavi lore, wherein the red planet—as the god Vahram—is identified as the fire-god par excellence.[645] Indeed, it was a

---

[641] E. von Weiher, *Der babylonische Gott Nergal* (Berlin, 1971), p. 80. Note that Nergal was also invoked as Girra, "fire." See F. Reynolds, "Unpropitious Titles of Mars in Mesopotamian Scholarly Tradition," in J. Prosecky ed., *Intellectual Life of the Ancient Near East* (Prague, 1998), p. 349.

[642] E. Reiner, *Astral Magic in Babylonia* (Philadelphia, 1995), p. 18.

[643] E. von Weiher, *op. cit.*, p. 80.

[644] F. Cumont, *Astrology and Religion Among the Greeks and Romans* (New York, 1960), p. 27.

[645] A. Scherer, *Gestirnnamen bei den indogermanischen Völkern* (Heidelberg, 1953), p. 88.

central tenet of Zoroastrian religion that the sacred fire itself represented Vahram/Bahram: "The king of fires is the Bahram fire, or sacred fire."[646]

Although the Greek and Pahlavi epithets attached to Mars could conceivably be attributed to the influence of Babylonian astronomical ideas, diffusion can hardly be the explanation for the presence of analogous epithets in the New World. Thus, the Crow Indians of the North American plains described the red planet as *Ihkawilée*, "Fire Star."[647] A similar name is attested among the Blackfeet, who knew Mars as the "Big Fire Star."[648] In Skidi Pawnee lore, according to Alice Fletcher, the red planet—explicitly identified as the "Morning Star"—was understood as the star of fire:

> The morning star is called *Ho-pi-ri-ku-tsu*. The word is made from *ho-pi-rit*, 'star;' *ko-ri-tu*, 'fire;' and *ku-tzu*, 'large, great, mighty.' The name signifies 'the mighty star of fire.'[649]

Similar conceptions are evident in China, a culture renowned for its ancient and systematic astronomical observations. Early texts describe the planet Mars by the name *huo hsing*, "Fire-Star":

> In classical Chinese the term *huo hsing* ('fire star') referred both to Antares...and to the planet Mars. Hence there was a natural affinity between Scorpio and Mars in astrological interpretations.[650]

In the face of such widespread and converging testimony, it stands to reason that the prototypical "Fire Star" was indeed the planet Mars. Thus, we would appear to be on firm ground in identifying such archetypal Fire-gods as Xiuhtecuhtli and Agni with the red planet. In this sense the Aztec Xiuhtecuhtli is best understood as representing a close structural analogue to the Pahlavi god Vahram—the planet Mars as the king of the prototypical fire: "The king of fires is the Bahram fire, or sacred fire."[651]

---

[646] A. Carnoy, "Iranian Views of Origins in connection with Similar Babylonian Beliefs," *JAOS* 36 (1917), p. 306.

[647] T. McCleary, *The Stars We Know* (Prospect Heights, 1997), p. 45.

[648] A. Kehoe, "Ethnoastronomy of the North American Plains," in V. Del Chamberlain et al eds., *Songs From the Sky* (Washington, D.C., 2005), p. 129.

[649] A. Fletcher, "Pawnee Star Lore," *The Journal of American Folklore* 16 (1903), pp. 11-12.

[650] K. T'ieh-fu, "A Summary of the Contents of the Ma-Wang-Tui Silk Scroll...," *Chinese Studies in Archaeology* 1 (1979), p. 69.

[651] A. Carnoy, "Iranian Views of Origins in connection with Similar Babylonian Beliefs," *JAOS* 36 (1917), p. 306.

To return to the Chinese traditions surrounding the so-called "Fire-star": According to several early texts, the Fire-star was intimately associated with the center of the cosmos. Witness the following quote from the Han period: "The central star (the Fire Star *Huo*), …."⁶⁵²

We would also draw attention to a recently discovered star chart adorning the ceiling of a tomb from the Former Han period.⁶⁵³ On the ceiling in question the Fire-Star is identified as the red star or "heart" of a celestial structure known as Green Dragon *(cang long)*, the latter deemed to be the most honored structure in the sky.⁶⁵⁴ As Xiaohchun and Kistemacher observe:

> The dragon's heart…was painted as the only red star on the chart, to indicate the Fire star *Huo*, one of the cardinal asterisms of the Canon of Yao. In the Yin time the appearance of *Huo* above the eastern horizon at dusk indicated the arrival of spring, the beginning of the year.⁶⁵⁵

As the "central" red star located within a greenish-colored dragon, the Chinese Fire-star offers an intriguing parallel to the Aztec god Xiuhtecuhtli who, it will be remembered, resided at the center or *navel* of the earth within a turquoise-colored enclosure known as the *xiuhtetzaqualko*. Recall again the ancient tradition preserved by Friar Sahagún:

> Mother of the gods, father of the gods, the old god spread out on the navel of the earth, within the circle of turquoise. He who dwells in the waters the color of the bluebird, he who dwells in the clouds. The old god, he who inhabits the shadows of the land of the dead, the Lord of fire and of time.⁶⁵⁶

Equally relevant is the fact that the Aztec fire-god was intimately associated with a turquoise-colored dragon known as Xiuhcoatl. Thus, Elizabeth Boone references an illustration of Xiuhtecuhtli in the *Codex Vaticanus A* (3738) which

---

⁶⁵² S. Xiaohchun & J. Kistemacher, *The Chinese Sky During the Han* (Leiden, 1997), p. 130.
⁶⁵³ See figure 6.1 on page 115 of S. Xiaochun & J. Kistemaker, *The Chinese Sky During the Han* (Leiden, 1997).
⁶⁵⁴ J. Majors, *Heaven and Earth in Early Han Thought* (Buffalo, 1993), p. 135: "Of those honored by the gods of Heaven, none is more honored than the Bluegreen Dragon. The Bluegreen Dragon is otherwise called the Heavenly Monad, or otherwise *taiyin*."
⁶⁵⁵ *Ibid.*, p. 114-115.
⁶⁵⁶ The *Florentine Codex* Chapter VI: 71v as translated in Miguel Leon-Portilla, *Aztec Thought and Culture* (Norman, 1963), p. 32.

shows the god "enveloped in the body of the fire serpent Xiuhcoatl."[657] As the archetypal fire-god enclosed within the body of the turquoise-colored serpent Xiuhcoatl, Xiuhtecuhtli offers a striking analogue to the Chinese Fire-Star *Huo*.

There is additional evidence that can be brought to bear on the question of the Chinese Fire-Star's celestial identification. Xiuhtecuhtli, as we have documented, was closely connected with ancient conceptions of sovereignty and kingship and was conceptualized as the archetypal sovereign. Here, too, there is some reason to believe that analogous conceptions were attached to the Chinese Fire-Star. Thus, according to Sima Qian's "Treatise on the Celestial Offices," the Fire-Star was identified as "the *Celestial King*."[658]

In addition to being described as a red star at the "center" or heart of a celestial dragon, the Chinese Fire-Star is expressly associated with spring and the origin of the year (the New Year often coincided with spring in numerous ancient cultures). Here, too, this thematic pattern is associated with the planet Mars around the globe, not Antares. In archaic Roman religion, for example, Mars was expressly identified as the god of spring: "Mars, moreover, was the god of the spring, the *ver*."[659]

The fact that Aboriginal cultures from Australia likewise attest to the intimate association between the red planet and spring attests to the archaic and *archetypal* nature of such widespread conceptions. Witness the following summary of the traditions of the Tanganekald tribe from South Australia:

> The 'red star' Mars (Waiyungari…) was seen to be responsible for spring and personified sexual activity and fertility.[660]

It goes without saying that, from the vantage point of modern astronomical science, the planet Mars has no conceivable relationship to the spring, sexual activity, or fertility. Indeed, this confluence of ideas would never occur to any sane sky-watcher given the present order of the solar system. Yet the very fact that analogous ideas are to be found around the globe strongly suggests that such ideas have a rational foundation in natural history—specifically, in the catastrophic planetary events reconstructed here.

---

[657] E. Boone, *Cycles of Time and Meaning in the Mexican Books of Fate* (Austin, 2007), p. 209. See also the discussion in B. Brundage, *op. cit.*, p. 69.
[658] D. Pankenier, *Astrology and Cosmology in Early China* (Cambridge, 2013), p. 73.
[659] H. Versnel, "Apollo and Mars one hundred years after Roscher," in *Visible Religion*, Vols. 4-5 (Leiden, 1985-1986), p. 140.
[660] D. Johnson, *Night Skies of Aboriginal Australia* (Sydney, 1998), p. 56.

Appendix Two

The question arises as to how we are to understand the primal sun's intimate association with the four cardinal directions? An evidence-based answer to this question, in turn, will clarify innumerable aspects of ancient symbolism.

In the present sky the cardinal directions are invisible to the human eye and devoid of tangible substance or structure. The familiar Sun, in turn, does not have any readily discernible relationship to the four cardinal directions. How, then, are we to explain the fact that cultures around the globe placed the primal sun at the central nexus of the four cardinal directions?

This question is inherently related to another mystery from the ancient world—namely, how to explain the curious fact that numerous cultures identified the four cardinal directions with the four winds?[661] So far as I know, it was Knut Tallqvist who first devoted a monograph to this subject. As Tallqvist documented, the idea that the four winds are to be identified with the four cardinal directions was widespread in the Old World:

> Sumerian *im*, Akkadian *šaru*, und Hebrew *ruah*, die alle eigentlich Wind aber auch Weltgegend bedeuten, nhd. *Windstrich*, Swedish *väderstreck*, Finnish *ilmansuunta* (eig. 'Luftrichtung'), English '*quarter of the wind* oder *the four winds*…und French *aire de vent* bezeugen endlich, dass Himmelsgegenden und Winde im Zusammenhang mit einander stehen.[662]

The very same belief-system is widespread among Amerindian cultures. Witness the findings of the early folklorist Harriet Converse:

> The American Indians of both continents personified the four winds…The four winds are usually regarded as the spirits of the four cardinal points, or the four corners of the earth…. In many of the American languages the names for the four directions are the names for the winds of these directions also. The Sioux call the

---

[661] The idea is already attested in Bronze Age China. See S. Allan, *The Shape of the Turtle* (Albany, 1981), p. 75.
[662] K. Tallqvist, "Himmelsgegenden und Winde," *Studia Orientalia* 2 (1928), p. 106.

four quarters of the globe, *ta-te-onye-toba*, which literally means, *whence four winds come*. Among the Mayas the names for the cardinal points are the names for the winds.[663]

Such conceptions were especially prominent among the aboriginal cultures of the American Northwest, as Franz Boas documented at the turn of the previous century: "The Winds live in the four corners of the world."[664] Alice Fletcher found the same to be true among the Skidi Pawnee: "The four winds guard the paths at the four quarters."[665] The Dakota, according to the renowned anthropologist James Dorsey, held that "the four primary winds and their respective quarters" were symbolized by a cross.[666]

Closer examination reveals a number of telltale clues that the four winds/directions emanated from the locus of the sunrise. This idea is most explicit in Aztec tradition, as reported by Sahagún:

> That which was known as [the wind] was addressed as Quetzalcoatl. From four directions it came, from four directions it traveled. The first place whence it came was the place from which the sun arose, which they named Tlalocan.[667]

This tradition finds a curious echo in Greek tradition. Thus it is that a magical papyrus invokes Helios as follows: "Thou who risest from the four winds."[668]

In short, it is at the nexus of the four corners/winds that the central fire or primal sun is to be found. Insofar as such traditions stand in glaring contradiction to the Sun's appearance in the present sky, they serve as compelling testimony that a different sun prevailed during the prehistoric period.

If we take the imagery from ancient pictographs and cylinder seals as relatively accurate portrayals of the ancient sky, it follows that the primal sun formerly resided at the center of a cross-like structure, the latter composed of radiating fiery filaments that spanned the visible heavens. There is much reason to believe that the luminous filaments in question—everywhere compared to radiating light, wind, lightning, flowing water, etc.—were plasma-based in nature and emanated

---

[663] H. Converse, *Myths and Legends of the New York Iroquois* (Albany, 1974), p. 37.
[664] F. Boas, "Tsimshian Mythology," *Bureau of American Ethnology* (Washington D.C., 1916), p. 455.
[665] A. Fletcher, "Pawnee Star Lore," *Journal of American Folk-Lore* 16 (1903), p. 12.
[666] J. Dorsey, "Indian Names for the Winds and Quarters," *The Archaeologist* 2 (1894), p. 42.
[667] B. Sahagún, *Florentine Codex: Book 7* (Sante Fe, 1953), p. 14.
[668] H. Leisegang, "The Mystery of the Serpent," in J. Campbell ed., *The Mysteries* (Princeton, 1955), p. 220, citing Pap. Bibl. Nat. suppl. Gr. 574.

outwards from the immediate vicinity of the primal sun, perhaps from Venus itself (the latter planet was positioned directly behind Mars at this time). Ancient traditions describing the fiery streamers as braided or rope-like in structure likewise point to plasma-based material as being responsible for the awe-inspiring display of pyrotechnics. A systematic review of the ancient writings will corroborate this point beyond any possible doubt.

Appendix Three

Xiuhtecuhtli was renowned for his turquoise headband—the *xiuhuitzolli*—the supreme symbol of kingship and sovereignty that ultimately came to serve as the Aztec ideogram for *tecuhtli*, "Lord or ruler."[669] Johannes Neuroth, in his comprehensive study of the *xiuhuitzolli*, observed: "It was a widespread emblem of royal power in Post-classic Central Mexico."[670]

At the same time, a number of indigenous sources report that the Aztec fire-god was intimately associated with a turquoise-colored serpent known as Xiuhcoatl. Alternately described as a comet-like celestial body[671] or as a "Fire Serpent" weaponized in the service of Xiuhtecuhtli or Huitzilopochtli, the Xiuhcoatl is commonly depicted as a sort of head-ornament or back-device adorning the Aztec fire-god (see figure one).[672] Yet as Justyna Olko has documented, there is some reason to believe that the Xiuhcoatl-serpent is to be identified as the celestial prototype for the turquoise headband (*xiuhhuitzolli*):

> Of particular importance is the link between Xiuhtecuhtli and the fire serpent Xiuhcoatl, for this creature appears to have been the most probable prototype of the *xiuhhuitzolli*. It was Beyer who first suggested that the *xiuhhuitzolli* was a schematic form of the head and tail of Xiuhcoatl…Although the idea linking the shape of the *xiuhhuitzolli* to the fire-serpent has not been developed or even accepted in any subsequent studies, there are good reasons to believe that it is valid.[673]

---

[669] On the crown as the ideogram for *tecuhtli*, see H. Nicholson, "A Royal Headband of the Tlaxcatleca," *Revista mexicana de estudios antropológicos* 21 (1964), p. 82.

[670] J. Neuroth, "*Xiuhuitzolli*—Motecuhzoma's Diadem of Turquoise, Fire, and Time," *Archiv für Völkerkunde* 46 (1982), p. 123. See especially D. Stuart's unpublished paper at https://mayadecipherment.com/2015/01/26/the-royal-headband-a-pan-mesoamerican-hieroglyph-for-ruler/

[671] M. Izeki, *Conceptions of 'xihuitl': History, Environment and Cultural Dynamics in Postclassic Mexica Cognition* (Oxford, 2008), p. 41 notes that "the depiction of Xiuhcoatl in the history sections of the codices are limited to scenes recording the observations of comets."

[672] J. Olko, *Insignia of Rank in the Nahua World* (Boulder, 2014), p. 54: "Xiuhtecuhtli and his fire-serpent manifestation [Xiuhcoatl] were believed to embody the celestial fire, also conceived as a dangerous weapon that could take the material form of turquoise."

[673] *Ibid.*, p. 128.

Figure one

To bring the argument full circle: In light of the fact that the turquoise enclosure served as a hearth in which the New Fire was drilled, it is significant to find that Aztec codices depict fire being drilled on the Xiuhcoatl serpent (see figure two).[674] Karl Taube called attention to this peculiar motif: "In many Late Postclassic Central Mexican representations of fire making, fire is drilled on the segmented, larval body of the Xiuhcoatl meteor serpent."[675] Although such imagery is wildly incongruous as a realistic depiction of fire's generation in the natural world, it makes perfect sense given the historical reconstruction offered here, which recognizes a fundamental structural affinity between the turquoise-colored Xiuhcoatl serpent and the turquoise-colored enclosure.

Figure two

---

[674] Adapted from K. Taube, "The Turquoise Hearth," in D. Carrasco ed., *Mesoamerica's Classic Heritage* (Boulder, 2000), figure 10:15:c.
[675] *Ibid.*, p. 294.

To summarize the argument to this point: Occam's razor suggests that the turquoise-colored headband associated with the Aztec fire-god Xiuhtecuhtli (*xiuhhuitzolli*) is identical in origin with the turquoise-colored enclosure (*xiuhtetzaqualco*) associated with the drilling of the New Fire. If the former object represented the royal crown marking Xiuhtecuhtli as the archetypal sovereign, the latter structure represented the cosmic hearth associated with the post-mortem transfiguration of Nanahuatl, the prototypical "sun" and "king" in Aztec cosmogony.

The key to understanding the Aztec traditions referencing a turquoise enclosure encircling the prototypical fire-god and serving as the god's hearth is a very real celestial structure that formerly spanned the heavens, the latter conceptualized as the crown of kingship *and* as a *kippatu* band encircling the sun.[676] According to the historical reconstruction offered here, these archaic mythological traditions encode astronomical events—specifically an extraordinary conjunction of planets in which the red planet Mars (Xiuhtecuhtli) was positioned in front of the much larger Venus (see figure three). The image presented by this spectacular conjunction of planets was closely modeled by the Egyptian shen-bond, in which a green band encircles a reddish orb. It is in this perfectly concrete sense, then, that we would understand the Skidi Pawnee report that a cosmic hearth associated with the planet Venus was the site of the prototypical drilling of fire by Mars.

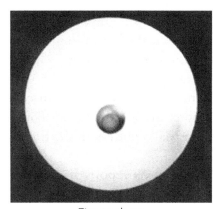

Figure three

---

[676] See the ground-breaking analysis in D. Talbott, *The Saturn Myth* (New York, 1980), pp. 145-171.

Appendix Four

> The mystery of Agni's birth is unquestionably the central motif of the Indo-Iranian mythology.[677]

> He who in birth (*jayamana*) opened out the earth.[678]

The birth of Agni forms a recurring theme in Vedic and post-Vedic literature. As a central mystery in Vedic cosmogonic myth—and the purported goal of sacrificial ritual—Agni's birth is extolled repeatedly in the extant sources, often in a riddling manner and in terms that are seemingly contradictory in nature.

Truth be told, there is no real mystery about the circumstances of Agni's birth: He was born from the navel of the earth. The supposed mystery only arises because all scholars and exegetes have assumed that the earth in question is terrestrial in nature and/or to be identified with the ritual landscape. Martin West, for example, in his survey of Indo-European mythological traditions, opined that the navel of the earth had reference to the local fire-pit: "It is not a remote, mythical location; it is the fire-pit at the place of sacrifice where Agni blazes and forms a link with heaven."[679]

This is wrong from A to Z: The navel of earth celebrated in Vedic cosmogonic myth is indeed a remote, mythical location. For all his erudition West has managed to confuse the terrestrial replica with the thing signified, in this case the primordial earth.[680]

Again and again the Vedic texts report that Agni was born in the highest heaven: "As he was being born in the highest heaven…"[681] So, too, the Vedic scribes are adamant that the earth's navel is to be found in the highest heaven: "That earth which formerly was water upon the ocean (of space)…whose heart is

---

[677] F. Kuiper, *Ancient Indian Cosmogony* (Delhi, 1983), p. 29.
[678] *AV* 13:2:20.
[679] M. West, *Indo-European Poetry and Myth* (Oxford, 2007), pp. 344-345.
[680] More sober-minded in this regard is the observation of Jamison and Brereton: "Thus 'our' just-born ritual fire is identified as both the first created thing and the creator itself, and ritual time, as so often, recapitulates cosmic time."
[681] *RV* 1:143:2.

in the highest heaven."[682] The same idea is evident in the following hymn: "Praised, the young one has flared up through his kindling, upon the summit of heaven and the navel of earth."[683] In perfect keeping with this testimony, Agni is celebrated as shining forth from the sky: "Agni glows from the sky, to Agni, the god, belongs the broad one."[684] The epithet "the broad one" points to the primordial earth, here localized in the sky.

Famously, the primordial earth is identified as a four-petaled lotus in Indian tradition.[685] And as the earth-born god *par excellence*, Agni is celebrated as lotus-born (*abja-ja*). "You, Agni, did Atharvan churn forth from the lotus," reads a hymn from the *Rig Veda*.[686] While such traditions will never be explained by fire's function in the familiar natural world, where the generation of fire has nothing whatsoever to do with the interior of a lotus flower, it conforms exactly with the historical reconstruction offered here, wherein the prototypical sun (=Agni) first appeared while in conjunction with a four-petaled flower. In this sense, the generation of Agni from within a lotus flower is functionally and structurally analogous to the appearance of the nascent sun Horus atop the lotus in Egyptian cosmogonical tradition.

Properly understood it is not the ritual generation of mundane fire that is translated into cosmogonic myth and projected onto the sky, rather the exact reverse: It is the extraordinary natural history of Creation as witnessed by prehistoric sky-watchers that is encoded in myth and reenacted in religious ritual.

---

[682] *AV* 12:1:8.
[683] *RV* 3:5:9.
[684] *AV* 12.1.20.
[685] H. Zimmer, *Myths and Symbols in Indian Art and Civilization* (Princeton, 1972), pp. 90-91.
[686] *RV* VI:16:13.

Appendix Five

At the time of Creation, if we are to believe the express testimony of sky-watchers around the globe, the nascent sun presented a flower-like appearance. Granted that there is some natural-historical basis for such archaic mythological traditions, it stands to reason that this singular situation would be reflected in ancient languages.

It is significant to note that a number of the world's major languages preserve an indissoluble connection between words denoting "to flower" or "blossom" and words signifying "to ignite" or "fire." Homer himself testifies to this belief-system in the *Iliad* when he speaks of the "flower of fire" (*puròs ánthos*).[687] So, too, Aeschylus likens the fire purloined by Prometheus to a flower in the following passage addressed to Hephaestus, the Greek god of fire: "For this is he who stole the flame of all-working fire, thy own bright flower, and gave to mortal men."[688]

It is the New World, however, which offers the most extensive database for such pyro-floral terminology. Thus it is that, when requesting coals of fire, the Zuni shaman employs the formulaic expression "Give us more beautiful flowers"—a striking parallel to Aeschylus.[689] According to the anthropologist Jane Hill, "The flower is symbolically associated with fire: fire 'blossoms,' and flowers 'burst into flame.'"[690] The same author documents the presence of this semantic field across the better part of Southwest America:

> The metaphoric association of flowers and flames is very widespread in Uto-Aztecan languages. The metaphor of the blooming flower as 'bursting into flame' can be reconstructed as a lexical item meaning 'blossom, bloom' for proto-southern Uto-Aztecan. Attestations include Nahuatl *xo-tla*, Yaqui *sew-ta*, and O'odham

---

[687] 9.212 as translated in J. Svenbro, *Phrasikleia* (Ithaca, 1993), p. 21: "But when the flower of fire had flown [*autàr epeì puròs ánthos apéptato*]."

[688] Line 7 as translated by Paul More, "Prometheus Bound," in W. Oates & E. O'Neill eds., *The Complete Greek Drama, Vol. 1* (New York, 1938), p. 127.

[689] M. Stevenson, "The Zuni Indians," *Bureau of American Ethnology* (Washington, 1904), p. 140.

[690] J. Hill, "The Flower World of Old Uto-Aztecan," *Journal of Anthropological Research* (1992), p. 122.

hio-ta, where the first element is the root meaning 'flower, bloom', and the second is the root for 'fire, flame'.[691]

Preserved in such terminology, like the DNA of a prehistoric insect entombed in amber, is an indelible fossilized record of a lost "sun" which blossomed forth into a heaven-spanning fire under cataclysmic circumstances. Although largely lost to history as currently conceptualized, the cataclysmic events in question were never wholly forgotten and still echo forth in the poetry, artworks, and dreams of modern human beings.

---

[691] *Ibid.*, p. 131.

Appendix Six

A globally attested tradition holds that Creation stemmed from the sexual union between the Thundergod and Earth, as a result of which all life was generated. This cosmogonic motif is alluded to in a passage quoted previously: "[Huracan] you who give abundance and new life, and you who give daughters and sons."[692] The word translated as "new life" here is *raxal*, literally "greenness/blueness" but by extension "life-giving," "new," and "prosperity."[693] Yet according to Thomás Coto's Cakchiquel (Maya) Vocabulary from 1651 *raxa* denotes the "flash of lightning" (*el resplandor del rayo*).[694] The original meteorological stimulus for such terminology and mytho-historical traditions, in our opinion, was the explosive appearance of four turquoise-colored "rays" or streamers emanating from the heart of the sun-cross as depicted in the cosmogram depicted in figure one. The turquoise-rays in question were not only conceptualized as "lightning" but also as the life-giving *tonalli* or élan vital that vitalized all living things (the *tonalli*, as we have seen, was explicitly likened to solar rays and described as turquoise in color). According to the historical reconstruction advanced by Talbott, Peratt, and myself, the heaven-spanning turquoise-colored structures in question were likely plasma-based in nature (lightning is a plasma).[695] Indeed, it is probable that it was the "life-like" appearance of the flowing plasma that inspired

---

[692] A. Christenson, *Popol Vuh* (New York, 2003), p. 289.
[693] *Ibid.*, p. 206. See also K. Hull, "Poetic Tenacity: A Diachronic Study of Kennings in Mayan Languages," in K. Hull & M. Carrasco eds., *Parallel Worlds* (Boulder, 2012), pp. 102-103.
[694] K. Bassie-Sweet, *Maya Sacred Geography and the Creator Deities* (Norman, 2010), p. 105.
[695] See especially A. Peratt, "Characteristics for the Occurrence of a High-Current, Z-Pinch Aurora as Recorded in Antiquity," *IEEE Transactions on Plasma Science* 31:6 (2003), pp. 1192-2014. See also the summary of Peratt's researches in D. Talbott & W. Thornhill, *Thunderbolts of the Gods* (Portland, 2005), pp. 1-29.

sky-watchers to imbue these extraterrestrial structures with biological properties in the first place.[696]

Figure one

The *Popol Vuh* contains other items of interest. Witness the following prayer to Huracan:

> May there be true life-giving roads and pathways. Give us steadfast light that our nation be made steadfast.[697]

Here, too, it is deducible that the "life-giving" (*raxal*) roads in question are identifiable with the four lightning-like structures emanating from the prototypical sun and extending to the four cardinal directions. The four directions feature prominently in the account of creation preserved in the *Popol Vuh* and, as such, form a central concept in Mesoamerican cosmology.[698] Mayan cities, in fact, were purposefully laid out with respect to the four cardinal directions as documented by Karen Bassie-Sweet and other Mayanists: "From the center of the world, four roads radiated out to the four directions."[699]

Note further that the verdant prosperity inherent in the term *raxal*—the term was employed by Christian Mayan writers to describe the Garden of Eden—is a patent reference to the luminous turquoise color of the lightning-like streamers

---

[696] M. A. van der Sluijs, *On the Origin of Myths, Vol. 1* (Vancouver, 2019), p. 89. Significantly, S. Houston, D. Stuart, and K. Taube, *op. cit.* p. 25 conclude: "In all likelihood, 'blue' or 'green' was associated in Maya thought with something 'fluid'."
[697] A. Christensen, *op. cit.*, p. 206.
[698] D. Tedlock, *op. cit.*, p. 243. See also L. Schele & D. Freidel, *A Forest of Kings* (New York, 1990), p. 66: "The four cardinal directions provided the fundamental grid for the Maya community and for the surface of the world."
[699] *Ibid.*, p. xi.

and, accordingly, forms a striking analogue to the "ever-green" prosperity associated with the Venus garden in Skidi cosmogony (the latter garden was remembered as the matrix from which "all life originates").[700]

Recall also the celestial garden of Enlil, described as follows in the Sumerian temple hymns: "The four corners of heaven became green for Enlil like a garden." Doubtless it is no coincidence that Sumerian hymns allude to a "garden of heavenly prosperity."[701] The modifying phrase here is $giri_{17}$-zal, commonly translated as "prosperity" or abundance and, as such, forms a probable semantic counterpart to the Mayan *raxal*.[702] It is this very same phrase that was employed to describe the luxuriant garden which sprang up in the wake of the *hieros gamos* between the planet Venus and Dumuzi.

---

[700] K. Hull, "Poetic Tenacity: A Diachronic Study of Kennings in Mayan Languages," in K. Hull & M. Carrasco eds., *Parallel Worlds* (Boulder, 2012), p. 102.
[701] C. Metcalf, *Sumerian Literary Texts in the Schoyen Collection*, Vol. 1 (University Park, 2019), p. ix.
[702] Lines 1-28 from "A dedication of a statue (Shulgi V)," *ETCSL*.

Appendix Seven: Earthborn Zeus

A remarkably uniform feature of Zeus' legend, as well as that of all divine children, speaks of the infant not as nurtured by his mother but by Mother Earth.[703]

Greek tradition is full of allusions to the fact that Zeus spent a portion of his infancy hidden deep within the earth. According to Hesiod, Zeus, together with the other gods, was secreted away within a dark cavern in order to escape the murderous designs of Kronos:

> So they sent her [Rhea] to Lyctus, to the rich land of Crete, when she was ready to bear great Zeus, the youngest of her children. Him did vast Earth receive from Rhea in wide Crete to nourish and to bring up. Thither came Earth carrying him swiftly through the black night to Lyctus first, and took him in her arms and hid him in a remote cave beneath the secret places of the holy earth on thick-wooded Mount Aegeum.[704]

The phrase translated as "secret places of the holy earth" by Evelyn-White is κεύθεσι γαίης. The Greek word *keuthesi*, in turn, is the plural of *keuthmōn*, "hiding place, hole."[705] It is the latter word that is employed elsewhere in the *Theogony* to describe the burial place employed by Ouranos in his attempt to dispose of his

---

[703] B. Dietrich, *The Origins of Greek Religion* (Berlin, 1974), p. 88.
[704] Lines 477-483 in *Theogony* as translated by H. Evelyn-White, *Hesiod, Homeric Hymns, Epic Cycle, Homerica* (Cambridge, 2002), p. 115.
[705] H. Liddell & R. Scott, *A Greek-English Lexicon* (Oxford, 1996), p. 944. See also the discussion in L. Muellner, *The Anger of Achilles* (Ithaca, 1996), pp. 69-77.

offspring: "And he used to hide them all away in a secret place of Earth so soon as each was born, and would not suffer them to come up into the light."[706] The original reference, without question, is to a dark "hole" within the Earth—hence the translation of Jan Bremmer: "the hiding of the first generation of gods in 'Gaia's hole' (Hesiod *Theogony* 158)."[707]

As for how we are to understand this remarkable state of affairs the evidence is clear: In ancient Greece, as in other cultures around the globe, the hole in the center of the earth was conceptualized as the Underworld. Thus it is that the terms *keuthmōn* and *keuthos* denote the underground hiding place of the dead in the *Iliad*, *Odyssey*, and Greek drama.[708] What the Greek traditions seem to be saying is that Zeus was at some point consigned to the Underworld.

As we have documented elsewhere, great gods everywhere are described as suffering a crisis in which they were hidden deep within the earth/underworld.[709] An interesting parallel is found in Mesoamerica, where Xiuhtecuhtli is described as follows: "Ayamictlan, Xiuhtecuhtli."[710] *Ayamictlan*, as noted previously, denotes "hidden" (*inaya*) in Mictlan (=Underworld).[711] At the same time, however, *Ayamictlan* is equated with the turquoise enclosure (=navel of the earth).

Zeus's earthborn status is also alluded to in Greek drama, albeit in rather cryptic fashion (pun intended). A recurring refrain in Aeschylus's *The Suppliants* includes the following plea: "O Earth, O my mother! O Zeus, thou king of the earth, and her child!"[712]

Apparent here is the archaic idea that Earth is the mother of all things and that Zeus is her child. And as the "king of the earth" Zeus is implicitly identified as Hades himself who, according to Homer, was conceptualized as living in the interior of earth.[713]

Zeus's chthonic past is also evident in the so-called *Dictaean Hymn to Kouros*, likely inscribed in the 3rd century AD but commonly held to preserve very archaic

---

[706] *Theogony* 158.

[707] J. Bremmer, *Greek Religion and Culture, the Bible and the Ancient Near East* (Leiden, 2008), p. 78.

[708] *Iliad* 20:482; *Odyssey* 24:204; *Prometheus* 220.

[709] E. Cochrane, "The Hidden God," an unpublished manuscript.

[710] *Florentine Codex: Book 6* (Santa Fe, 1969), p. 89.

[711] Florentine Codex 71v-72 r as translated in A. Austin, *op. cit.*, "The Masked God of Fire," in E. Boone ed., *The Aztec Templo Mayor* (Washington D.C., 1987), p. 267.

[712] Lines 890-892 as translated in W. Oates & E. O'Neill, *The Complete Greek Drama, Vol. 1* (New York, 1938), p. 37.

[713] *Iliad* 20:61; *Odyssey* 9:524. See also M. West, *op. cit.*, p. 158: "From Homer to Nonnus we are confronted by the remarkable fact that the lord of the underworld, the consort of Persephone-Kore in Hades, is Zeus—often distinguished by the epithet (κατα)χθόνιος, but nevertheless Zeus."

traditions. Here the god appears in the guise of the Cretan Zeus, hidden by the Kouretes:

> O most mighty, Thou, Kouros, son of Kronos,…sing it standing around your well-walled altar, o most mighty etc. (str. 2) for here it was that the Kouretes took Thee, immortal child, from Rhea, and hid Thee, dancing with their shields around you, o most mighty etc. (str. 3)…[714]

In the hymn in question Zeus is depicted as an agent of fertility, whom Martin West likened to an Adonis-like figure. Witness the following passage in which the Greek god was urged to "leap" (θόρε) in order to promote fertility: "O [lord, spring up in the wine-j]ars and spring in the fleecy [flocks, and in the crop]s of the fields spring up…"[715] Jan Bremer discussed this motif in his commentary on the *Hymn*:

> The conclusion is justified that this θόρε is an indication of a very early stage of Greek, if not pre-hellenic, religious sentiment. This god, who is supposed to leap, to mount as a bull does, is evidently not the father of gods and men, the cloud-gatherer and Olympic supergod, but a young god who—probably in connexion with (subordination to?) a Mother-goddess—has absolute power (παγκρατής) over vegetation, fertility and the 'brightness and splendour' that accompany them.[716]

Unlike Bremmer, we see no reason to distinguish between the King of the Gods and the youthful paramour of the Mother Goddess. It is the Olympian god that is described as hidden in the innermost earth and implored to leap forth and bring fertility (recall the Aztec traditions describing Tezcatlipoca as leaping forth from the earth). In this understanding the verdant "brightness and splendor" (*ganos*) associated with Zeus's emergence from the earth is analogous to the verdant greenery (giri$_{17}$-zal) that sprung up in the wake of the *hieros gamos* involving Inanna/Venus and Dumuzi. Indeed, the radiant sheen and "joy" inherent in the Greek term is also inherent in the Sumerian term and encodes a radiance that is otherworldly and stellar in origin.[717]

---

[714] J. Bremer, "Greek Hymns," in H. S. Versnel, *Faith, Hope, and Worship* (Leiden, 1981), p. 206.
[715] Lines 57-59 as translated in M. West, "The Dictaean Hymn to the Kouros," *Journal of Hellenic Studies* 85 (1965), p. 150.
[716] J. Bremer, *op. cit.*, p. 206.
[717] H. G. Liddell & R. Scott, *A Greek-English Lexicon* (Oxford, 1996), p. 338.

Appendix Eight

Greek tradition appears to have preserved a vestigial memory of the archaic mytheme of the primordial earth's fixing at the time of Creation. According to Pindar's account of Apollo's birth in the *Hymn to Zeus*, the blessed event occurred on the island Delos. Prior to the archer-god's delivery by Leto, the rocky outcrop was said to be wandering about the Mediterranean, buffeted by swirling winds. It is the god's birth that serves to "fix" the island securely in place:

> For before, it was tossed on the waves by the blasts of all sorts of winds. But when Leto, the daughter of Coeus, raging with agony of imminent labour, set foot on her, then it was that the four straight pillars with adamantine bases rose from the roots of the earth, and on their capitals held up the rock, where she gave birth, and beheld her blessed offspring…[718]

It will be noted that the four straight pillars (τέσσαρες ὀρθαὶ) which serve to fix the floating island in place are said to have come "from the roots of the earth" (τρέμνων ὄρουσαν χθονίων). The parallel with regard to the four posts which serve to fix the earth and/or uphold the heavens in Amerindian cosmogonic traditions is evident at once.[719]

There is reason to believe, moreover, that in this particular instance Pindar has adapted or reworked traditions originally associated with the primordial earth in order to localize his account of Apollo's birth.[720] This is most evident when he describes the diminutive Delos as "unmoved marvel of the broad earth" (χθονὸς εὑρεί/-ας ἀκίνητον τέρας) in a contiguous fragment from the same *Hymn*:

> Hail, O heaven-built one, most lovely branch for the children of shining-haired Leto, O daughter of the sea, unmoved marvel of the broad earth, called Delos by mortal men, but by the blessed

---

[718] Fragment 33d as translated in I. Rutherford, "Pindar on the Birth of Apollo," *The Classical Quarterly* 38 (1988), p. 74.

[719] As in Chorti tradition, for example. See also the Jewish tradition in *b. Óag 12a*: "As to the earth, on what does it stand? On pillars: 'Who shakes the earth out of her place and the pillars thereof tremble' (*Job 9:6*)."

[720] S. Montiglio, *Wandering in Ancient Greek Culture* (Chicago, 2005), p. 15 notes: "The myth of Apollo's birth draws on the widespread identification of earth and mother."

ones of Olympus known as the far-shown star of the dark-blue earth…[721]

The epithet "broad"—Greek εὐρεί/-ας—is a familiar epithet of the primordial earth, as noted earlier. But it is the epithet "unmoved" (ἀκίνητον) that serves as a dead giveaway with respect to the traditional origins of the poet's imagery insofar as analogous epithets were employed to describe the primordial earth by poets around the globe. Hesiod can be called as a witness here: "Verily at the first Chaos came to be, but next wide-bosomed Earth, the ever-sure foundation of all."[722] A very similar tradition is preserved in the *Rig Veda*: "When you spread out the immovable foundation [=earth], you set the airy realm on the doorposts of heaven with your lofty power."[723]

Equally revealing is the designation of Delos as the "far-shown star of the dark-blue earth" (τήλέΦατον κυανέας χθονὸς ἀστρον). On what possible grounds can an inconspicuous rock in the Aegean sea to be compared to a brilliant star?

In Greek tradition, Delos was originally a star (*astron*) fallen from heaven—hence its name *Asteria*, translated as "Star-Island" by Classicists. Indeed, later chroniclers understood the phrase "unmoved marvel" (ἀκίνητον τέρας) to mean "fixed star of the earth."[724]

The Hellenistic poet Callimachus redeployed the same traditional material some two centuries after Pindar in his hymn *To Delos*. As in Pindar, Delos is said to have been "swept by wind and wave" prior to the birth of Apollo.[725] So, too, Callimachus reiterates that Delos was a star fallen from heaven: "Your name in that olden time was Asterië, who shot like a star from heaven into the deep."[726] And once again it is the archer-god's birth that served to "fix" the island in place: "But once you had offered ground for Apollo to be born on, sailors called you Delos, fittingly: for then, no longer sailing out of sight, you let your feet take root in the Aegean Sea, and there you stayed."[727]

---

[721] Fragment 33c as translated in I. Rutherford, "Pindar on the Birth of Apollo," *The Classical Quarterly* 88 (1988), p. 74.

[722] *Theogony* 116-117 as translated in H. Evelyn-White, *Hesiod, Homeric Hymns, Epic Cycle, Homerica* (Cambridge, 1936), p. 87.

[723] *RV* 1:56:5.

[724] D. Robinson, *Pindar, a Poet of Eternal Ideas* (Baltimore, 1936), p. 249. So, too, the term *astron* employed by Pindar likewise alludes to a "fixed star." See the discussion in A. Kampakoglou, *Studies in the Reception of Pindar in Ptolemaic Poetry* (Berlin, 2019), p. 319.

[725] Line 17 as translated in F. Nisetich, *The Poems of Callimachus* (Oxford, 2001), p. 37.

[726] Lines 51-54 as translated in *Ibid.*, p. 38.

[727] Lines 74-79 as translated in *Ibid*, p. 39.

It will be noted that, while Pindar made four straight pillars fix the island in place, Callimachus attributes the fixing to Delos' "feet" (ποδῶν).

The *Homeric Hymn to Apollo* offers additional data of interest. There, too, it is reported that Apollo's birth stabilizes the island. Yet it is the claim that, as soon as he was born, Apollo started walking with firm steps (ἐβίβασκεν) over the wide-pathed earth that warrants our attention: "So said Phoebus, the long-haired god who shoots afar and began to walk upon the wide-pathed earth."[728] Silvia Montiglio summarized these events as follows: "Apollo's steady walking fixes his authority over the island that his birth has rooted and, from there, over the world."[729] Here it is likely that Apollo's "steady walking" represents an analogue to the Egyptian and Indic traditions reporting that the ancient sun-god's striding ordered the cosmos (the Egyptian texts proclaim that the sun god was a walker already on the day of his birth).[730]

Suffice it to note that millennia-old memories echo here and doubtless much eludes us still. Future generations, aided perhaps by unforeseen archaeological finds revealing prehistoric civilizations offering a more or less contemporary account of the unfolding of Creation, will hopefully help fill in some of the details.

---

[728] Lines 133-134 as translated in H. Evelyn-White, *Hesiod, Homeric Hymns, Epic Cycle, Homerica* (Cambridge, 1936), p. 333.
[729] S. Montiglio, *op. cit.*, p. 15.
[730] J. Zandee, *Der Amunshymnus des Papyrus Leiden I 344 verso*, Vol. 1 (Leiden, 1992), p. 323: "Läufer (*phrrw*) schon am Tage seiner Geburt." J. Assmann, *Egyptian Solar Religion in the New Kingdom* (London, 1995), p. 112, translates the passage as "circulating [*phrrw*] on the day of his birth."

Appendix Nine: The World Tree

> Formerly sky and earth were connected by a big tree.[731]

> The soma mythologem was part and parcel of the basic cosmogonic myth.[732]

> Its [Soma's] identity still is shrouded in mystery.[733]

Students of ancient myth and religion have long recognized that archaic conceptions of the World Tree interface with and mirror the imagery attached to the World Pillar. It is Mircea Eliade, perhaps, who has done the most to elucidate the symbolism in question:

> The symbolism of the World Tree is complementary to that of the Central Mountain. Sometimes the two symbols coincide; usually they complement each other. But both are merely more developed mythical formulations of the Cosmic Axis (World Pillar, etc.).[734]

Inasmuch as the World Tree is a globally-attested mythologem, it constitutes an invaluable mnemonic fossil offering a wealth of insight with regards to the visual appearance, structure, and history of the polar configuration. While multiple volumes would be required to properly document the manifold symbolism attached to the Tree, the following brief summary must suffice for our purposes here.

---

[731] J. Wilbert & K. Simoneau, *Folk Literature of the Mataco Indians* (Los Angeles, 1982), p. 46.
[732] N. Lidova, "Indramahotsava in the Late Vedic and Early Epic Traditions," *Journal of the Asiatic Society of Mumbai* 76-78 (2002-2003), p. 99.
[733] M. Witzel, *The Origins of the World's Mythologies* (Oxford, 2012), p. 159.
[734] M. Eliade, *Myths, Rites, and Symbols* (New York, 1975), p. 380.

The Vedic Soma plant offers a classic example of the World Tree. Like the World Pillar, the Soma plant was thought to uphold heaven and buttress the cosmos. The following passage from the *Rig Veda* is representative in this regard: "The (soma) plant, the prop and buttress of heaven, which, when well extended and fully filled, encompasses in every direction."[735]

It will be noted that the Soma plant is identified as the sky-prop (*skambha*) and said to extend in every direction (*visvatah*).

In an earlier hymn from the same text the plant is said to be located on the navel of the earth: "On the navel of the earth is the buttress of great heaven."[736] Here, too, the Soma plant is described as the buttress (*dharúno*) upholding or otherwise supporting heaven.

The World Tree plays a central role in the cosmogonic traditions of Mesoamerican cultures as well.[737] For the Maya, the Tree was known as *Yax Che*, literally "green tree." According to indigenous accounts, the *Yax Che* was erected *in illo tempore* at the navel of the earth.[738] Walter Lamb documented this idea among the Tzotzil:

> Some Tzotzil preserve the belief that at the center of the Earth, associated thus with the color green (Holland 1964: 14-16), there looms a huge ceiba tree that connects the heavens…The ceiba or *yaxte*' 'green tree' is the very tree of life.[739]

To this day Maya tribes preserve the tradition that the *Yax Che* was explicitly associated with the four cardinal directions. Witness the following anthropological report: "[The ceiba tree] had four branches, one for each of the cardinal points."[740] And as a four-branched tree, the *Yax Che* was commonly represented as a cruciform structure in ancient Maya cities:

---

[735] *RV* 9:74:2. P. Horsch, "From Creation Myth to World Law: The Early History of 'Dharma'," *Journal of Indian Philosophy* 32 (2004), p. 433 translates as follows: "The supporting separator of heaven."

[736] *RV* 9:72:7.

[737] See especially the works of Linda Schele and David Freidel: *A Forest of Kings* (New York, 1990), pp. 66-77; and *Maya Cosmos* (New York, 1995), p. 53-55.

[738] See R. Roys, *The Book of Chilam Balam of Chumayel* (Washington D.C., 1933), pp. 99-100: "The final act of this phase of creation was to raise the Yax Che, or 'green tree,' at the center of the world."

[739] W. Lamb, "Tzotzil Maya Cosmology," in V. del Chamberlain, J. Carlson & J. Young, *Songs From the Sky* (College Park, 2005), p. 165.

[740] A. Tozzer, *A Comparative Study of the Mayas and the Lacandones* (London, 1907), p. 154.

> The cross and ceiba tree were used interchangeably in ancient Maya art to represent the *axis mundi* of the cosmos…Contemporary Maya continue to use many of these symbols…Sacred places in Zinacantan are marked by shrines with blue/green crosses. These crosses are called the *yax che* 'green tree.' *Yax che*' is also the modern Maya word for ceiba tree, and these cross shrines still mark the center of the cosmos. In Zinacantan, this is the *mixik balamil* or 'navel of the world'.[741]

The Maya *Yax Che* finds a striking parallel in the Egyptian Ished-tree, remembered as being present at the Beginning.[742] It was from the midst of this turquoise-colored tree that the sun-god first appeared or was "born." The following solar hymn is representative in this regard: "I know this sycamore of turquoise, out of whose middle Re comes forth."[743]

Although such archaic traditions are exceedingly difficult to explain by reference to the familiar sky, wherein a turquoise-colored tree is nowhere to be found, they offer a close mythopoeic parallel to the aforementioned traditions wherein Horus-Re was born from a lotus flower *in illo tempore*.[744] To point out the obvious: The Ished-tree and the primeval lotus can be traced to the very same celestial phenomenon—specifically, a turquoise-colored cruciform structure centered upon the primal sun (see the cosmogram depicted in figure one). And so it is that, in the hieroglyphic writing systems of ancient Egypt as well as Mesoamerica, the lotus/rosette is interchangeable with the cross.[745]

Norse lore also preserves memory of a heaven-spanning tree. There the World Tree was known as Yggdrasil: "Its branches spread out over the whole world and reach up over heaven."[746] According to the account of creation preserved in the Old Norse (Icelandic) *Völupsá* 17, the Yggdrasil was located in close proximity

---

[741] F. Salamone & W. Adams eds., *Explorations in Anthropology and Theology* (New York, 1997), p. 178.
[742] J. Zandee, *Der Amunshymnus des Papyrus Leiden I 344 verso, Vol. 1* (Leiden, 1992), p. 414: "Der Isched-Baum stand an der Urstätte der Welt, wo der Sonnengott am Anbeginn erschienen war."
[743] *Ibid.*, p. 416: "Ich kenne diese Sykomore aus Turkiš, aus deren Mitte Re hervorgehen." Author's translation.
[744] *Ibid.*, p. 413: "Der Isched-Baum als Gebärmutter des Sonnengottes ist mit der Vorstellung vom 'Gott auf der Blume' vergleichbar."
[745] In Egypt, for example, the *wn*-glyph (M42) is interchangeable with the cross (Z11). See J. Allen, *Middle Egyptian* (Cambridge, 2014), p. 486.
[746] Translated by J. Young in *The Prose Edda of Snorri Sturlson* (Berkeley, 1960), p. 42. On the Yggdrasil as World Tree, see P. Terry, *Poems of the Elder Edda* (Philadelphia, 1990), p. 9: "Yggdrasil, is also called the World Tree."

to the celebrated spring of Urd: "It stands ever green over Urd's spring."⁷⁴⁷ As the "ever green" Tree, the Yggdrasil naturally recalls the Maya *Yax Che* and the Egyptian Ished-tree.

The same basic memory is attested in ancient Mesopotamia, where we find mention of the turquoise-colored *Kiškanu* tree.⁷⁴⁸ According to an early Assyrian text, the *Kiškanu* tree was located near the apsu, the latter described as the cosmic waters beneath the primordial earth:

> In Eridu a *kiškanû*-tree was created in a pure place; its radiance of pure lapis lazuli stretches forth into the Apsû. The way of Ea is full of abundance, and his dwelling is the place of the underworld.⁷⁴⁹

Elsewhere in Mesopotamia the World Tree was known as the Mes-tree. According to the Sumerian epic *Enmerkar and the Lord of Aratta*, the Mes-tree "links heaven and earth."⁷⁵⁰ The same tree was celebrated as follows in *The Poem of Erra*:

> Where is the Mesu tree, the flesh of the gods, the ornament of the king of the universe? That pure tree…whose roots reached as deep down as the bottom of the underworld…whose top reached as high as the sky of Anum?⁷⁵¹

A number of early Sumerian kings likened themselves to the Mes tree. A royal hymn from the reign of Shulgi (2100 BCE) is instructive in this regard:

> On the day of his elevation to kingship,/ He radiated like a fertile mes-tree; watered by fresh water,/ Extending (his) blossoming branches toward the pure watercourse;/ Upon his blossoming branches, Utu conferred the (following) blessing:/ Being a fertile mes-tree, he has borne pure fruit,/ Šulgi, the righteous shepherd of Sumer, will truly spread abundance!⁷⁵²

---

⁷⁴⁷ Translated by J. Young in *The Prose Edda of Snorri Sturlson* (Berkeley, 1960), p. 46.
⁷⁴⁸ S. Tharapalan, *The Meaning of Color in Ancient Mesopotamia* (2019), p. 362: "The earlier Sumerian version 'a *Kiškanu*-tree whose appearance was zagindaru (i.e., light blue/turquoise)."
⁷⁴⁹ M. Geller, "A Middle Assyrian Tablet of Utukku Lemnutu, Tablet 12," *Iraq* 42 (1980), p. 34.
⁷⁵⁰ Line 520 as translated in H. Vanstiphout, *Epics of Sumerian Kings* (Leiden, 2004), p. 87.
⁷⁵¹ L. Cagni, *The Poem of Erra* (Malibu, 1977), pp. 74-75.
⁷⁵² Lines 59-64 of Shulgi F as translated in J. Klein, *The Royal Hymns of Shulgi King of Ur* (Philadelphia, 1981), p. 24.

As one of the world's earliest literary accounts describing the World Tree, the Shulgi hymn warrants close scrutiny because it appears to preserve a number of tell-tale lexical clues that point to a celestial prototype. Witness the reference to the Tree's "blossoming branches": The Sumerian adjective translated as "blossoming" here is mul-mul, a word derived from mul "star." According to the translator Jacob Klein, the literal meaning of mul is "shining."[753] Note further that Shulgi—who frequently compared himself to the sun—is here said to rise brilliantly, wherein the expression dalla mu-e$_3$ clearly evokes celestial imagery (the latter phrase commonly describes the prototypical sunrise).[754] It stands to reason, therefore, that Shulgi is identifying himself with the radiant World Tree that became manifest with the prototypical sunrise.

In our discussion of the Rajasuya rite in a previous chapter, we noted that royal accession rites typically reenacted cosmogonic myth. Thus it is that the Indic king stretched forth his arms upon assuming the throne, seemingly in a purposeful attempt to emulate the erection of the World Tree *in illo tempore*. Analogous rites are evident in ancient Mesoamerica, where the ruler was commonly depicted as the World Tree.[755] Such is the case among the Classic Maya, for example: "The Classic Maya king is routinely portrayed as the World Tree (*yax te* [*che*], green/central/first tree."[756] Shulgi's manifestation as the supremely fertile Mes-tree on the day of his accession likely encodes the same archaic symbolism. Absent a clearly visible celestial prototype, it is extremely difficult to imagine why cultures around the globe would have their rulers emulate a tree-like structure supporting—but also separating—heaven and earth.

---

[753] J. Klein & Y. Sefati, "The 'Stars (of) Heaven' and Cuneiform Writing," in L. Sassmannshausen ed., *He Has Opened Nisaba's House of Learning* (Leiden, 2014), p. 96 note: "The stars serve primarily as similes for shining or glittering (astral) goddesses; and the only meaning for mul as a verb or verbal adjective is 'to shine', 'to glitter' and the like, qualifying gods, goddesses, persons or objects."

[754] As in line 71 from Shulgi R. See also J. Polonsky, *The Rise of the Sun-God and the Determination of Destiny in Ancient Mesopotamia*. Ph.D. dissertation, University of Philadelphia (2002), p. 244.

[755] B. Fagan & N. Durrani, *People of the Earth* (London, 2014), p. 434: "The [Maya] ruler was often depicted as the World Tree."

[756] A. Demarest, *Ideology and Pre-Columbian Civilizations* (Santa Fe, 1992), p. 120. The royal iconography at Copan associated with a fellow named 18 Rabbit offers a case in point: "The lower portion of the east side of Stela C positions 18 Rabbit as the World Tree that supports the cosmos…By costuming himself in attributes of the World Tree on both sides of Stela C, 18 Rabbit placed himself literally at the center of the universe, or the axis mundi." See discussion in L. Foster, *Handbook to Life in the Ancient Maya World* (Oxford, 2005), pp. 182-183.

Appendix Ten

The testimony of ancient Mesopotamia with respect to the ordering of the cosmos at the time of Creation is in basic agreement with that from Vedic India and Egypt. Thus it is that the Sumerian sun-god Utu is celebrated as the "King of justice," wherein the latter word translates nig$_2$-si$_2$-sa, literally "to be straight" or be in order.[757] Of Utu it was said: "[To carry out] right [and justice] is yours."[758] Justice itself, moreover, was first rendered by Utu at the time of the prototypical sunrise.[759]

The Sumerian king, as the incarnation of the Sun, was conceptualized as the paragon of justice. Thus the ruler is commonly invoked as lugal nig$_2$-si-sa$_2$, "king of justice" or as lugal si-sa$_2$, "just king," where si-sa$_2$ denotes "justice."[760] Again and again Sumerian rulers are compared to Utu in their capacity for rendering justice: "The king, who like Utu, renders the just verdict."[761] Such statements, as Janice Polonsky points out, serve to identify the ruler with the sun-god himself: "The just ruler is envisioned as the rising sun god, a powerful icon of judgment and decision-making."[762]

---

[757] Line 5 from "An adab (?) to Utu for Shulgi (Shulgi Q)," *ETCSL*. See also Mark Cohen, *An Annotated Sumerian Dictionary* (University Park, 2023), p. 1090.
[758] M. Cohen, "Another Utu Hymn," *ZA* 67 (1977), p. 7.
[759] J. Polonsky, "ki-^{d}utu-è-a," in L. Milano ed., *Landscapes: Territories, Frontiers and Horizons in the Ancient Near East* (Padova, 1999), p. 96: "At the moment of sunrise, Utu is seen as emerging with truth (ni-zi-da; *kittu*) on his right side and justice (ni-si-sá; *mišaru*) at his left."
[760] M. Cohen, *An Annotated Sumerian Dictionary* (University Park, 2023), p. 1090. See also J. Polonsky, *The Rise of the Sun-God and the Determination of Destiny in Ancient Mesopotamia*. Ph.D. dissertation, University of Philadelphia (2002), p. 493.
[761] *Ibid.*, p. 499.
[762] *Ibid.*, p. 500.

Sumerian kings routinely credit Utu with endowing them with justice. The following inscription of Išme-Dagan is representative in this regard: "Utu put justice and reliable words in my mouth."[763] Anticipating Hesiod's extolling of Zeus's "straight judgment" thousands of years later, the Sumerian ruler Išme-Dagan proclaimed: "When like Utu I decide a just verdict," wherein the word translated as "just" is si sa$_2$, literally "straight."[764] Evident in this language is the archaic conception that it was the prototypical sun-god Utu who first proffered *straight* judgments at the time of Creation.

In addition to "straight" and "to be in order," the Sumerian word si also denotes solar "ray" or "beam of light," thereby paralleling the situation with respect to the Egyptian *Maat* and Vedic *rájas*.[765] Thus it is no accident that the establishment of justice is explicitly compared to radiance: "In the land you have caused order to be resplendent," wherein "order" is nig$_2$-si-sa$_2$.[766] It will be noted that order/justice is here said to "shine" (dalla ba-e-e$_3$). The same idea is evident in a praise poem offered to Ur-Namma: "I make justice apparent," wherein apparent is pa e$_3$, the latter being the very expression employed to describe the sunrise.[767] A similar sentiment is expressed in Hammurabi's Shamash hymn, wherein the sun-god is invoked as follows: "You blaze abroad the judgments."[768]

The fact that the same phrase occurs in early Sumerian names for "wind"—witness the word ^{tumu}si-sa$_2$, "straight wind"—encodes the close connection between solar "radiance" and solar "wind" in the minds of the ancient sky-watchers.[769] In this sense the Sumerian term mirrors the role of *m3ꜥ* in ancient Egypt which, in addition to signifying a solar ray, also denotes "fair" or straight or orderly wind.[770]

---

[763] Line 90 in "A praise poem of Išme-Dagan (Išme-Dagan A + V)," *ETCSL*.

[764] Line 226 from "A praise poem of Išme-Dagan (Išme-Dagan A + V)," *ETCSL*.

[765] M. Cohen, *An Annotated Sumerian Dictionary* (University Park, 2023), p. 1146. The same author references line 232 from "Lugalbanda in the mountain cave," *ETCSL*: "The youth Utu extended from heaven his lustrous sunbeams."

[766] Lines 57-58 in "A praise poem of Enlil-bani (Enlil-bani A)," *ETCSL*.

[767] Line 38 in "A praise poem of Ur-Namma (Ur-Namma C)," *ETCSL*.

[768] Line 58 as translated in E. Reiner, *Your Thwarts in Pieces, Your Mooring Rope Cut* (Ann Arbor, 1985) p. 72.

[769] W. Horowitz, *op. cit.*, p. 197.

[770] D. Kurth, "Wind," *LÄ* VI (1990), col. 1269.

Appendix Eleven: A Baptism by Fire

At that time all of the common folk came to the flame, hurled themselves at it, and blistered themselves as fire was taken.[771]

The primeval is that which is most alive—in fact, it alone is truly alive. It is not the subjective talent of the artist which gives the creations of Greek myth their incomparable vitality, quickening man's pulse as they have through the ages; but it is the appearance of the primeval world, which these creations have been able to evoke.[772]

A widespread custom among indigenous peoples found parents placing their children in or near the hearth fire in order to empower them and ensure their good health. Such rites were conspicuous in the pre-Columbian cult of Xiuhtecuhtli, for example:

> He was the most ancient and venerable of all the gods and sacrifices were always made to him first…Newborn children were commonly passed through the flames of the hearth and lightly singed as a form of baptism and an acknowledgment of their filiation with the fire god.[773]

---

[771] *Florentine Codex: Book 6* (Santa Fe, 1969), p. 29.
[772] W. Otto, *Dionysos* (Bloomington, 1965), p. 120.
[773] B. C. Brundage, *The Fifth Sun* (Norman, 1979), p. 22. See also B. de Sahagún, *Book 2: The Ceremonies* (Santa Fe, 1981), p. 165: "Thereupon they took each of the children to singe them [in the fire]."

Far from being confined to the New World, analogous rituals are attested around the globe. In his monumental *Golden Bough* and other works, James Frazer provided a wealth of documentation that "the practice of passing children over fire was in all times much practiced amongst heathen nations, and that it is even now practiced in China and other places."[774] Citing the Greek festival known as the Amphidromia, in which a newborn child of five days old was carried around the central hearth-fire, Frazer offered the following observation:

> The ancient Greek practice of running around the central hearth with an infant on the fifth or seventh day after birth may have been a substitute for an older custom of passing the child over the fire, for such a custom has been practiced from superstitious motives by many peoples, both savage and civilized, in many lands. In the Highlands of Scotland, to quote a single case, 'it has happened that, after baptism, the father has placed a basket filled with bread and cheese on the pot-hook that impended over the fire in the middle of the room, which the company sit around; and the child is thrice handed across the fire, with the design to frustrate all attempts of evil spirits or evil eyes.'[775]

The Old Testament testifies to similar practices having once prevailed in the ancient Near East. Jeremiah railed against the notorious rites performed in the Valley of Ben Hinnom: "They have built the high places of Topheth in the Valley of Ben Hinnom to burn their sons and daughters in the fire…to sacrifice their sons and daughters to Molech."[776] Maimonides points to vestiges of analogous practices among Jewish celebrants during the Medieval period. Witness the following commentary with regards to the passing of infants through the fire:

> We still see the midwives wrap newborn children in swaddling bands, and, after putting foul-smelling incense on the fire, move the children to and fro over the incense on the fire.[777]

The mythological traditions of numerous cultures likewise tell of placing children within the hearth fire in order to garner them god-like powers or immortali-

---

[774] J. Frazer, *Fastorum libri sex* (London, 1929), p. 315.
[775] *Ibid.*, p. 296.
[776] *Jeremiah* 7:31.
[777] J. Frazer, *Fastorum libri sex* (London, 1929), p. 314.

ty.⁷⁷⁸ This idea is most familiar from the Greek myth of Demeter and Demophon, in which the Mother of the Gods is reputed to have concealed the infant in the fire in order to make him immortal. The story is told most fully in *The Homeric Hymn to Demeter*:

> At night she hid him like a firebrand in the blazing fire, secretly from his dear parents. To them it was a miracle how he blossomed forth and looked like the gods.⁷⁷⁹

Alas, the experiment did not end well. Upon being discovered by the infant's horrified mother in the act of curing him in the fire, the goddess became incensed and flew into a rage:

> In anger at her [the boy's mother, Metanira], bright-crowned Demeter snatched from the flames with immortal hands the dear child…and, raging terribly at heart, cast him away from herself to the ground.⁷⁸⁰

As the charter myth for the Eleusinian mysteries, it is commonly agreed that *The Homeric Hymn to Demeter* managed to preserve very archaic traditions.⁷⁸¹ Be this as it may, the account of Demophon recalls analogous traditions surrounding Achilles, Jason, Triptolemos, and other Greek heroes.⁷⁸²

In ancient Rome the god Mars was represented as receiving a baptism by fire at the hands of Minerva (see figure one). This scene, which appears on a Praenestan cista dating to the fourth century BCE, has generated a good deal of discussion and speculation as to its meaning. Wilhelm Roscher, followed by Henk Versnel, saw in it a "rejuvenation" of Mars and compared the cista's imagery to Jason's magical rejuvenation in Medea's cauldron.⁷⁸³

---

⁷⁷⁸ See the masterful discussion in J. Frazer, "Putting Children on the Fire," in *Apollodorus: The Library, Vol. 2* (London, 1921), pp. 311-317.
⁷⁷⁹ Lines 239-245 as translated in A. Athanassakis, *The Homeric Hymns* (Baltimore, 1976), p. 8.
⁷⁸⁰ Lines 251-254 as translated in H. Foley, *The Homeric "Hymn to Demeter"* (Princeton, 1994), p. 14.
⁷⁸¹ W. Burkert, *Greek Religion* (Oxford, 1985), p. 159. See also E. Håland, *Greek Festivals, Modern and Ancient, Vol. 2* (Cambridge, 2017), p. 167; R. Seaford, *Euripides: Bacchae* (Oxford, 1996), p. 197.
⁷⁸² Jason is said to have been rejuvenated by Medea, who plunged him into a fiery cauldron. See the Scholiast to Aristophanes' *Knights* 1321; scholiast to Lycophron 1315. See also S. Spence, *The Image of Jason in Early Greek Myth* (Lulu, 2010), pp. 122-125.
⁷⁸³ W. Roscher, "Mars," *Ausführliches Lexikon der griechischen und römischen Mythologie* (Leipzig, 1884-1937), col. 2408. H. Versnal, *Inconsistencies in Greek and Roman Religion, Vol. 2* (Leiden, 1993), p. 324 compared Mars' firing to that of Demophon. With regards to the many

Figure one

Possible insight into the scene on the Praenestine cista is provided by a story told by Aelianus (*Var. Hist.* 9, 16), himself of Praenestine origin. Wagenvoort's commentary on Aelianus is relevant here:

> According to Aelianus Mares dies at the age of 123, i.e. at the end of an Etruscan *saeculum*, but he comes to life again. If we are right in supposing him to be identical with Mars, then the Etruscans must have made him, in imitation of Greek and Oriental nature gods, into a dying and resuscitated divinity: each saeculum stands therefore under the sway of a new Mars (the ritual with the vessel of boiling water may also remind us of a rejuvenating process…in which case Mars did not die but was changed from a senile greybeard at the end of the period into a baby boy).[784]

A tale told by Plutarch shares several features in common with the Demophon myth. There the roasted child is the son of the king of Byblos and the attendant goddess is Isis, still mourning the loss of her husband Osiris:

---

interpretations offered, H. Versnel, "Apollo and Mars One Hundred Years after Roscher," *Visible Religion* 4 (1986), p. 147 writes: "The most attractive seem to be those which connect the immersion with death and rebirth, or rejuvenation."

[784] H. Wagenvoort, *Studies in Roman Literature, Culture and Religion* (Leiden, 1956), pp. 229-230.

> Now the name of the king was Malcander, and the name of the queen was Astarte…So Isis nursed the child, giving him her finger to suck instead of her breast; but at night she burned away all of him that was mortal, and turning herself into a swallow, she fluttered twittering mournfully about the house, in which the coffin with the dead body of Osiris was enclosed. But when the queen saw her child burning in the fire, she cried out, and so prevented him from becoming immortal.[785]

As various scholars have pointed out, behind the name Malcander we should probably recognize Melqart, the tutelary god of Byblos (and Tyre) who was renowned in the ancient world for suffering cremation on a great funeral pyre. Although Melqart's cult is of untold antiquity—certainly extending back well into the second millennium BCE—much of our information about it comes from brief allusions in the Old Testament and later Greek and Christian writers.[786] According to the Pseudo-Clementines, people used to speak of a place near Tyre where Melqart had been immolated and, in fact, representations of the god at Pyrgi show him enveloped in flames.[787] From Menander by way of Josephus, we learn that Hiram, a king of Tyre mentioned in the Old Testament account of Solomon, erected a temple to Melqart and his consort Astarte in the tenth century BCE.[788] The same source reports that it was customary every spring to celebrate the "awakening" (*egersis*) of Melqart.[789] Although the nature of the Tyrian rite remains obscure, it appears to have involved a resurrection of the god through a sacred marriage with Astarte. Sergio Ribichini summarized the evidence as follows:

> Other references in classical literature inform us about this annual festival, which from many points of view recalls analogous cultic situations in honour of other dying and rising gods (cf. Adonis

---

[785] Plutarch, *Isis et Osiris*, 16, as translated in J. Frazer, *Fastorum Libri Sex, Vol. 3* (London, 1929), p. 295.

[786] *I Kings* 18:27; *Ezekiel* 28:2. For a summary of the available evidence see S. Ribichini, "Melqart," in K. van der Toorn et al eds., *Dictionary of Deities and Demons in the Bible* (Leiden, 1995), cols. 1053-1058.

[787] *Recogn. Clem.* X, 24, P.G. 1, 1434 as cited in R. de Vaux, *The Bible and the Ancient Near East* (Garden City, 1971), p. 250. See also W. Burkert, "Oriental and Greek Mythology: The Meeting of Parallels," in J. Bremmer ed., *Interpretations of Greek Mythology* (Totowa, N.J., 1989), p. 36.

[788] *Antiquities*, 8:5:3; contra *Apionem* 1, 17f.

[789] W. Burkert, *op. cit.*, p. 36, citing Menander, *Fragment* 783 F 1.

and Eshmun). It was probably the greatest festival of Melqart: the god, burnt with fire, as the Greek hero [Heracles], was brought to life by means of a hierogamic rite with his divine partner Astarte, through the participation of a particular celebrant, the *mqm ʿlm*, 'awakener of deity'…The myth runs parallel to this rite, describing the god's disappearance and return (Athenaeus IX 392 D and Zenobius, *Cent*. V 56).[790]

The Phoenician Melqart, in turn, has long been suspected as being the god concealed behind the peculiar Greek traditions surrounding the child hero named Melikertes, the subject of several lost Greek tragedies whom the Greeks themselves compared with Demophon.[791] Apollodorus reports that Ino-Leukothea, upon being stricken with a terrible madness, plunged Melikertes into a cauldron of boiling water and leapt into the sea with the infant.[792] According to various accounts, the boy's body was subsequently brought to shore on the back of a dolphin, whereupon it was properly buried at the Isthmus of Corinth. Shortly thereafter the Ishtmian athletic games were instituted to honor the boy, now named Palaimon.[793] Other ancient authorities report that Melikertes was resurrected in some manner.[794]

Alas, there are hints that the child-hero was not the innocent babe portrayed by Apollodorus.[795] According to Callimachus and other ancient authorities, the cult of Melikertes was fêted with child-sacrifices on the Aegean island Tenedos, thereby reminding us of similar sacrifices within the Phoenician religious sphere, where Melqart was the leading god.[796]

In addition to his resemblance to Demophon and Melqart, Melikertes also appears to share a certain affinity with Heracles as well. We have seen that the

---

[790] S. Ribichini, *op. cit.*, col. 1055.
[791] C. Pache, *Baby and Child Heroes in Ancient Greece* (Urbana, 2004), p. 77: "The link between Melikertes and Demophon is actually made explicit in the scholia." On Melikertes' affinity with Melqart, see M. Astour, *Hellenosemitica* (Leiden, 1967), pp. 204-212.
[792] 3:4:3. Ino's affinity with Aphrodite is commonly acknowledged, some scholars viewing her as a hypostasis of *Urania*. See the discussion in L. Farnell, *The Cults of the Greek States*, Vol. II (New Rochelle, 1977), pp. 637-638; H. Güntert, *Kalypso* (Halle, 1919), pp. 190-191.
[793] *Apollodorus* 3.4.3. See also Plutarch, *Theseus* 25.5. See also Ovid, *Fasti* 6.501-502.
[794] *Eudoxus* fragment 284. See here the discussion in W. Burkert, *op. cit.*, p. 188. C. Pache, *op. cit.*, p. 386 speaks of the "death and coming back to life of the hero Melikertes."
[795] See the discussion in E. Cochrane, *Martian Metamorphoses* (Ames, 1997), pp. 45-48.
[796] Callimachus *Aitia* 4. Lykophron, *Alexandria* 229 describes Melikertes as a child-slayer. A scholiast (*Alexandra* 229) adds: "Palaimon is Melikertes, the son of Ino. He is especially honored in Tenedos, and there they even sacrifice babies to him." See here the discussion in C. Pache, *op. cit.*, pp. 141-143. See also D. Hughes, *Human Sacrifice in Ancient Greece* (London, 1991), p. 134.

child-hero was identified with the chthonic god Palaimon.⁷⁹⁷ Yet *Palaimon* was also an epithet of the Greek strongman.⁷⁹⁸ The founding of the athletic games at Isthmus in honor of Melikertes, likewise, recalls Heracles' role as the founder of the Olympic games—not to mention Demophon's role in the founding of the athletic games at Eleusis. So, too, Melikertes' reputation as a child-slayer—the god was described with the epithet *Brephoktonos,* "Baby Slayer" by Callimachus—recalls Euripides' disturbing account of Heracles' slaying of his own children during a bout of sudden madness (according to Pherekydes, the infant children were "thrown into the fire by their father").⁷⁹⁹

Heracles himself suffered death by immolation, not unlike Melqart and Melikertes. According to Greek lore, Heracles' fiery death on Mt. Oeta paved the way for his apotheosis and rejuvenation.⁸⁰⁰ Our primary source for the circumstances attending the hero's demise is Sophocles' oft-macabre *The Trachiniae.* There it is related that Heracles was driven to commit suicide because his body was corroding away as a result of donning a robe laced with the Hydra's poison, the latter a gift from Deianeira. A pathetic and pitiable figure by the end of the play, Heracles is made to announce: "Glued to my sides, it [the garment] hath eaten my flesh to the inmost parts…already it hath drained my fresh life-blood, and my whole body is wasted."⁸⁰¹

That there was, in fact, a ritual celebrating Heracles' cremation has only recently been confirmed. In 1920, archaeologists working at a site upon Mt. Oeta discovered effigy-like figurines of the great hero that had apparently been subjected to repeated firings.⁸⁰² Judging from the artifacts found at the site, the cult persisted from at least the 6th century BCE well into Roman times.⁸⁰³ Referencing the discovery of the Oetean cult, Nilsson opined that the archaic rite had given rise to the myth of the hero's cremation:

---

⁷⁹⁷ *Fabula* 2. See here C. Pache, *op. cit.*, p. 150. On Palaimon's cult, see W. Burkert, *Homo Necans* (Berkeley, 1983), pp. 196-204.
⁷⁹⁸ Lykophron, *Alex.* 663.
⁷⁹⁹ E. Stafford, *Herakles* (Oxford, 2010), p. 89. See also E. Cochrane, *Martian Metamorphoses* (Ames, 1997), pp. 45-48.
⁸⁰⁰ B. Currie, *Pindar and the Cult of Heroes* (Oxford, 2005), p. 377: "Herakles' fiery death on Oeta led to his translation to Olympus and his cult on earth as a god or hero."
⁸⁰¹ 1051-1057.
⁸⁰² H. Shapiro, "*Hêrôs Theos*: The Death and Apotheosis of Herakles," *Classical World* 77:1 (1983), p. 15.
⁸⁰³ J. Croon, "Artemis Thermia and Apollo Thermios (With an excursus on the Oetean Heracles-Cult)," *Mnemosyne* 9 (1956), p. 212. J. Boardman, "Heracles in Extremis," in K. Schauenberg, *Studien zur Mythologie und Vasenmalerei* (Berlin, 1986), p. 129 would place the origin of the Oetean cult "long before the sixth century."

Such a bonfire was kindled on the top of Mount Oeta and the figure burned on the pyre was called Heracles. This is proved by early inscriptions and statuettes of Heracles. So the myth of Heracles' death in the flames of the pyre on Mount Oeta was created and connected with the magnificent but late myth of Deianeira.[804]

Greek artworks depicting Heracles' cremation make a special point of alluding to his rejuvenation after the experience atop Mt. Oeta (see figure two). John Boardman describes three Attic vases from about 470-450 BCE depicting the hero's apotheosis and rejuvenation:

> On two of the three Attic vases with the pyre and chariot Herakles is shown as a young man…The young Herakles has clearly been rejuvenated by his experience in the pyre and leaves behind only the muscle-corselet. It is difficult not to take this piece of armour, which appears on all three vases, as an indication of the mortality which Herakles has shed, as a snake sloughs its skin. The concept is one which occupies later writers and was perhaps somehow made explicit in other works of art…Whatever the service of the pyre in burning away his mortality and whatever its possible debts to eastern beliefs and practices…the concept does seem to determine this feature on the Classical vases.[805]

Figure two

---

[804] M. Nilsson, *The Mycenaean Origin of Greek Mythology* (New York, 1963), p. 205.
[805] J. Boardman, "Herakles in Extremis," in K. Schauenberg ed., *Studien zur Mythologie und Vasenmalerei* (Berlin, 1986), pp. 128-129.

That Heracles experienced rejuvenation in the wake of his immolation is also implied by Nonnus in his *Dionysiaka*. Insofar as the poet from Panopolis is renowned for having preserved archaic details of myth, otherwise lost, his magnificent hymn comparing Heracles' post-mortem rejuvenation with that of the Phoenix is of interest here:

> Starclad Heracles, lord of fire, prince of the universe!...On thy fragrant altar, that thousand-year wise bird the phoenix lays sweets-melling woods with his curved claw, bringing the end of one life and the beginning of another; for there he is born again, self-begotten, the image of equal time renewed—he sheds his old age in the fire, and from the fire takes in exchange youthful bloom.[806]

The reference to the fire-transfigured hero's "youthful bloom" (*anthos hebe*) is telling, an apparent allusion to the rejuvenation of Heracles and/or the Phoenix in the wake of his immolation (the hero's post-mortem *hieros gamos* with Hebe, herself a personification of youth, encodes the same metamorphosis). *Anthos hebe* was a proverbial expression in ancient Greek epic poetry for youthful vigor and warrior-prowess. In the *Iliad*, for example, Aeneas is described as follows: "the flower of youth is his, where man's strength is highest."[807] It will be remembered here that Demophon was described in very similar terms in the Homeric hymn—as "blossoming forth" or blooming (*prothales*) as a result of his roasting in the hearth-fire. And granted the likelihood that Nonnus was presenting an admixture of traditions surrounding the Greek strongman and the Tyrian god Melqart, it is significant to find that the child hero Melikertes was also described in floral terminology.[808] Witness the testimony of the Roman author Aelius Aristides regarding his transfixion before a picture of the child hero:

> It is good to talk about Palaimon and say his name and swear his oath, as well as to take part in the initiation ritual (*teletê*) and the celebration of secret rites (*orgiasmos*) in his honor, also—so great is the desire (*himeros*) attached to the boy—to see in the picture the bloom and freshness and flower of the boy when he is on the back

---

[806] Nonnus, *Dionysiaca* 40: 369-401.

[807] *Iliad* 13.484. See here the discussion in J-P. Vernant, *Mortals and Immortals* (Princeton, 1991), p. 61.

[808] On the possibility that Nonnus's account is referring to Melqart, see M. Otlewska-Jung, "Orpheus and Orphic Hymns in the *Dionysiaca*," in K. Spanoudakis ed., *Nonnus of Panopolis in Context* (Berlin, 2014), p. 80.

of the sea, and when he is in his mother's arms. For these are the sweetest of sights to see and to hear.[809]

As Corinne Pache pointed out in her comprehensive analysis of Melikertes' mythus, Aelius's report underscores the sublime beauty traditionally accorded the child-hero. Yet there is also a peculiar emphasis on the child's capacity for sprouting forth like a flower: "Aristides uses a series of adjectives associated with youth to describe Palaimon in his mother's arms: *thalos, hôran, anthos*, all belong to the metaphorical world of flowers and spring, and draw attention to Palaimon's youth and beauty."[810]

Confronted with the striking parallels between Demophon, Melikertes, and Heracles it is difficult to avoid the suspicion that there is some deeper significance behind their peculiar metamorphoses. Yet how is it possible to understand the mysterious phenomenon whereby a hero suddenly *blossoms* or becomes beautified and/or rejuvenated upon being incinerated in fire?

Truth be told, the peculiar traditions surrounding Heracles' fiery death, apotheosis, and rejuvenation have drawn relatively little attention from comparative scholars. The few scholars who have addressed the matter have focused upon terrestrial rituals and settled upon diffusion as the most likely source for the shared thematic patterns in question. Walter Burkert's discussion is representative in this regard:

> The complex of immolation and apotheosis recalls Near Eastern tradition, even if it remains a mystery how this came to be associated with the peak fire on Mount Oita. At Tarsos in Cilicia a pyre is prepared every year for a god who is called Heracles in Greek and Sandes or Sandon in the local languages…and the Hittite kings, as we learn, were made gods by extravagant cremation.[811]

Burkert's analysis of the Greek hero's immolation, which has since been endorsed by Martin West, is erudite and insightful, as is typically the case with this distinguished scholar. Yet the mere fact that analogous traditions will be found around the globe strongly suggests that diffusion from the ancient Near East cannot be the sole explanation for the Greek strongman's apotheosis and rejuvenation on the funeral pyre.[812]

---

[809] 46.40 as translated in C. Pache, "Singing Heroes," in G. Nagy ed., *Greek Literature in the Roman Period and Late Antiquity* (New York, 2001), p. 387.
[810] *Ibid.*, p. 387.
[811] W. Burkert, *Greek Religion* (Oxford, 1985), p. 210.
[812] See the discussion in E. Cochrane, *Starf*cker* (Ames, 2006), pp. 56-64, 140-144.

For our purposes here, it is significant to note that Heracles' incendiary metamorphosis on Mt. Oeta finds a striking parallel in Mesoamerica, where the immolation of Nanahuatl forms the decisive event in the Aztec myth of Creation, recounting the "birth" of the sun (see the account in Chapter five). Nanahuatl, like Heracles himself, was notorious for his skin disease and described as a dwarf.[813] How interesting, then, to find it reported that he suddenly "blossomed" (*cuecueponi*) upon being incinerated in the turquoise enclosure that constituted his funeral pyre: "Like so he burns, he blossoms, his flesh sizzles."[814]

In addition to "blossoming" forth into a sun-like god, it is elsewhere reported that Nanahuatl was beautified as a result of his experience in the hearth. The pustuluous hero's beautification is the subject of a Nahua myth recorded by Hernando Ruiz de Alarcon and published in 1629:

> But the God insisted that he was talking to him, persuading him to run through the middle of everyone and quickly throw himself into the fire. With this, the poor sick person—pustulous and scabby—resolved to undergo the rigorous test [at which point various others try and stop him several times, but he persists]. Immediately the sick man courageously threw himself into the midst of the furious fire, with whose force and flames he purged and purified all his sickness and sores and became beautiful and shining and was converted into the sun, which is the most resplendent of the planets, and this as a prize for the test of his courage and suffering, for which he deserved the said transmutation and to climb to the sky and be adored as a god.[815]

Nanahuatl's fire-induced blossoming and beautification naturally recalls the dramatic metamorphoses experienced by Demophon and Heracles/Melqart in the wake of their immolations and begs the following question: How is it possible to understand such traditions from the standpoint of natural history? It is Nanahuatl's identification with the nascent "sun" of Creation that provides the all-important clue: For the fact is that ancient sky-watchers

---

[813] Pseudo-Aristotle, *Problemata physica* 953a references "the eruption of ulcers prior to his [Heracles'] disappearance at Oeta." See also See J. Frazer, *Adonis, Attis, Osiris* (London, 1907), p. 175, who notes that "'The itch of Hercules' was a Greek term for someone with skin diseases."

[814] As translated in K. Read, *Time and Sacrifice in the Aztec Cosmos* (Bloomington, 1998), p. 53. See also K. Read & J. Gonzalez, *Mesoamerican Mythology* (Oxford, 2000), p. 100.

[815] Hernando Ruiz de Alarcon, *Treatise on the Heathen Superstitions that Today Live Among the Indians Native to this New Spain*, 1629 (Norman, 1984), p. 71.

conceptualized the prototypical sun as a "blossoming," flower-like form (see the discussion in chapter three).

Properly understood, the Aztec myth of Nanahuatl's blossoming and beautification will provide us with the natural-historical context necessary to decipher the curious traditions attached to Demophon and the other child-heroes from ancient Greece. It is precisely because the nascent "sun" presented a "flower-like" appearance that ancient myths around the globe describe mythical heroes as suddenly "blossoming" into a "new" or radically different "god-like" form. In the case of Demophon, it is his hiding or emplacement within the hearth fire that facilitates the infant's transfiguration into a god-like form (*daimoni isos*). Recall again the Homeric poet's description of Demeter's charge in the wake of his immolation: "To them it was a miracle how he blossomed forth and looked like the gods." This, in essence, is the story of the Aztec Nanahuatl: Upon mounting the pyre and being enveloped in flames, the hitherto diminutive and pustulous hero suddenly "blossoms" and becomes transfigured into a beautiful god-like form—i.e., the new "sun." In short, we would recognize a common natural history behind the mysterious metamorphoses associated with the various mythological characters discussed in this chapter: It is the "blossoming" or florification of the child within the hearth-fire that marks his new status as a *daemon* (Demophon) or "sun" (Nanahuatl).

Conclusion

We began this chapter by reviewing the curious practice of passing infant children through fire. As documented by James Frazer and other anthropologists, analogous customs have been practiced since time immemorial by cultures around the globe, often in conjunction with sacred rituals of initiation.[816] Such rites do not arise spontaneously, much less by imaginative impulse. Rather, they are best interpreted as deadly serious and purposeful attempts to simulate or recreate an extraordinary and awe-inspiring astronomical event—in this case, the glorious nova-like appearance of the nascent sun at the time of Creation.

According to a widespread mythological interpretation of the natural events in question, the nascent sun was rejuvenated or otherwise beautified as a result of its immolation on a funeral pyre or hearth. The extraordinary beauty of the hero/god undergoing immolation is a frequent point of emphasis, as is the hero's "blossoming"—the latter, in the final analysis, being inseparable from his apotheosis into a star while in conjunction with the floral-shaped Venus. Such is the Aztec myth of Nanahuatl as reported by Sahagún and other indigenous sources.

---

[816] M. Eliade, *Rites and Symbols of Initiation* (New York, 1958), p. 99: "Among some tribes, the initiation also includes the novice's being 'roasted' in or at a fire."

The strange constellation of traditions attached to Heracles' immolation and transfiguration would appear to reflect the same natural history. The hideously deformed and ulcerous Heracles, like Nanahuatl, is rejuvenated and/or "divinized" as a result of his experience on the pyre at Oeta. Indeed, the apotheosis of Heracles is a direct result of his immolation, much as Nanahuatl's immolation leads to his apotheosis as the prototypical "sun" in Aztec lore.

The Greek myth of Demophon's roasting by Demeter evidently represents a vestigial remnant or reminiscence of this same tradition and, much like the ritual passing of children through fire, stands as an enduring testament to the profound and life-altering impact the referenced astronomical events had on our prehistoric forebears, many of whom sought to empower their own children through similar pyrotechnics—i.e., by means of sympathetic magic (via the so-called law of similarity). The Aztec custom of purposefully blistering themselves and their children during the New Fire ritual offers a paradigmatic example of this belief-system and is best interpreted as an attempt to emulate or re-enact Nanahuatl's exploits and transfiguration at the time of Beginning.

Appendix Twelve: Sky-God or Thundergod?

In the first volume of this work I endeavored to show that Zeus, the Greek sky-god, was originally just the bright or day-light sky conceived as alive and operant...Zeus, then, was primarily god of the bright sky. But the sky is not always bright.[817]

The gods, then, or any rate those designated by this word [*diw/ dyu* whence Zeus], were literally 'the celestials'; they belonged to the sky.[818]

Zeus is the Greek god *par excellence* and yet he remains elusive—an Olympus-sized enigma, as it were. Witness the confession of ignorance by his biographer Ken Dowden: "As the mountain of data grows, it becomes harder and harder to get a clear idea of Zeus, particularly if one must now abandon Victorian ideas like nature and evolution as a means of patterning the information."[819] That said, it stands to reason that a satisfactory understanding of Greek religion and culture is bound to remain elusive apart from additional insight into the god's original nature and *modus operandi*.

In addition to his preeminent position in Greek religion, Zeus represents a pivotal figure in the history of comparative mythology. It was the discovery of cognate names in ancient Vedic and Latin texts— *Dyaus Pitar* and **Diove Pater* respectively—that originally led William Jones (1786) to propose the common Indo-Germanic ancestry of the three languages in question. It was this finding, in turn, that almost single-handedly launched the modern scientific investigation of

---

[817] A. B. Cook, *Zeus, Vol. 2* (Cambridge, 1925), p. 1.
[818] M. West, *Indo-European Poetry and Myth* (Oxford, 2007), p. 120.
[819] K. Dowden, *Zeus* (London, 2006), p. 14.

ancient myth and the two complementary fields of comparative mythology and comparative linguistics.[820]

It follows, accordingly, that the etymology of the god's name looms large in any analysis of his cult. For Walter Burkert, the Greek god is best understood as a god of the bright sky and the "flash of daylight." With a nod towards Jones' monumental discovery, Burkert observed:

> Zeus is the only name of a Greek god which is entirely transparent etymologically, and which indeed has long been paraded as a model case in Indo-European philology...Zeus is therefore the Sky Father, the luminous day sky.[821]

Linguists are agreed that the root meaning of Zeus points to a celestial agent associated with light. Edgar Polomé summarized the evidence as follows:

> From the discredited etymological method precious little survived except for one solid comparison: Ved. *Dyaus pitā*=Gk. *Zeus patêr*=Lat. *Juppiter* reflecting an IE **dyéus* 'god of the luminous sky,' whose name has also survived in Germanic **Tîwaz*, contained in *Tuesday* and reflected in Old Norse by the name of the Eddic deity *Tyr*.[822]

There is much reason to believe, moreover, that at some point in the prehistoric past the King of the Gods became conceptualized as the archetypal god *par excellence*. This development was also encoded in language, as documented by Burkert:

---

[820] J. Puhvel, *Comparative Mythology* (Baltimore, 1987), p. 13 calls this development "one of the greatest discoveries of modern times." On William Jones, see B. Feldman & R. Richardson, *The Rise of Modern Mythology* (Bloomington, 1972), pp. 267-275.

[821] W. Burkert, *Greek Religion* (Cambridge, 1985), p. 125

[822] E. Polomé, "Some Thoughts on the Methodology of Comparative Religion, with Special Focus on Indo-European," in E. Polomé ed., *Essays in Memory of Karl Kerényi* (Washington, D.C., 1984), p. 10. See also S. Jamison & J. Brereton, *The Rigveda* (Austin, 2014), p. 50: "One of the most remarkable and satisfying phrasal equations across the older Indo-European languages is that of Vedic *dyaús pita* 'father Heaven' with Greek Zeus Pater and Latin Jupiter, thus attesting to a deified paternal Heaven for Proto-Indo-European as well as the older daughter languages. Ironically, perhaps, the Vedic god, the meaning of whose name is still transparent and lexically additive, is far less important in the Vedic pantheon than his correspondents in the Classical languages, where the original semantics have become attenuated or have disappeared entirely."

This root *dieu/deiw-* also survived in Greek in words such as εὐδία 'fine weather', ἔνδιος 'in the light of day', and in the adjective δῖος 'brilliant', besides the well-known *Zeus*. The Greek vocabulary, parallel to Latin *deus-dies*, thus conveys a special message of the Indo-european concept of 'god': 'God' belongs to the sky and the flash of daylight.[823]

Granted that Zeus's fundamental affinity with the bright sky and ancient conceptions of divinity is reflected in his name, how are we to understand the god's manifold connections with lightning and thunder? Meteorological phenomena, after all, are alluded to in some of the god's most archaic epithets: *Terpikeraunos*, "rejoicing in lightning"; *Astrapios*, "sender of lightning," and *Ergidoupos*, "very thundering." Indeed, in Homer a whopping 26 of the god's epithets commemorate his meteorological functions.[824] Burkert himself never managed to resolve the natural-historical basis of the connection: "The association remained uncertain; Weather God and Sky God could not be reconciled."[825]

Remarkably, most modern scholars deny an inherent connection between Zeus and his Thundergod characteristics. For Martin West, Jaan Puhvel and other eminent authorities Zeus's association with lightning and thunder is best understood as a secondary development and hence ultimately unrelated to the original conception of the god:

> The Indo-European *Dyeus was essentially the bright sky of day. We saw in Chapter 4 that his Indic and Greek representatives could fertilize Earth with rain. But this peaceful conjugal relationship, of which we are the incidental offspring, is complete in itself. Thunderous electrical rages directed (in most mythologies) against demons or dragons cannot be considered an organic part of it. And the specialist storm-gods have a distinctive character of their own; they are more like each other than they are like the god of the sky, where he can still be made out. So it seems altogether more likely that Zeus and Jupiter have appropriated the functions of a separate storm-god who has faded from sight than that they alone preserve the integrity

---

[823] W. Burkert, "From Epiphany to Cult Statue: Early Greek *Theos*," in A. Lloyd ed., *What is a God?* (Swansea, 1997), p. 15.
[824] K. Dowden, *Zeus* (London, 2006), p. 46. See also W. Burkert, *Greek Religion* (Cambridge, 1985), p. 126.
[825] *Ibid.*, p. 126.

of *Dyeus' personality, the other traditions having conspired to create a separate thunderer.[826]

Here, in plain English, is summarized perhaps the single-most important question in comparative mythology: Is the greatest god of the Indo-European pantheon best understood by a uniformitarian understanding of the day sky and not by any reference to stormy weather and catastrophe-bringing thunderbolts? As near as I can discern, West's position is wholly untenable.

The "peaceful conjugal relationship" between Father Sky and Mother Earth referenced by West is a figment of his imagination. The esteemed Classicist has conveniently ignored the fact that it was as a fiery thunderbolt (*keraunós*) that Zeus inseminated Earth, as illustrated by his incendiary coupling with Semele.[827] The Sky-god's thunderbolting of Semele, in turn, offers a close parallel to Perkunas's striking of the close cognate Zemyna in Baltic cosmogonic myth. Recall again Gimbutas's formulation, quoted earlier: "The earth is barren until the Thunder strikes her in the springtime—until in his epiphany of thunder Perkunas weds the Mother Earth, Zemyna."

Equally relevant is the fact that Zeus's stormy hierogamy with Semele offers a close thematic parallel to the *hieros gamos* between Heaven and Earth in archaic Mesopotamian creation accounts, which typically occurs in a general context of Sturm und Drang.[828] The account from the Barton cylinder (ca. 2400 BCE) is representative in this regard:

> On that far-away day…Then a gale was really blowing unceasingly, there were really flashes of lightning continuously. Near the sanctuary of Nippur a gale was really blowing unceasingly, there were really flashes of lightning continuously. An-heaven is shouting together with Ki-earth.[829]

As is evident in the Barton cylinder and a number of other archaic Mesopotamian texts, the roaring storm and "thunderous electrical rages" are part and parcel

---

[826] M. West, *Indo-European Poetry and Myth* (Oxford, 2007), pp. 238-239.

[827] J. Puhvel, *Comparative Mythology* (Baltimore, 1989), p. 228 calls it a "fulgural hierogamy that 'got out of hand'."

[828] A. George, "Cosmogony in Ancient Mesopotamia," p. 6 speaks of a "violent storm" attending the primordial coupling of Heaven and Earth. Note: This is an English reprint of the author's "Die Kosmogonie des alten Mesopotamien," in M. Gindhart & T. Pommerening eds., *Anfang & Ende: vormoderne Szenarien von Weltentstehung und Weltuntergang* (Darmstadt, 2016), pp. 7-25.

[829] Translation per J. Lisman, *At the Beginning: Cosmogony, Theogony and Anthropogeny in Sumerian texts of the Third and Second Millennium BCE* (Leiden, 2013), p. 30.

of the primeval *hieros gamos* between the Sky-god and Mother Earth.[830] In overlooking such imagery, Martin West has effectively emasculated Zeus and offered a fundamentally misleading conception of the god.

Implicit in Euripides' account of Zeus's amorous encounter with Semele is the idea that the god was believed to be incarnate in the fiery thunderbolt (ἀστραπηφόρῳ πυρί): "Semele brought to bed by the lightning-fire."[831] Louis Farnell made much the same point more than a century ago while discussing Zeus's epithet *Kappotas*, "falling":

> The descending Zeus is the Zeus that descends in the rain or lightning…This naïve belief that the god himself came down in the lightning or the meteor is illustrated by the story which Pausanias found in the neighborhood of Gythium about a sacred stone, a λίθος ἀργός, on which Orestes sat and was cured of his madness, and which the country people called Zeus καππῶτας…There is much to be said for the view that the term means 'the falling god,' …We are here touching on a stratum of thought infinitely older than the Homeric.[832]

The sacred stone in question—*lithos argos*, conventionally translated "unwrought stone"—was thought to embody Zeus. The inescapable conclusion is that the Greek Sky-god was formerly conceptualized as a descending stone or meteor. And as Pausanias pointed out in his *Geography*, such religious conceptions are of extreme antiquity in Old Europe: "In the olden time, all the Greeks worshipped unwrought stones instead of images."[833]

A similar belief-system is attested in the Latin cult of Jupiter, where solemn oaths were sworn under the name of *Iuppiter Lapis*, "Jupiter present in the thunderstone."[834] As Cyril Bailey observed well over a century ago, Jupiter's epithet evidently describes the god as a stone-like object:

---

[830] Y. Chen, *The Primeval Flood Catastrophe* (Oxford, 2014), p. 113: "In Sumerian mythological prologues, stormy weather is used metaphorically to depict the cosmic union or reproduction (cosmogony), as seen in mythological compositions from the Early Dynastic III Period such as the Barton Cylinder." E. Håland, *Greek Festivals, Modern and Ancient, Vol. 2* (Cambridge, 2017), p. 121: "The marriage of the Sky Father with the Earth Mother also takes place in the thunderstorm."

[831] Line 3 as translated in A. B. Cook, *op. cit.*, p. 28.

[832] L. Farnell, *The Cults of the Greek States, Vol. I* (New Rochelle, 1977), p. 46.

[833] Pausanias VII.22.4 as translated in W. Ridgeway, *The Early Age of Greece, Vol. II* (Cambridge, 1931), pp. 422-423.

[834] P. Chemery, "Meteorological Beings," in M. Eliade ed., *The Encyclopedia of Religion, Vol. 16* (1987), p. 491. See also G. Dumézil, *Archaic Roman Religion, Vol. 1* (Baltimore, 1966), p. 179.

Here no doubt the underlying notion is not merely symbolical, but in origin the stone is itself the god, an idea which later religion expressed in the cult-title specially used in this connection, *Iuppiter Lapis*.[835]

To reiterate: "In origin the stone is itself the god." Exactly.

The idea that the Sky-god or his thunderbolt descended as a stone-like object is of untold antiquity and will be found among indigenous cultures around the globe.[836] The evidence was compiled by Christopher Blinkenberg well over one hundred years ago:

> The thunderstone falls down from the sky in thunderstorms or, more accurately, whenever the lightning strikes. The stroke of the lightning, according to this view, consists in the descent of the stone; the flash and the thunder-clap are mere after-effects or secondary phenomena.[837]

Meteors, in accordance with this archaic belief-system, were widely identified with thunderbolts and/or lightning. According to G. A. Wainwright, whose primary area of focus was ancient Egypt, the thunderbolt was simply a rock hurled from heaven: "In religion the meteorite and the thunderbolt are the same thing."[838] The very same conception is attested in the New World: "In Mesoamerica meteors and fireballs are viewed as a kind of lightning."[839]

Students of ancient myth and religion have long struggled to explain the thunderbolt's underlying connection with a meteor or stone-like object. Since this idea does not make sense from the vantage point of modern astronomy and meteorology, Classicists dismiss it as nonsense. Albert Cook, surveying the evidence for such beliefs surrounding Zeus and the

---

[835] C. Bailey, *The Religion of Ancient Rome* (London, 1907), p. 7. See also R. Janko, *The Iliad: A Commentary* (Oxford, 1994), p. 230.

[836] C. Blinkenberg, *The Thunderbolt in Religion and Folklore* (Cambridge, 1911), p. 32: "The lightning, then, is produced by a stone which shoots down from heaven to earth." See also M. West, *op. cit.*, p. 254: "The thunderbolt is everywhere conceived as being due to the impact of a solid object."

[837] *Ibid.*, p. 1. For analogous conceptions from indigenous Africa, see S. Lagercrantz, "Der Donnerkeil im afrikanischen Volksglauben," *Etnologiska Studier* 10 (1940), pp. 1-40.

[838] G. A. Wainwright, "Letopolis," *Journal of Egyptian Archaeology* 18 (1932), p. 161.

[839] J. Staller & B. Stross, *Lightning in the Andes and Mesoamerica* (Oxford, 2013), p. 199. See also K. Bassie-Sweet & N. Hopkins, "Ancient Thunderbolt and Meteor Deities," in K. Bassie-Sweet ed., *The Ch'ol Maya of Chiapas* (Norman, 2015), p. 128: "Fiery meteors and meteor showers were considered cognates of thunder and lightning in Maya world view."

other great Thundergods, offered the following disclaimer with regards to the *keraunós*:

> This is usually translated by the word 'thunderbolt,' but must not be taken to denote a solid missile of any sort. It means nothing more than the bright white flash in its destructive capacity.[840]

Ken Dowden offered a very similar opinion in his recent monograph on Zeus. Witness the statement: "There is no such thing as a thunderbolt, because lightning is not an object that is thrown…"[841]

It is Jane Harrison, perhaps, who has devoted the most ink to Zeus's thunderbolt. She too would deny that the all-powerful *keraunós* ever actually existed:

> Here and elsewhere we have three factors in a thunderstorm, thunder itself, the noise heard (βροντή), lightning, the flash seen (στεροπή), and a third thing, κεραυνός, which we translate 'thunderbolt.' All three are shafts, κῆλα, of mighty Zeus. Mighty Zeus we may dismiss. He is the product of a late anthropomorphism, but the three sorts of 'shaft' mentioned are interesting. Thunder is a reality, a sound actually heard, lightning no less a reality, actually seen, but the third shaft—the thunderbolt? There is no such thing. Yet by a sort of irony it is the non-existent thunderbolt that Greek art most frequently depicts.[842]

These pronouncements from the hallowed halls of academia are thoroughly misguided and form the modern equivalent of Thomas Jefferson denying the possibility that stones (meteors) could fall from the sky simply because he couldn't imagine such a thing.[843] Such skepticism involves nothing less than turning a deaf ear to the express testimony of ancient sky-watchers around the globe (Sumerian sky-watchers had warned of the dire consequences of stones/meteorites falling from the planet Mars from time immemorial). Truth be told, the ancient sky-watchers and mythmakers did not wake up one prehistoric morning and suddenly decide to honor their greatest gods by arbitrarily inventing imaginary constructs like Zeus's meteor-like thunderbolt.

---

[840] A. B. Cook, *Zeus, Vol. II* (New York, 1965), p. 11.
[841] K. Dowden, *Zeus* (London, 2006), p. 56.
[842] J. Harrison, *Epilegomena to the Study of Greek Religion* (New York, 1962), p. 88.
[843] O. Farrington, *Meteorites* (Chicago, 1915), p. 12: "The possibility of such an occurrence was at that time [1807] scarcely believed and the general opinion was expressed by the President of the United States, Thomas Jefferson, in a remark that it was easier to believe that Yankee professors would lie than to believe that stones would fall from heaven."

The agnosticism of Cook, Dowden, and Harrison is also at loggerheads with the linguistic evidence. Thus it is well known that a number of Indo-European languages describe thunderbolts by terminology signifying "stone" or meteorite.[844] The heaven-hurled weapon of the Vedic Indra, for example, was known as *ásman*, "rock, thunderbolt."[845] This word finds a close cognate in Lithuanian, where *akmuô*, "stone," denotes Perkunas's thunderbolt. Thor's thunderbolt, in turn, was known by the cognate term *hamarr*, "stone." The fact that Hesiod employs the Greek cognate *akmon* in the sense of "meteorite" or "stone" likely encodes the same natural-historical reality: The Thundergod's fiery "bolt" was a heaven-hurled stone or bolide.[846]

To bring the argument full circle: It is well-known that a number of these same words denote "sky/heaven" as well as stone and thunderbolt. The Vedic *ásman* and Avestan *asman* are two such terms, but there are others as well, including Greek *akmon*.[847] With reference to the latter word, David Johnson observes: "Indo-European cognates mean 'stone' but also 'sky,' 'meteorite,' and 'thunderbolt'."[848] The original historical stimulus for this archaic language, in our view, was the archetypal Sky-god himself—Zeus, conceptualized at once as a stone (*lithos argos*), thunderbolt (*keraunós*), and sky/heaven (*diw/dyu*). Far from representing a conundrum, Zeus's inherent connection with the sky, thunderbolt, and stone is actually the starting point for a unified interpretation of Greek religion. Simply stated: From the outset, Zeus was conceptualized as a stone—as a planet or planet-sized meteor.

Conclusion

Ken Dowden begins his recent monograph on Zeus by asking the following question: "How could the Greeks have worshipped such an empty god?"[849] And then he gets downright dismissive and condescending:

> From beginning to end Zeus has been unseen, operating the causal system of the universe in mysterious ways, and underlying every event…The mythology was only a way of talking about Zeus, a

---

[844] R. Janko, *The Iliad: A Commentary, Vol. 4* (Cambridge, 1994), p. 230.

[845] R. Beekes, "Stone," in J. Mallory & D. Adams, *Encyclopedia of Indo-European Culture* (London, 1997), p. 547.

[846] J. Puhvel, *op. cit.*, p. 227. See also C. Whitman, "Hera's Anvils," *Harvard Studies in Classical Philology* 74 (1970), p. 40.

[847] See the discussion in A. Panaino, *A Walk Through the Iranian Heavens* (Oxford, 2019), pp. 59ff.

[848] D. Johnson, "Hesiod's Description of Tartarus," *Phoenix* 53 (1999) p. 13.

[849] K. Dowden, *Zeus* (London, 2006), p. 3.

façon de parler. No one believed that the gods actually had a palace at the top of a mountain in Thessaly. Mythology was always a parable, a transposition of the mysterious into another language.[850]

Talk about hubris! Talk about blasphemy! Such are the armchair musings of a modern scholar who is totally alienated from the natural-historical context and cognitive reality of the Greek sky-watchers and mythmakers—so alienated, in fact, that, like Oedipus, he is incapable of seeing or understanding what lies right before his face. The parable-spinning mythmakers whom Dowden derides here, it will be noted, include the likes of Homer, Hesiod, Heraclitus, Aeschylus, Euripides, Sophocles, and Plato—in short, some of the greatest poets and philosophers the human race has yet produced. If we are to believe Dowden, such men were either hopelessly deluded or hell-bent on deceiving their countrymen with fanciful stories regarding the blustering bogeyman Zeus.

More to the point: Dowden is wrong on every single score here. Far from being a mere *façon de parler* or figure of speech, the mythological traditions attached to Zeus were the product of an empirically-based reality—in this case, a direct confrontation with a god who took the form of a towering planetary orb hovering in the circumpolar heavens, a perfectly visible source of fire, lightning, and thunder. When Heraclitus described the fundamental power behind the Universe as Zeus or *keraunós* he was not engaging in metaphysical speculation but drawing upon millennia-old traditions of a heaven-spanning power akin to the image depicted in figure one. Indeed, Heraclitus's famous dictum that "the *keraunós* steers everything" finds a striking parallel in the cult of the Semitic thundergod Adad, who was invoked as: "Lord of lightning, whose glow illuminates the universe" (*Bel birqi ša šarurušu unammaru kibrati*).[851] Such formulaic expressions, properly understood, describe a prodigious lightning-like structure as personally witnessed by prehistoric sky-watchers the world over. In this sense Zeus himself was every bit as real as the *keraunós* and yet Dowden denies the reality of both! In the face of such myopia, is it any wonder that modern Classicists have so little to say that is of interest about how and why the ancient gods and myths inspired the Greek masters to create their tragedies and other timeless works of art?

---

[850] *Ibid.*, pp. 3-4.
[851] D. Charpin, "Solar Aspects of Royal Power in Old Babylonian Mesopotamia," in J. Hill et al eds., *Experiencing Power, Generating Authority* (Philadelphia, 2013), p. 81.

Figure one

To return to the debate over Zeus's status as the archetypal Thundergod: Far from "appropriating" or "annexing" the functions of a separate storm-god, as per the thesis of Martin West and other noted authorities, the evidence of comparative mythology and comparative linguistics supports the conclusion that Zeus was from the very beginning a celestial agent intrinsically associated with the "flash of lightning" as well as with the "flash of daylight" and bright sky. Walter Burkert let the cat out of the bag when, in a magisterial discussion of the etymology of the god's name, he observed: "For the practically minded man the day sky is admittedly of no great interest."[852] This is exactly correct. The uneventful day sky could never produce an awe-inspiring, terrifying Colossus like Zeus, a *mysterium tremendum* for the ages. It is only a cataclysmic sky, one filled with planet-sized bolides and heaven-spanning thunderbolts, that could inspire the mighty deity described by Homer, Hesiod, and the other Greek poets.

---

[852] W. Burkert, *Greek Religion* (Cambridge, 1985), p. 126.

Bibliography

Hernando Ruiz de Alarcon, *Treatise on the Heathen Superstitions that Today Live Among the Indians Native to this New Spain*, 1629 (Norman, 1984).

H. B. Alexander, "Latin American Mythology," in L. Gray ed., *The Mythology of All Races,* Vol. 11 (New York, 1964).

_____, "North American," in L. Grey ed., *The Mythology of All Races, Vol. 10* (Boston, 1917).

S. Allan, *The Shape of the Turtle* (Albany, 1981).

J. Allen, *Genesis in Egypt* (New Haven, 1988).

_____, *Middle Egyptian* (Cambridge, 2014).

C. Ambos, "Temporary Ritual Structures and Their Cosmological Symbolism," in D. Ragavan ed., *Heaven and Earth* (Chicago, 2013), pp. 245-258.

P. Amiet, *La glyptique mésopotamienne archaique* (Paris, 1961).

E. Anati, *Camonica Valley* (New York, 1961).

J. Assmann, *The Search for God in Ancient Egypt* (Ithaca, 2001).

_____, *The Mind of Egypt* (Cambridge, 1996).

_____, *Egyptian Solar Religion in the New Kingdom* (London, 1995).

_____, "Solar Discourse," *Deutsche Vierteljahrsschrift für Literaturwissenschaft und Geistesgeschicte* 4 (1994), pp. 107-123.

M. Astour, *Hellenosemitica* (Leiden, 1967).

A. Athanassakis, *The Homeric Hymns* (Baltimore, 1976).

N. Ayali-Darshan, "The Other Version of the Story of the Storm-god's Combat with the Sea in the Light of Egyptian, Ugaritic, and Hurro-Hittite Texts," *Journal of Ancient Near Eastern Religions* 15 (2015), pp. 36ff.

C. Bailey, *The Religion of Ancient Rome* (London, 1907).

E. Baird, "Stars and War at Cacaxtla," in R. Diehl & J. Berlo eds., *Mesoamerican After the Decline of Teotihuacan...* (Washington D.C., 1989), pp. 117ff.

James Baldwin, "The White Man's Guilt," in *Ebony* 20:10 (August, 1965), pp. 65ff.

W. Barta, "Der Königsring als Symbol zyklischer Wiederkehr," *Zeitschrift* für Ägyptische *Sprache und Altertumskunde* 98 (1970), pp. 5-13.

K. Bassie-Sweet, *Maya Sacred Geography and the Creator Deities* (Norman, 2008).

K. Bassie-Sweet & N. Hopkins, "Ancient Thunderbolt and Meteor Deities," in K. Bassie-Sweet ed., *The Ch'ol Maya of Chiapas* (Norman, 2015), p. 128ff.

M. Beard, *Re-Reading (Vestal) Virginity* (London, 1995).

S. Beaulieu, *Eve's Ritual: The Judahite Sacred Marriage Rite* (Montreal, 2007).

R. Beekes, "Stone," in J. Mallory & D. Adams, *Encyclopedia of Indo-European Culture* (London, 1997), pp. 547ff.

M. Bender & A. Wuwu, *The Nuosu Book of Origins* (Seattle, 2019).

A. Bernabé, "The question of the Origin: Cosmogony—Introduction," in S. Fink & R. Rollinger eds., *Conceptualizing Past, Present and Future* (Münster, 2018), pp. 366ff.

R. Bielfeldt, "Sight and light: reified gazes and looking artefacts in the Greek cultural imagination," in M. Squire ed., *Sight and the Ancient Senses* (London, 2016), pp. 124ff.

J. Bierhorst, *Four Masterworks of American Indian Literature* (Tucson, 1974).

_____, translator. *History and Mythology of the Aztecs: The Codex Chimalpopoca* (Tucson, 1992).

_____, *A Nahuatl-English Dictionary and Concordance to the Cantares Mexicanos* (Stanford, 1985).

J. Black & A. Green, *Gods, Demons and Symbols of Ancient Mesopotamia* (London, 1992).

J. Black et al, *The Literature of Ancient Sumer* (Oxford, 2004).

J. Black, *Reading Sumerian Poetry* (London, 1998).

_____, "The Sumerians and Their Landscape," in T. Abusch ed., *Riches Hidden in Secret Places* (Winona Lake, 2002), pp. 56ff.

A. Blackman & H. Fairman, "The Myth of Horus at Edfu—II," *Journal of Egyptian Archaeology* 29 (1943), pp. 12ff.

C. J. Bleeker, *Hathor and Thoth* (Leiden, 1973).

C. Blinkenberg, *The Thunderbolt in Religion and Folklore* (Cambridge, 1911).

M. Bloomfield, *Hymns of the Atharva-Veda* (Oxford, 1897).

J. Boardman, "Heracles in Extremis," in K. Schauenberg, *Studien zur Mythologie und Vasenmalerei* (Berlin, 1986), pp. 129ff.

F. Boas, "Tsimshian Mythology," *Bureau of American Ethnology* (Washington D.C., 1916), pp. 455ff.

E. Boot, "Loanwords, 'Foreign Words,' and Foreign Signs in Maya Writing," in A. de Voogt & I. Finkel eds., *The Idea of Writing* (Leiden, 2010), pp. 156ff.

J. Borghouts, *Book of the Dead [39]: From Shouting To Structure* (Wiesbaden, 2007).

A. Bowles, Dharma, *Disorder and the Political in Ancient India* (Leiden, 2007).

M. Boyce & F. Grenet, *A History of Zoroastrianism* (Leiden, 1991).

P. Boylan, *Thoth: The Hermes of Egypt* (Oxford, 1922).

J. Bremer, "The Meadow of Love," *Mnemosyne* 28 (1975), pp. 269ff.

———, "Greek Hymns," in H. S. Versnel, *Faith, Hope, and Worship* (Leiden, 1981), pp. 206ff.

J. Bremmer, *Greek Religion and Culture, the Bible and the Ancient Near East* (Leiden, 2008).

M. Brennan, *The Stones of Time* (Rochester, 1994).

J. Brereton, "Dharman in the Rgveda," *Journal of Indian Philosophy* 32 (2004), pp. 449-489ff.

H. Breuil & H. Obermaier, *The Cave of Altamira* (Madrid, 1935).

L. Brisson, *Plato the Mythmaker* (Chicago, 2000).

B. Brundage, *The Fifth Sun* (Austin, 1979).

E. Brunner, "Die Grüne Sonne," in M. Görg & E. Pusch eds., *Festschrift für Elmar Edel* (Wiesbaden, 1979), pp. 54-59ff.

F. Bruschweiler, *Inanna la déesse triomphante et vaincue dans la cosmologie sumérienne* (Leuven, 1988).

R. Bunzel, "Introduction to Zuni Ceremonialism," *Annual Report of the Bureau of American Ethnology* 47 (1929-1930), pp. 514ff.

E. van Buren, "The Sacred Marriage in Early Times in Mesopotamia," *Orientalia* 13 (1944), pp. 1ff.

———, "The Rosette in Mesopotamian Art," *Zeitschrift für Assyriologie XI* (1939), pp. 99-107.

W. Burkert, "Jason, Hypsipyle, and New Fire at Lemnos," *Classical Quarterly* 20 (1970), pp. 4ff.

———, *Greek Religion* (Cambridge, 1985).

———, "Oriental and Greek Mythology: The Meeting of Parallels," in J. Bremmer ed., *Interpretations of Greek Mythology* (Totowa, N.J., 1989), pp. 36ff.

———, *Homo Necans* (Berkeley, 1983).

———, "From Epiphany to Cult Statue: Early Greek *Theos*," in A. Lloyd ed., *What is a God?* (Swansea, 1997), p. 15ff.

———, *Structure and History in Greek Mythology* (Berkeley, 1982).

C. Burland, *The Gods of Mexico* (New York, 1967).

T. Burrow, "Sanskrit rájas," *Bulletin of the School of Oriental and African Studies* 12 (1948), pp. 648ff.

D. Burton, "Nike, Dike and Zeus at Olympia," in J. McWilliam et al eds., *The Statue of Zeus at Olympia* (Cambridge, 2011), pp. 52ff.

L. Cagni, *The Poem of Erra* (Malibu, 1977).

D. Carballo, *Collision of Worlds* (Oxford, 2020).

J. Carlson, "Transformations of the Mesoamerican Venus Turtle Carapace War Shield," in V. del Chamberlain, J. Carlson, & M. Young eds., *Songs From the Sky* (Washington, D.C., 2005), pp. 115ff.

D. Carrasco, *City of Sacrifice: The Aztec Empire and the Role of Violence in Civilization* (Boston, 1999).

D. Carrasco & S. Sessions, *Daily Life of the Aztecs* (London, 1998).

G. Catlin, *O-kee-pa: A Religious Ceremony* (Lincoln, 1976).

V. del Chamberlain, *When Stars Came Down to Earth* (College Park, 1982).

V. del Chamberlain & P. Schaafsma, "Origin and Meaning of Navajo Star Ceilings," in V. del Chamberlain, J. Carlson, & J. Young eds., *Songs From the Sky* (Washington D.C., 1987), pp. 91ff.

D. Charpin, "Solar Aspects of Royal Power in Old Babylonian Mesopotamia," in J. Hill et al eds., *Experiencing Power, Generating Authority* (Philadelphia, 2013), pp. 65-96.

P. Charvát, *The Birth of the State* (Prague, 2013).

P. Chemery, "Meteorological Beings," in M. Eliade ed., *The Encyclopedia of Religion, Vol. 16* (1987), pp. 491ff.

Y. S. Chen, *The Primeval Flood Catastrophe* (Oxford, 2014).

A. Christenson, *Popol Vuh* (New York, 2003)

_____, *Art and Society in a Highland Maya* Community (2010).

R. T. Clark, *Myth and Symbol in Ancient Egypt* (London, 1959).

R. Clifford, *Creation Accounts in the Ancient Near East* (Washington, D.C., 1974).

E. Cochrane, *On Fossil Gods and Forgotten Worlds* (Ames, 2010).

_____, "Ladder to Heaven," *Aeon* 6:5 (2004) pp. 55-76.

_____, "Suns and Planets in Neolithic Rock Art," in *Martian Metamorphoses* (Ames, 1997), pp. 194-214.

_____, "Thundergods and Thunderbolts," *Aeon* 6:1 (2001), pp. 102ff.

_____, "Anomalies in Ancient Descriptions of the Sun-God," *Chronology & Catastrophism Review* (2016), pp. 3-12.

_____, *Phaethon: The Star That Fell From Heaven* (Ames, 2017)

_____, *Starf*cker* (Ames, 2010).

_____, *Martian Metamorphoses* (Ames, 1997).

_____, "Written in the Stars," available online at https://www.maverick-science.com/wp-content/uploads/Written-in-the-Stars.pdf

M. Cohen, "Another Utu Hymn," *ZA* 67 (1977), pp. 7ff.

D. Collon, "Mond," *RA* 8 (Berlin, 1993-1997).

_____, *First Impressions* (London, 1987).

A. Coomaraswamy, "An Indian Temple," in R. Lipsey ed., *Coomaraswamy: Selected Papers* (Princeton, 1977), pp. 3-12.
H. Converse, *Myths and Legends of the New York Iroquois* (Albany, 1974).
A. B. Cook, *Zeus, Vol. 1* (Cambridge, 1914).
_____, *Zeus, Vol. II* (New York, 1965).
G. Cook & T. Offit, *Indigenous Religion and Cultural Performance in the New Maya World* (Albuquerque, 2013).
J. Croon, "Artemis Thermia and Apollo Thermios (With an excursus on the Oetean Heracles- Cult)," *Mnemosyne* 9 (1956), pp. 212ff.
E. Csapo, "Star Choruses: Eleusis, Orphism, and the New Musical Imagery and Dance," in M. Revermann & P. Wilson, *Performance, Iconography, Reception* (Oxford, 2008), pp. 271ff.
G. Curtis, *The Cave Painters* (New York, 2006).
N. Curtis, *The Indians' Book* (New York, 1907).
B. Currie, *Pindar and the Cult of Heroes* (Oxford, 2005).
R. Dandekar, "Universe in Vedic Thought," in J. Ensink & P. Gaeffke ed., *India Maior* (Leiden, 1972), pp. 98ff.
A. Demarest, *Ideology and Pre-Columbian Civilizations* (Santa Fe, 1992).
M. Dexter, "Earth Goddess," in J. Mallory & D. Adams eds., *Encyclopedia of Indo-European Culture* (Chicago, 1997), pp. 174ff.
B. Dietrich, *The Origins of Greek Religion* (Berlin, 1974).
B. Dippie, *Catlin* (Lincoln, 1990).
D. Disterheft, M. Huld & J. Greppin et al eds., *Studies in Honor of Jaan Puhvel* (Washington, D.C., 1997).
G. Dorsey, *Traditions of the Skidi Pawnee* (Boston, 1904).
J. Dorsey, "Indian Names for the Winds and Quarters," *The Archaeologist* 2 (1894), pp. 247ff.
K. Dowden, *Zeus* (London, 2006).
P. Dronke, *Fabula* (Leiden, 1985).
G. Dumézil, *Archaic Roman Religion, Vol. 1* (Baltimore, 1966).
Alan Dundes, "Madness in Method Plus a Plea for Projective Inversion in Myth," in L. Patton & W. Doniger eds., *Myth and Method* (London, 1996), pp. 147ff.
J. Eggeling, *The Satapatha Brahmana* (New Delhi, 1990).
M. Eliade, *Rites and Symbols of Initiation* (New York, 1958).
_____, *History of Religious Ideas*, Vol. 1 (Chicago, 1978).
_____, *Myth and Reality* (New York, 1963).
_____, *The Forge and the Crucible* (New York, 1962).
_____, *Myths, Dreams, and Mysteries* (New York, 1960).

_____, *Myths, Rites, and Symbols* (New York, 1975).

_____, *The Sacred and Profane* (New York, 1959).

D. Evans, "Dodona, Dodola, and Daedala," in G. Larson ed., *Myth in Indo-European Antiquity* (Berkeley, 1974), pp. 116ff.

H. Evelyn-White, *Hesiod, Homeric Hymns, Epic Cycle, Homerica* (Cambridge, 2002).

B. Fagan & N. Durrani, *People of the Earth* (London, 2014).

L. Farnell, *The Cults of Greek States, Vol.* 1 (New Rochelle, 1977).

_____, *The Cults of the Greek States, Vol. II* (New Rochelle, 1977).

O. Farrington, *Meteorites* (Chicago, 1915).

R. Faulkner, *The Ancient Egyptian Coffin Texts* (Oxford, 1973).

_____, "Astarte and the Insatiable Sea," in W. Simpson, ed., *The Literature of Ancient Egypt* (New Haven, 2003), pp. 109ff.

W. Faulkner, *Requiem for a Nun* (New York, 1950).

B. Feldman & R. Richardson, *The Rise of Modern Mythology* (Bloomington, 1972).

R. Finnestad, *Image of the World and Symbol of the Creator* (Wiesbaden, 1985).

A. Fischer, "Twilight of the Sun-God," *Iraq* 64 (2002), pp. 125ff.

A. Fletcher, "Pawnee Star Lore," *Journal of American Folk-Lore* 16 (1903), pp. 12ff.

H. Foley, *The Homeric Hymn to Demeter* (Princeton, 1994).

R. J. Forbes, *Studies in Ancient Technology* (Leiden, 1966).

A. Ford, *Homer: The Poetry of the Past* (Ithaca, 2019).

B. Foster, *The Age of Agade* (London, 2016).

_____, *Before the Muses* (Bethesda, 2005).

L. Foster, *Handbook to Life in the Ancient Maya World* (Oxford, 2005).

D. Foxvog, "Astral Dumuzi," in M. Cohen ed., *The Tablet and the Scroll* (Bethesda, 1993), pp. 103-108.

E. Frahm, "Rising Suns and Falling Stars," in J. Hill ed., *Experiencing Power, Generating Authority* (Philadelphia, 2013), pp. 97-120.

H. Frankfort, *Kingship and the Gods* (Chicago, 1948).

_____, *The Art and Architecture of the Ancient Orient* (1954).

D. Frayne, "Notes on The Sacred Marriage Rite," *Bibliotheca Orientalis* 42:1/2 (1985), cols. 11ff.

J. Frazer, *Myths of the Origin of Fire* (London, 1930).

_____, *Adonis, Attis, Osiris* (New Hyde Park, 1961).

_____, *The Golden Bough: The Magic Art*, Vol. II (London, 1911).

_____, *Fastorum libri sex* (London, 1929).

———, "Putting Children on the Fire," in *Apollodorus: The Library*, Vol. 2 (London, 1921), pp. 311-317.

———, *The Magic Art and the Evolution of Kings*, Vol. II (London, 1911).

W. Gaerte, "Kosmische Vorstellungen im Bilde prähistorischer Zeit: Erdberg, Himmelsberg, Erdnabel und Weltenströme," *Anthropos* 9 (1914), pp. 978ff.

M. Gagarin, "Dike in Archaic Greek Thought," *Classical Philology* 69 (1974), pp. 193ff.

T. Gamkrelidze & V. Ivanov, *Indo-European and the Indo-Europeans* (Berlin, 1995).

K. Geldner, *Der Rig-Veda* (Cambridge, 2003).

M. Geller, "A Middle Assyrian Tablet of Utukku Lemnutu, Tablet 12," *Iraq* 42 (1980), pp. 34ff.

A. George, *Babylonian Topographical Texts* (Leuven, 1992)

———, "Die Kosmogonie des alten Mesopotamien," in M. Gindhart & T. Pommerening eds., *Anfang & Ende: vormoderne Szenarien von Weltentstehung und Weltuntergang* (Darmstadt, 2016), pp. 6ff.

E. Gifford & G. Block, *Californian Indian Nights* (Lincoln, 1930).

M. Gimbutas, "Perkunas/Perun: The Thunder God of the Balts and Slavs," *Journal of Indo-European Studies* 1 (1973), pp. 475ff.

M. Gindhart & T. Pommerening eds., *Anfang & Ende: vormoderne Szenarien von Weltentstehung und Weltuntergang* (Darmstadt, 2016).

J. Gonda, *Some Observations on the Relations Between "Gods" and "Powers" in the Veda* ('s-Gravenhage, 1957).

———, *Aspects of Early Visnuism* (Utrecht, 1954).

———, *Ancient Indian Kingship from the Religious Point of View* (Leiden, 1969).

M. Graulich, "Aztec Human Sacrifice as Expiation," in J. Bremmer ed., *The Strange World of Human Sacrifice* (Leuven, 2007), pp. 15ff.

———, *Myths of Ancient Mexico* (Norman, 1997).

M. Green, *The Sun-Gods of Ancient Europe* (London, 1991).

D. Grene in D. Grene & R. Lattimore, *Greek Tragedies, Vol. 1* (Chicago, 1960).

R. Griffith, *The Texts of the White Yajurveda* (Benares, 1899).

J. Grimm, *Teutonic Mythology, Vol. 2* (Gloucester, 1976).

G. Grinnell, *The Cheyenne Indians* (Bloomington, 2008).

H. Güntert, *Kalypso* (Halle, 1919).

W. Guthrie, *A History of Greek Philosophy*, Vol. 1 (Cambridge, 1962).

B. Haile, *Starlore Among the Navaho* (Santa Fe, 1947).

P. Hajovsky, *On the Lips of Others: Moteuczoma's Fame in Aztec Monuments and Rituals* (Austin, 2015).
E. Håland, *Greek Festivals, Modern and Ancient*, Vol. 2 (Cambridge, 2017).
W. Halbfass, *India and Europe* (Delhi, 1990).
R. Hall, *An Archaeology of the Soul* (Urbana, 1997).
W. Hallo & J. van Dijk, *The Exaltation of Inanna* (New Haven, 1968).
J. Halloran, *Sumerian Lexicon* (Los Angeles, 2006).
J. Hani, *Sacred Royalty* (Paris, 2011).
R. Hannig, Ägyptisches *Wörterbuch I* (Mainz, 2003).
P. Harper et al eds., *The Royal City of Susa* (New York, 1992), p. 34ff.
J. Harrison, *Epilegomena to the Study of Greek Religion* (New York, 1962).
J. Hayes, *A Manual of Sumerian Grammar and Texts* (Malibu, 2000).
A. Headrick, "Gardening with the Great Goddess at Teotihuacan," in A. Stone ed., *Heart of Creation* (Tuscaloosa, 2002), pp. 88ff.
J. Heesterman, *The Ancient Indian Royal Consecration* (Leiden, 1957).
W. Heimpel, "Mythologie A.1," in E. Ebeling & B. Meissner, *Reallexikon der Assyriologie, Vol. 8* (Berlin, 1993-1997), pp. 539ff.
R. Heizer & C. Clewlow, *Prehistoric Rock Art of Californ*ia (Ramona, 1973
J. Henderson, *Aristophanes* (Cambridge, 2000).
N. Henne, *Reading Popol Wuj* (Tucson, 2020).
J. Hill et al eds., *Experiencing Power, Generating Authority* (Philadelphia, 2013).
_____, "The Flower World of Old Uto-Aztecan," *Journal of Anthropological Research* (1992), pp. 122ff.
J. Horne, *A Basic Vocabulary of Scientific and Technological German* (Oxford, 1969).
E. Hornung, *Conceptions of God in Ancient Egypt* (Ithaca, 1982).
_____, "Ancient Egyptian Religious Iconography," in J. Sasson ed., *Civilizations of the Ancient Near East, Vol. 3/4* (Farmington Hills, 1995), pp. 1729ff.
W. Horowitz, *Mesopotamian Cosmic Geography* (Winona Lake, 1994).
P. Horsch, "From Creation to World Law: The Early History of *Dharma*," in P. Olivelle, *Dharma* (Delhi, 2004), pp. 12ff.
B. Hruška, "Das spätbabylonische Lehrgedict 'Inannas Erhöhung," *Archiv Orientalni* 37 (1969), pp. 482ff.
D. Hughes, *Human Sacrifice in Ancient Greece* (London, 1991).
K. Hull, "Poetic Tenacity: A Diachronic Study of Kennings in Mayan Languages," in K. Hull & M. Carrasco eds., *Parallel Worlds* (Boulder, 2012), pp. 102ff.
H. Hunger, "Kosmologie," in J. Hazenbos & A. Zgoll eds., *Das geistige Erfassen der Welt im Alten Orient* (Wiesbaden, 2007), pp. 222ff.

T. Irstam, *The King of Ganda* (Stockholm, 1990).

M. Izeki, *Conceptions of 'xihuitl': History, Environment and Cultural Dynamics in Postclassic Mexica Cognition* (Oxford, 2008).

T. Jacobsen, *Treasures of Darkness* (New Haven, 1976).

R. Jacobson, "Linguistic Evidence in Comparative Mythology," in S. Rudy ed., *Selected Writings, Vol. VII* (Berlin, 1985), pp. 20ff.

E. O. James, *Creation and Cosmology* (Leiden, 1969).

S. Jamison, *The Ravenous Hyenas and the Wounded Sun* (Ithaca, 1991).

S. Jamison & J. Brereton, *The Rigveda* (Austin, 2014).

R. Janko, *The Iliad: A Commentary* (Oxford, 1994).

_____, *Aristotle: Poetics* (Cambridge, 1987).

M. Jansen & G. Jimenez, *Time and the Ancestors* (Leiden, 2017).

R. Jebb, "Oedipus at Colonus," in W. Oates & E. O'Neill, *The Complete Greek Drama, Vol. One* (New York, 1938), pp. 638ff.

A. Jeremias, "Schamasch," in W. Roscher ed., *Ausführliches Lexikon der griechischen und römischen Mythologie, Vol. 4* (Leipzig, 1965), col. 555ff.

_____, *Handbuch der altorientalischen Geisteskultur* (Berlin, 1929).

D. Johnson, "Hesiod's Description of Tartarus," *Phoenix* 53 (1999) pp. 13ff.

P. Jones, "Mesopotamian Sacred Marriage Hymn Iddin-Dagan A," *Journal of the American Oriental Society* 123:2 (2003), pp. 295ff.

J. Jurewicz, "The Concept of *ṛtá* in the *Ṛgveda*," in R. Seaford ed., *Universe and Inner Self in Early Indian and Early Greek Thought* (Cambridge, 2010), pp. 34ff.

S. Kallen, *Native Peoples of the Subartic* (Minneapolis, 2017).

A. Kampakoglou, *Studies in the Reception of Pindar in Ptolemaic Poetry* (Berlin, 2019).

W. Kirfel, *Die Kosmographie der Inder* (Bonn, 1920).

K. Kitchen, "Maat," in T. Longman & P. Enns, *Dictionary of the Old Testament* (Downer's Grove, 2008), pp. 448ff.

J. Klein, *The Royal Hymns of Shulgi King of Ur* (Philadelphia, 1981).

J. Klein & Y. Sefati, "The 'Stars (of) Heaven' and Cuneiform Writing," in L. Sassmannshausen ed., *He Has Opened Nisaba's House of Learning* (Leiden, 2014), pp. 96ff.

G. Komoróczy, "The Separation of Heaven and Earth," *Acta Antigua Academiae Scientiarum Hungaricae* 21 (1973), pp. 36ff.

S. Kramer, *From the Poetry of Sumer* (Berkeley, 1979).

S. Kramrisch, *The Hindu Temple, Vol. 1* (New Delhi, 1976).

W. Kristensen, *The Meaning of Religion* (The Hague, 1960).

E. Krupp, *Beyond the Blue Horizon* (New York, 1991).

F. Kuiper, *Ancient Indian Cosmogony* (Delhi, 1983).

D. Kurth, *Den Himmel Stützen* (Brussels, 1975).

_____, "Wind," *LÄ* VI (1990), cols. 1269ff.

R. Kutscher, "The Cult of Dumuzi/Tammuz," in J. Klein ed., *Bar-Ilan Studies in Assyriology* (New York, 1990), pp. 41ff.

S. Kyeyune, *Shaping the Society, Vol. II* (Bloomington, 2012).

S. Lagercrantz, "Der Donnerkeil im afrikanischen Volksglauben," *Etnologiska Studier* 10 (1940), pp. 1-40.

W. Lamb, "Tzotzil Maya Cosmology," in V. del Chamberlain, J. Carlson & J. Young, *Songs From the Sky* (College Park, 2005), pp. 165ff.

W. Lambert, "Kosmogonie," in E. Ebeling & B. Meisnner eds., *Reallexikon der Assyriologie, Vol. 6* (Berlin, 1980-1983), pp. 219ff.

J. Langbein, *Torture and the Law of Proof* (Chicago, 2006).

P. Lapinkivi, *The Sumerian Sacred Marriage* (Helsinki, 2004)

P. Lapinkivi, "The Sumerian Sacred Marriage and Its Aftermath in Later Sources," in M. Nissinen & R. Uro eds., *Sacred Marriages* (Winona Lake, 2008), pp. 14ff.

G. Leick, *Sex and Eroticism in Mesopotamian Literature* (London, 1994).

H. Leisegang, "The Mystery of the Serpent," in J. Campbell ed., *The Mysteries* (Princeton, 1955), pp. 220ff.

M. León-Portilla, *Time and Reality in the Thought of the Maya* (Norman, 1998).

M. León-Portilla & E. Shorris eds., *In the Language of Kings: An Anthology of Mesoamerican Literature* (New York, 2001).

H. G. Liddell & R. Scott, *A Greek-English Lexicon* (Oxford, 1996).

N. Lidova, "Indramahotsava in the Late Vedic and Early Epic Traditions," *Journal of the Asiatic Society of Mumbai* 76-78 (2002-2003), pp. 99ff.

R. Linton, "The Thunder Ceremony of the Pawnee," *Field Museum of Natural History* (1922), pp. 5ff.

_____, "The Sacrifice to Morning Star by the Skidi Pawnee," *Leaflet Field Museum of Natural History, Department of Anthropology* 6 (1923), pp. 5ff.

_____, "The Origin of the Skidi Pawnee Sacrifice to the Morning Star," *American Anthropologist* 28 (1928), p. 457ff.

J. Lisman, *At the Beginning: Cosmogony, Theogony and Anthropogeny in Sumerian texts of the Third and Second Millennium BCE* (Leiden, 2013).

H. Lloyd-Jones, *Aeschylus: The Oresteia* (London, 2014).

M. Looper & J. Kappelman, "The Cosmic Umbilicus in Mesoamerica: A Floral Metaphor for the Source of Life" *Journal of Latin American Lore* 21 (2000), pp. 14ff.

L. Lujan, *The Offerings of the Templo Mayor of Tenochtitlan* (Albuquerque, 2005).

K. McCaffery, "The Sumerian Sacred Marriage: Texts and Images," in H. Crawford, *The Sumerian World* (New York, 2013), pp. 227ff.
A. Macdonell, *Vedic Mythology* (Strassburg, 1897).
_____, *A Practical Sanskrit Dictionary* (Delhi, 2004).
M. Macri & M. Looper, *The New Catalog of Maya Hieroglyphs* (Norman, 2003).
H. McKillop, *The Ancient Maya* (Santa Barbara, 2004).
J. Maffie, *Aztec Philosophy* (Boulder, 2014).
S. Maul, "Die altorientalische Hauptstadt—Abbild und Nabel der Welt," in G. Wilhelm ed., *Die orientalische Stadt* (Saarbrücken, 1997), pp. 112ff.
_____, "Der assyrische König—Hüter der Weltordnung," in K. Watanabe eds., *Priests and Officials in the Ancient Near East* (Heidelberg, 1999), pp. 201-214.
_____, "Walking Backwards into the Future," in T. Miller ed., *Given World and Time* (Budapest, 2008), pp. 15-24.
J. Mallory & D. Adams, *Encyclopedia of Indo-European Culture* (London, 1997).
_____, *The Oxford Introduction to Proto-Indo-European and the Proto-Indo-European World* (Oxford, 2006).
O. Mazariegos, *Art and Myth of the Ancient Maya* (New Haven, 2017).
C. Metcalf, *Sumerian Literary Texts in the Schoyen Collection*, Vol. 1 (University Park, 2019).
S. Milbrath, "The Many Faces of Venus in Mesoamerica," in G. Villalobos & D. Barnhart eds., *Archaeoastronomy and the Maya* (Oxford, 2014), pp. 126ff.
R. van der Molen, *A Hieroglyphic Dictionary of Egyptian Coffin Texts* (Leiden, 2000).
S. Montiglio, *Wandering in Ancient Greek Culture* (Chicago, 2005).
U. Moortgart-Correns, "Die Rosette—ein Schriftzeichen?" in *Altorientalische Forschungen* 21 (1994), pp. 369ff.
Paul More, "Prometheus Bound," in W. Oates & E. O'Neill eds., *The Complete Greek Drama, Vol. 1* (New York, 1938), pp. 127ff.
M. Aguilar-Moreno, *Handbook to Life in the Aztec World* (Oxford, 2006).
J. de Morgan, *Memoires, Vol. 12* (Paris, 1912).
L. Muellner, *The Anger of Achilles* (Ithaca, 1996).
J. Muir, *Original Sanskrit Texts, Vol. 2* (London, 1874).
C. Müller-Winkler, "Schen-Ring," *Lexikon der Ägyptologie V* (Wiesbaden, 1984), cols. 578ff.
M. Munn, *The Mother of the Gods, Athens, and the Tyranny of Asia* (Berkeley, 2006).
J. Murdoch, *Vedic Hinduism and the Arya Samaj* (London, 1902).
J. Murie, "Ceremonies of the Pawnee," *Smithsonian Contributions to Anthropology* 27 (Cambridge, 1981), pp. 39ff.

G. Murray, *The Collected Plays of Euripides* (London, 1954).
G. Nagy, *The Ancient Greek Hero* (Cambridge, 2013).
_____, *Greek Mythology and Poetics* (Ithaca, 1990).
_____, "Perkunas and Perun," *Innsbrucker Beiträge zur Sprachwissenschaft* 12 (1974), pp. 113ff.
M. Naylor ed., *Authentic Indian Designs* (New York, 1975).
J. Neuroth, "Xiuhuitzolli—Motecuhzoma's Diadem of Turquoise, Fire, and Time," *Archiv für Völkerkunde 46* (1982), pp. 123ff.
H. B. Nicholson, "Religion in Pre-Hispanic Central Mexico," in R. Wauchope ed., *Handbook of Middle American Indians, Vol. 10* (Austin, 1971), pp. 413ff.
_____, "A Royal Headband of the Tlaxcatleca," *Revista mexicana de estudios antropológicos* 21 (1964), pp. 82ff.
_____, *Topiltzin Quetzalcoatl* (Boulder, 2001).
_____, "The Birth of the Smoking Mirror," *Archaeology* 7:3 (1955), pp. 170ff.
M. Nilsson, *The Mycenaean Origin of Greek Mythology* (New York, 1963).
F. Nisetich, *The Poems of Callimachus* (Oxford, 2001).
W. Oates & E. O'Neill, *The Complete Greek Drama, Vol. 1* (New York, 1938).
P. Olivelle ed., *Dharma* (Delhi, 2009).
G. Olivier, *Mockeries and Metamorphoses of an Aztec God* (Boulder, 2003).
J. Olko, *Turquoise Diadems and Staffs of Office* (Warsaw, 2005).
_____, *Insignia of Rank in the Nahua World* (Boulder, 2014).
F. Olquin, "Religion," in E. Moctezuma & H. Burden eds., *Aztecs* (London, 2002), pp. 225ff.
A. Oppenheim, "Man and Nature in Mesopotamian Civilization," in C. Gillispie ed., *Dictionary of Scientific Biography, Vol. 15* (New York, 1981), pp. 634ff.
A. Oppenheim et al eds., *The Assyrian Dictionary, Vol. K* (Chicago, 1971).
M. Otlewska-Jung, "Orpheus and Orphic Hymns in the *Dionysiaca*," in K. Spanoudakis ed., *Nonnus of Panopolis in Context* (Berlin, 2014), pp. 80ff.
W. Otto, *Dionysus* (Bloomington, 1965).
C. Pache, *Baby and Child Heroes in Ancient Greece* (Urbana, 2004).
_____, "Singing Heroes," in G. Nagy ed., *Greek Literature in the Roman Period and Late Antiquity* (New York, 2001), pp. 387ff.
A. Panaino, *A Walk Through the Iranian Heavens* (Oxford, 2019), pp. 59ff.
T. Papadopoulou, *Aeschylus: Suppliants* (London, 2011).
Robert Parker, *On Greek Religion* (Ithaca, 2011).
A. Parpola, *The Roots of Hinduism* (Oxford, 2015).
S. Parpola, "Excursus: The Substitute King Ritual," in S. Parpola, *Letters From Assyrian Scholars to the Kings Esarhaddon and Assurbanipal, Part II* (Winona Lake, 2007), pp. XXII-XXXII.

A. Peratt, "Characteristics for the Occurrence of a High-Current, Z-Pinch Aurora as Recorded in Antiquity," *IEEE Transactions on Plasma Science* 31:6 (2003), pp. 1192-2014.

E. Polomé, "Some Thoughts on the Methodology of Comparative Religion, with Special Focus on Indo-European," in E. Polomé ed., *Essays in Memory of Karl Kerényi* (Washington, D.C., 1984), pp. 10ff.

J. Polonsky, "ki-ᵈutu-è-a," in L. Milano ed., *Landscapes: Territories, Frontiers and Horizons in the Ancient Near East* (Padova, 1999), pp. 96ff.

_____, *The Rise of the Sun-God and the Determination of Destiny in Ancient Mesopotamia*. Ph.D. dissertation, University of Philadelphia (2002).

B. Pongratz-Leisten, "When the Gods are Speaking," in M. Köckert & M. Nissinen eds., *Propheten in Mari, Assyrien, und Israel* (Göttingen, 2003), pp. 144.

M. Preuss, "A Study of Jurakán of the *Popol Vuh*," in E. Magana & P. Mason eds., *Myth and the Imaginary in the New World* (Amsterdam, 1986), pp. 360ff.

B. Pritzker, *A Native American Encyclopedia* (Oxford, 2000).

J. Puhvel, *Comparative Mythology* (Berkeley, 1987).

S. Pyne, *Vestal Fire* (New York, 2011).

S. Quirke, *Ancient Egyptian Religion* (London, 1992).

D. Ragavan, "Heaven on Earth: Temples, Ritual, and Cosmic Symbolism in the Ancient World," in D. Ragavan ed., *Heaven and Earth* (Chicago, 2013), pp. 13ff.

_____, "Entering Other Worlds," in *Ibid.*, *Heaven and Earth* (Chicago, 2013), pp. 202ff.

K. Read, *Time and Sacrifice in the Aztec Cosmos* (Bloomington, 1998).

K. Read & J. Gonzalez, *Mesoamerican Mythology* (Oxford, 2000).

Adrián Recinos in D. Goetz & S. Morley, *Popol Vuh* (Norman, 1950), pp. 80ff.

G. Reichel-Dolmatoff, *Amazonian Cosmos* (Chicago, 1971).

F. Reilly, "The Landscape of Creation," in A. Stone ed., *Heart of Creation* (Tuscaloosa, 2002), pp. 58ff.

E. Reiner, *Your Thwarts in Pieces, Your Mooring Rope Cut* (Ann Arbor, 1985).

D. Reisman, "Iddin-Dagan's Sacred Marriage Hymn," *Journal of Cuneiform Studies* 25 (1973), pp. 186-191.

L. Reitzammer, *The Athenian Adonia in Context* (Madison, 2016).

S. Ribichini, "Melqart," in K. van der Toorn et al eds., *Dictionary of Deities and Demons in the Bible* (Leiden, 1995), cols. 1053-1058.

W. Ridgeway, *The Early Age of Greece, Vol. II* (Cambridge, 1931).

H. Ringgren, "Light and Darkness in Ancient Egyptian Religion," in *Liber Amicorum* (Leiden, 1969), pp. 144ff.

D. Robinson, *Pindar, a Poet of Eternal Ideas* (Baltimore, 1936).

F. Rochberg, "Heaven and Earth," in S. Noegel & J. Walker eds., *Prayer, Magic, and the Stars in the Ancient and Late Antique World* (University Park, 2003), pp. 174ff.

W. Roscher, *Die Gorgonen und Verwandtes* (Leipzig, 1879).

_____, "Mars," *Ausführliches Lexikon der griechischen und römischen Mythologie* (Leipzig, 1884-1937), cols. 2408ff.

R. Roys, *The Book of Chilam Balam of Chumayel* (Washington D.C., 1933).

C. Lopez-Ruiz, *When the Gods Were Born: Greek Cosmogonies and the Near East* (Cambridge, 2010).

I. Rutherford, "Pindar on the Birth of Apollo," *The Classical Quarterly* 38 (1988), pp. 74ff.

B. de Sahagún, *Book 2: The Ceremonies* (Santa Fe, 1981).

_____, *Book 4—The Soothsayers* and *Book 5—The Omens* (Santa Fe, 1979).

_____, *Florentine Codex: Book 1* (Sante Fe, 1953).

_____, *The Florentine Codex: Book 7* (Santa Fe, 1953).

F. Salamone & W. Adams eds., *Explorations in Anthropology and Theology* (New York, 1997).

S. Sanders, *From Adapa to Enoch* (Tübingen, 2017).

L. Schele & D. Freidel, *A Forest of Kings* (New York, 1990).

T. Schneider, "Das Schriftzeichen 'Rosette' und die Göttin Seschet," *Studien zur Altägyptischen Kultur* 24 (1997), pp. 249ff.

J. Scurlock, "Images of Dumuzi," in J. Hill et al eds., *Experiencing Power, Generating Authority* (Philadelphia, 2013), pp. 151-184.

R. Seaford, *Euripides: Bacchae* (Oxford, 1996).

_____, *Dionysos* (London, 2006).

Y. Sefati, *Love Songs in Sumerian Literature* (Jerusalem, 1998).

C. Segal, *Dionysiac Poetics and Euripides' Bacchae* (Princeton, 1982).

A. Seidenberg, "The Separation of Sky and Earth at Creation (II)," *Folklore* 80 (1969), pp. 194ff.

E. Seler, *Codex Fejérváry-Mayer* (Berlin, 1901/2).

_____, *Codex Vaticanus No. 3773* (Berlin, 1903).

G. Selz, "Five Divine Ladies," *NIN* 1 (2000), pp. 31ff.

_____, "Early Dynastic Vessels in 'Ritual' Contexts," *Wiener Zeitschrift für die Kunde des Morgenlandes* 94 (2004), pp. 277ff.

_____, "The Tablet with 'Heavenly Writing', or How to Become a Star," in A. Panaino ed., *Non licet stare caelestibus* (Milano-Udine, 2014), pp. 55ff.

_____, "Plant Metaphors: On the Plant of Rejuvenation," in S. Gaspa et al eds., *From Source to History* (Munster, 2014), pp. 664ff.

J. Serrano, "Origin and Basic Meaning of the Word ˙*nmmt* (The So-Called 'Sun-Folk')," *Studien zur Altägyptischen Kultur* 27 (1999), pp. 366ff.

H. Shapiro, "*Hêrôs Theos*: The Death and Apotheosis of Herakles," *Classical World* 77:1 (1983), pp. 15ff.

D. Silverman ed., *Ancient Egypt* (London, 1997).

E. Simpson, *The Gordion Wooden Objects, Vol. 1* (Leiden, 2010).

Å. Sjöberg, "Hymns to Meslamtaea, Lugalgirra and Nanna-Suen in Honour of King Ibbisuen (Ibbisin) of Ur," *OrSuec* 19-20 (1970-71), pp. 169ff.

_____, "In the Beginning," in T. Abusch ed., *Riches Hidden in Secret Places* (Winona Lake, 2002), pp. 238ff.

K. Slanski, "The Mesopotamian 'Rod and Ring'," *Proceedings of the British Academy* 136 (2007), pp. 41ff.

M. A. van der Sluijs, *On the Origin of Myths, Vol. 1* (Vancouver, 2019).

_____, *On the Origin of Myths in Catastrophic Experience, Vol. 1* (Vancouver, 2019).

_____, *Traditional Cosmology, Vol. 3* (London, 2011).

_____, *Traditional Cosmology, Vol. 5* (Vancouver, 2018).

S. Spence, *The Image of Jason in Early Greek Myth* (Lulu, 2010).

I. Sprajc, "The Venus-Maize Complex in the Mesoamerican World View," *Journal of the History of Astronomy* 24 (1993), pp. 35ff.

D. Srinivasan, *Many Heads, Arms and Eyes* (Leiden, 1997).

E. Stafford, *Herakles* (Oxford, 2010).

J. Staller & B. Stross, *Lightning in the Andes and Mesoamerica* (Oxford, 2013).

P. Steinkeller, "Of Stars and Men," in W. Moran & A. Gianto eds., *Biblical and Oriental Essays in Memory of William L. Moran* (Rome, 2005), pp. 18ff.

_____, "Priests and Sacred Marriage," in K. Watanabe ed., *Colloquium on the Ancient Near East* (Heidelberg, 1999), pp. 136ff

_____, "On Stars and Stripes in Ancient Mesopotamia," *Iranica Antiqua* 37 (2002), pp. 363ff.

J. Steele, *Ancient Astronomical Observations and the Study of the Moon's Motion (1691-1757)* (London, 2012).

M. Stevenson, "The Zuni Indians," *Bureau of American Ethnology* (Washington, 1904), pp. 140ff.

H. Stewart, "Traditional Egyptian Sun Hymns of the New Kingdom," *Bull. Inst. Arch.* 6 (1967), pp. 52ff.

V. Straizys & L. Klimka, "The Cosmology of the Balts," *Journal of the History of Astronomy* 22 (1997), pp. 57-81.

B. Stross, "Venus and Sirius: Some Unexpected Similarities," *Kronos* XII:1 (1987), pp. 26ff.

U. Strutynski, "Ares: A Reflex on the Indo-European War God?," *Arethusa* 13 (1980), pp. 227ff.

A. Sugi, "The Iconographical Representation of the Sun God in New Kingdom Egypt," in Z. Hawass ed., *Egyptology at the Dawn of the Twenty-first Century, Vol. 2* (Cairo, 2003), pp. 515ff.

T. Sullivan, "Tlazolteotl-Ixcuina: The Great Spinner and Weaver," in E. Boone ed., *The Art and Iconography of Late Post-Classic Central Mexico* (Austin, 1990), p. 14ff.

J. Svenbro, *Phrasikleia* (Ithaca, 1993).

K. Szarzynska, "Offerings for the goddess Inana," *Revue d'assyriologie et d'archéologie orientale* 87 (1993), pp. 7ff.

_____, "Cult of the Goddess Inana in Archaic Uruk," in *Sumerica* (Warsaw, 1997), pp 147ff.

J. Taggart, *Nahuat Myth and Social Structure* (Austin, 1983).

Gabor Takács, *Etymological Dictionary of Egyptian, Vol. 3* (Leiden, 2008).

D. Talbott, *The Saturn Myth* (New York, 1980).

D. Talbott & W. Thornhill, *Thunderbolts of the Gods* (Portland, 2005).

K. Tallqvist, "Himmelsgegenden und Winde," *Studia Orientalia* 2 (1928), pp. 106ff.

K. Taube, *The Major Gods of Ancient Yucatan* (Washington D.C., 1992).

_____, "The Jade Hearth: Centrality, Rulership, and the Classic Maya Temple," in S. Houston ed., *Function and Meaning in Classic Maya Architecture* (Cambridge, 1998), pp. 429ff.

_____, "Structure 10L-16 and Its Early Classic Antecedents," in E. Bell et al eds., *Understanding Early Classic Copan* (Philadelphia, 2004), pp. 266ff.

_____, "Creation and Cosmology: Gods and Mythic Origins in Ancient Mesoamerica," in D. Nichols & C. Pool eds., *The Oxford Handbook of Mesoamerican Archaeology* (Oxford, 2012), pp. 741-751.

_____, "At Dawn's Edge: Tulúm, Santa Rita, and Floral Symbolism…," in G. Vail & C. Hernández eds., *Astronomers, Scribes, and Priests* (Washington, D.C., 2010), pp. 162ff.

_____, "The Turquoise Hearth," in D. Carrasco ed., *Mesoamerica's Classic Heritage* (Boulder, 2000), pp. 292ff.

B. Tedlock, "The Road of Light," in A. Aveni ed., *The Sky in Mayan Literature* (Oxford, 1992), pp. 28ff.

D. Tedlock, *Popol Vuh* (New York, 1985).

_____, *2000 Years of Mayan Literature* (Berkeley, 2010).

_____, *Breath on the Mirror* (Albuquerque, 1993).
B. Teissier, *Ancient Near Eastern Cylinder Seals* (Berkeley, 1984).
_____, *Egyptian Iconography on Syrian-Palestinian Cylinder Seals of the Middle Bronze Age* (Fribourg, 1996)
P. Terry, *Poems of the Elder Edda* (Philadelphia, 1990).
S. Tharapalan, *The Meaning of Color in Ancient Mesopotamia* (2019).
J. Thompson, *A Catalog of Maya Hieroglyphs* (Norman, 1962).
S. Thompson, "Myth and Folktales," in T. Sebeok, *Myth: A Symposium* (Bloomington, 1955), pp. 173ff.
_____, *Tales of the North American Indians* (Bloomington, 1966).
O. Topcuoglu, "Iconography of Protoliterate Seals," in C. Woods ed., *Visible Language* (Chicago, 2015), pp. 29-32.
A. Tozzer, *A Comparative Study of the Mayas and the Lacandones* (London, 1907).
E. Twohig, *The Megalithic Art of Western Europe* (London, 1981).
M. de Vaan, *Etymological Dictionary of Latin and the other Italic Languages* (Leiden, 2008).
H. Vanstiphout, *Epics of Sumerian Kings* (Leiden, 2004).
R. de Vaux, *The Bible and the Ancient Near East* (Garden City, 1971).
J-P. Vernant, *Mortals and Immortals* (Princeton, 1991).
_____, *The Universe, the Gods, and Men* (New York, 2001).
H. S. Versnel, "Apollo and Mars One Hundred Years After Roscher," *Visible Religion* IV/V (1985/6), pp. 154ff.
_____, *Inconsistencies in Greek and Roman Religion, Vol. 2* (Leiden, 1993).
_____, "Apollo and Mars One Hundred Years after Roscher," *Visible Religion* 4 (1986), pp. 147ff.
C. & J. Villacorta, *The Dresden Codex* (Walnut Creek, 1930).
H. Wagenvoort, *Studies in Roman Literature, Culture and Religion* (Leiden, 1956).
G. A. Wainwright, "Letopolis," *Journal of Egyptian Archaeology* 18 (1932), pp. 161ff.
W. Waitkus: "Die Geburt des Harsomtus aus der Blüte," *SAK* 30 (2002), pp. 377ff.
Y. Wang, H. Liu & Z. Sun, "Lamarck rises from his grave: parental environment-induced epigenetic inheritance in model organisms and humans," *Biological Reviews* 92:4 (2017), pp. 2084ff.
K. Watanabe eds., *Priests and Officials in the Ancient Near East* (Heidelberg, 1999).
C. Watkins, *How to Kill a Dragon* (Oxford, 1995).
G. Weltfish, *The Lost Universe* (New York, 1965).

A. J. Wensinck, "The Semitic New Year and the Origin of Eschatology," *Acta Orientalia* 1 (1923), pp. 169ff.
L. Werr, *Studies in the Chronology and Regional Style of Old Babylonian Cylinder Seals* (Malibu, 1988).
M. West, *Indo-European Poetry and Myth* (Oxford, 2007).
_____, *Theogony* (Oxford, 1966).
_____, "The Dictaean Hymn to the Kouros," *Journal of Hellenic Studies* 85 (1965), pp. 150ff.
J. Westenholz, "King by Love of Inanna," in *NIN 1* (2000), pp. 75-82ff.
_____, "Heaven and Earth," in J. Stackert & T. Abusch eds., *Gazing on the Deep* (Bethesda, 2010), pp. 293ff.
P. Wheatley, *The Pivot of the Four Quarters* (Chicago, 1971).
Grace White, *The Religious Iconography of Cappadocian Glyptic in the Assyrian Colony Period...* Dissertation for the University of Chicago (1993).
C. Whitman, "Hera's Anvils," *Harvard Studies in Classical Philology* 74 (1970), pp. 40ff.
W. Whitney & C. Lanman, *Atharva-Veda Samhita, Part 2* (Cambridge, 1905).
F. Wiggermann, "Scenes From the Shadow Side," in M. Vogelzang & H. Vanstiphout eds., *Mesopotamian Poetic Language: Sumerian and Akkadian* (Groningen, 1996), pp. 209ff.
J. Wilbert & K. Simoneau, "Sun and Moon," in *Folk Literature of the Sikuani Indians* (Los Angeles, 1992), pp. 25-28.
_____, *Folk Literature of the Mataco Indians* (Los Angeles, 1982).
R. Wilkinson, *Reading Egyptian Art* (London, 1992).
T. Wilkinson, *Early Dynastic Egypt* (London, 1999).
A. Willi, "Demeter, Gê, and the Indo-Europeans word(s) for 'earth'," *Historische Sprachforschung* 120 (208), pp. 171ff.
A. Willcox, *The Rock Art of Africa* (Kent, 1984).
G. Williams, *African Designs* (New York, 1971).
M. Williams, *A Sanskrit-English Dictionary* (Oxford, 1872).
R. Williamson, *Living the Sky* (Norman, 1984).
M. Wiltshire, *Ascetic Figures Before and in Early Buddhism* (Berlin, 1990).
Eva Wilson, *Ancient Egyptian Designs* (London, 1986).
F. Windels, *The Lascaux Cave Paintings* (London, 1949).
M. Witzel, *The Origins of the World's Mythologies* (Oxford, 2012).
R. Woodard, "Hesiod and Greek Myth," in R. Woodard ed., *The Cambridge Companion to Greek Mythology* (Cambridge, 2007), p. 83-165.
_____, *Indo-European Sacred Space* (Urbana, 2006).
C. Woods, "At The Edge of the World," *JANER* 9:2 (2009), pp. 186ff.

———, "Sons of the Sun: The Mythological Foundations of the First Dynasty of Uruk," *JANER* 12 (2012), pp. 90ff.

B. Wright, *Pueblo Shields* (Flagstaff, 1976).

J. Young, *The Prose Edda of Snorri Sturlson* (Berkeley, 1960).

J. Zandee, *Der Amunshymnus des Papyrus Leiden I 344 verso, Vol. 1* (Leiden, 1992).

H. Zimmer, *Myths and Symbols in Indian Art and Civilization* (Princeton, 1972).

Index

A

Abbild   159, 229
abdomen   97
ability   10, 19, 145
abja-ja   177
abject   35
abogado 61
Aboriginal   169, 171
Abusch   8, 11, 86, 101-102, 109, 112, 220, 233, 236
academia 215
Academiae   109, 129, 227
Academy 48, 233
Achilles   5, 183, 198, 229
Adapted   16, 18, 22-26, 32, 43-44, 46, 49, 81, 83, 88, 104, 119, 144, 174, 186
Adonia   107, 231
Adonis   71, 200, 206, 224
Adrián   125, 231
adrmhad 142
Adventure   9
Aegean   187, 201
Aegeum   183
Aelianus   199
Aelius   204-205
Aeneas   204
Aeschylus   106, 117, 120-121, 178, 184, 217, 228, 230
affairs   23, 102, 110, 120, 184
Africa   16, 18, 103, 152, 214, 236

African   24, 136, 221, 236
Aftermath   74, 150, 228
Agamemnon   117
Ägyptische   47, 219
Aitareya   102
akisizza   152
Akkade   24
Akkadian   11, 26, 46, 140, 159, 170, 236
Alarcon   206, 219
Albany   170-171, 219, 223
albedo   162
Albert   214
Alexander   57, 118, 124, 151, 219
Alexandra   201
Alexandria   201
alienated 217
all-seeing 120-121
allusion   87, 89, 110, 204
allusions 73, 86, 92, 183, 200
Altamira 15-16, 19, 221
Amazonian   55, 58, 123, 231
America 60, 65, 108, 178
American   26, 33, 38, 44-45, 57, 63-66, 69, 84-85, 89, 103, 114, 118, 124, 140, 167, 170-171, 178, 219-221, 224, 227-228, 230-231, 233, 235
Americas 57, 65, 103
Amerindian   36, 45-46, 60, 100, 103, 170, 186
Amicorum   53, 232
amoenus 75
amorous 8, 75, 213
amorphous   109
Amsterdam   95, 231
analogical   109, 129, 148
analogue 18, 105, 167, 169, 182, 188
analogues   119
analogy   114
Anbeginn   29, 191
ancestors 7-8, 65, 100, 227
ancestral   105
ancestry   209
Ancient   3, 5, 7-8, 10-12, 14-15, 17-28, 30-32, 34, 38-41, 43-46, 48-49, 51-54, 56, 58, 70-74, 76, 81-84, 87, 89, 92-95, 99, 102-103, 108, 112, 115, 118-125,

127, 130, 134, 136-137, 139-146, 149-150, 152-155, 157-162, 166-172, 176, 178, 184, 186, 188-198, 200-201, 204-207, 209-215, 217, 219-222, 224-226, 228-236
ancients 21, 101, 117
Anfang 112, 212, 225
Angeles 60, 77, 189, 226, 236
angespielt 126
Angirases 54
An-heaven 109, 112, 212
animal 72
animals 61, 70, 102
Annotated 77, 164, 194-195
Anomalies 25, 222
anomalous 8, 19-20, 25, 84, 88, 122, 130
anomaly 15, 20, 24, 113
Antares 167, 169
Anthology 42, 61, 228
Anthony 5, 129, 161
anthos 204-205
ánthos 178
Anthropos 46, 128, 225
Antigua 109, 129, 227
Antiqua 87, 233
Antique 23, 232
Antiquity 22, 71, 107, 127, 162, 180, 200, 205, 213-214, 224, 230-231
Anvils 216, 236
anxiety 54, 160
apéptato 178
Aphrodite 106, 201
Apionem 200
Apocalypto 35
Apollo 56, 169, 186-188, 199, 202, 223, 232, 235
apotheosis 202-203, 205, 207-208, 233
apotropaic 153
apparition 47, 119
apposition 137
aprathaya 137
Arabia 22
Aratta 77, 90-91, 111, 192
arcane 27
archaic 8, 10-12, 15, 24, 30-31, 36, 38, 40,
47, 51, 53, 56, 58-59, 69, 71-72, 79, 82, 84, 86, 88-90, 92, 105-108, 110, 114, 117-118, 120, 124-125, 128, 133, 138, 140, 143, 145-146, 153, 155, 164, 166, 169, 175, 178, 184, 186, 189, 191, 193, 195, 198, 202, 204, 211-214, 216, 223, 225, 234
archaique 22, 219
archer-god 186-187
archetypal 31, 39, 51, 54, 57, 62, 78, 85-86, 96-97, 107, 125, 138, 153-155, 164, 166-167, 169, 175, 210, 216, 218
archetype 37-38, 47, 135
Archiv 80, 173, 226, 230
Arethusa 10, 234
Ariadne 13
Aristides 204-205
Aristotle 161, 227
armchair 217
armour 203
Artemis 202, 223
Arunta 7
Ascetic 139, 236
Asiatic 189, 228
Aspects 67, 95, 170, 217, 222, 225
assailants 161
Assmann 28-29, 31, 130-131, 147, 188, 219
Assyrian 44, 48-49, 153, 192, 225, 230, 236
Assyrien 77, 231
assyrische 142, 146, 229
astabhayah 137
Astarte 127, 200-201, 224
Asteria 187
Asterië 187
asterisms 168
asterope 120
Astour 201, 219
astral 23-24, 71, 76, 79, 89, 166, 193, 224
astrape 120
Astrapios 211
Astrology 166, 169
astron 120, 187
astronomer 68
Astronomy 22, 45, 60, 166, 214, 233
Atharva 93, 124, 126-127, 132, 136, 142
Atharvan 177
Athenaeus 106, 201

239

Athenian 107, 161, 231
Athens 107, 229
athletic 201-202
Atlantic 163
atmosphere 132, 137
August 111, 165, 219
Aurora 162, 180, 231
auroral 14
Ausdruck 125
Austin 38, 43, 55, 59, 96, 102, 112-114, 124, 136, 145, 169, 184, 210, 221, 226-227, 230, 234
Australia 169
Australian 7
Authentic 46, 230
Authority 23, 48, 142, 153, 155, 158, 188, 217, 222, 224, 226, 232
avatars 96
Avestan 216
Avraamides 5
axe-like 96
Ayamictlan 37, 184
Aztecan 160
Aztecs 36, 41, 43, 45, 47, 54-55, 57-58, 62, 83, 98, 113, 156, 160, 220, 222, 230

B

babies 201
Babylonia 166
Babylonian 21-23, 25-26, 49, 70-71, 90, 118-119, 159, 166-167, 217, 222, 225, 236
Bacchae 9, 104, 116-117, 198, 232
Badtibira 75
ba-e-e 195
Bahram 167
Bailey 213-214, 219
balamil 191
balbale 75, 80
Baldwin 165, 219
Balken 127
Baltic 45, 92, 97, 104-105, 212
Baltimore 56, 187, 198, 210, 212-213, 219, 223, 232
banished 56

baptism 4, 160, 196-198
Barbara 125, 229
Bar-Ilan 71, 228
barley 75
Barnhart 61, 229
Barton 26, 103, 111-113, 212-213
basket 197
battle 116
battles 116
Beaulieu 73, 220
beautified 110, 205-207
beautiful 29, 31, 65, 76, 178, 206-207
beauty 15, 86, 88-89, 205, 207
bedchamber 104
bedeuten 170
Beekes 216, 220
Beiträge 114, 230
belief 36, 54, 57, 64, 70, 95, 105, 109, 153, 155, 190, 213
beliefs 12, 54-55, 92, 127, 167, 203, 214
believers 6
Benares 144, 225
Bender 108, 130, 220
Bering 65
Berkeley 17, 44, 105, 107-108, 143, 161, 191-192, 202, 221, 224, 227, 229, 231, 234-235, 237
Berlin 23, 31, 42, 55, 76, 86, 93, 131, 134, 139, 166, 183, 187, 202-204, 220, 222-223, 225-228, 230, 232, 236
Bernabé 129, 220
Bernardino 36
Bethesda 8, 11, 89, 109, 141, 224, 236
Bhrgus 39
Biblical 21, 233
Bielfeldt 122, 220
Bierhorst 41, 63, 98, 103, 113-114, 122, 220
Biography 21, 62, 102, 120, 230
Biological 164, 181, 235
biology 123, 155
Birgit 5, 33, 137
birthplace 21, 47
bizarre 37, 67, 131, 160-161
Blackfeet 167
Blackman 157, 220
blasphemy 217
Bleeker 101, 220

Bloomfield 93, 126, 136, 220
Bluegreen 168
blueness 180
Boardman 202-203, 220
bodies 8, 15, 22-24, 49, 89, 109, 153
Boeotia 116
Boeotian 105, 121
bogeyman 217
bolide 216
bolides 218
bonfire 203
Borbonicus 38, 98
Borghouts 30, 220
Borgia 49
Boston 35-36, 43, 100, 108, 118, 219, 222-223
bottle 20
Boulder 35-36, 41, 43, 61, 84, 97, 173-174, 180, 182, 226, 229-230, 234
Bouleus 108
bounty 89
Bowles 142, 220
Boylan 31, 220
Brahmana 102, 125-126, 144, 223
Brahmanas 126
braided 48, 172
Breath 100, 114, 235
Bremer 110, 185, 221
Bremmer 60, 184-185, 200, 221, 225
Brennan 18, 221
Brereton 38-41, 102, 112, 131, 136, 142, 145, 154, 176, 210, 221, 227
Breuil 16, 221
bridegroom 76
brilliance 72-73, 91
brilliant 53, 59, 77, 148, 187, 211
Brisson 6, 221
British 48, 233
Bronze 32, 81, 84, 119, 170, 235
Brundage 42, 55, 59-60, 113, 169, 196, 221
Brunner 30, 221
Brussels 134, 228
bubonous 60
Budapest 157, 159, 229
Buddhism 139, 236
buffalo 65, 78, 168

Buganda 152
Bulletin 136, 221
Bunzel 140, 221
Burden 52, 62, 156, 230
Bureau 140, 171, 178, 220-221, 233
burial 183
buried 10, 201
Burkert 12, 35, 117, 160-161, 198, 200-202, 205, 210-211, 218, 221
Burland 57, 221
Burrow 136-137, 143, 221
Burton 143, 221
bushes 94
buttress 145, 190
Byblos 199-200

C

Cacaxtla 83, 219
Caddoan 65
Caeculus 155
Cakchiquel 180
calendric 38
California 17-18, 46, 132, 226
Calvert 12
Cambridge 7, 28, 65, 92, 102, 107-108, 112, 115-117, 120, 124, 126-127, 132, 136-137, 141, 143, 146, 149, 155, 161, 169, 183, 187-188, 191, 198, 209-211, 213-214, 216, 218-221, 223-227, 229-232, 234, 236
Camonica 17-19, 219
Campbell 171, 228
campsite 66
Canada 65
Canadian 118
canoes 65
Cantares 41, 122, 220
capitals 135, 186
Carapace 44, 222
Carballo 160, 221
cardinal 42, 44-45, 51, 82, 125-128, 134, 136-138, 143-145, 148-150, 160, 163, 168, 170-171, 181, 190
Carlson 44-45, 190, 222, 228
Carnoy 167

241

Carrasco 35-36, 41, 43, 100, 174, 180, 182, 222, 226, 234
carvings 19
castration 161
cataclysm 57
cataclysms 57, 157
Catalog 44, 83, 229, 235
cátasra 126
catharsis 161
Catlin 161, 222-223
caturanga 46, 133
cauldron 160, 198, 201
cavern 183
cavity 36, 67, 79
Ceilings 45, 222
celebrant 201
celebrants 197
celestial 15-17, 19-20, 22-24, 26, 29, 31, 35-36, 40-41, 45, 47, 49, 53, 59-63, 68-69, 74, 76-79, 81, 83, 85, 87, 89, 94, 109, 111, 119-121, 123, 127-129, 131, 133-136, 138, 144, 146, 150, 153-154, 156, 160-164, 168-169, 173, 175, 182, 191, 193, 210, 218
center 17, 19, 23-24, 33, 35, 37, 39-44, 49, 83, 93, 105, 107, 113, 124, 133, 140, 155, 163, 168-169, 171, 181, 184, 190-191, 193
Centrality 127, 234
centre 39-40, 140
centuries 9, 11, 24, 142, 163, 187
century 6, 37, 48, 65, 87, 107, 120, 132, 171, 184, 198, 200, 202, 213, 234
Ceremonies 7, 64-65, 68, 155, 196, 229, 232
ceremony 35-36, 61, 68, 71-72, 78, 93, 98, 100, 140, 161-162, 222, 228
certain 7, 23-24, 30, 34, 58, 65, 119-120, 127, 147, 158, 161, 201
chamber 89, 118
chants 54
chaotic 135
chariot 80, 104, 114, 203
Charles 10
Charpin 217, 222
charter 198
Charvát 82, 222

cheese 197
Chemery 213, 222
Cheyenne 45, 127, 225
Chiapas 214, 219
Chicago 6, 10, 22, 29, 40, 44, 49, 55, 57-58, 68, 93, 101, 104, 123, 128, 135, 142, 153, 159, 186, 215, 219, 221, 223-225, 228-231, 235-236
Chilam 33-34, 125, 190, 232
child-hero 201-202, 205
Chinese 130, 149, 167-169
Chorti 127, 186
Choruses 120, 223
Christian 181, 200
chronicled 151
Chronology 8, 22-23, 25, 119, 222, 236
chthonic 184, 202
Chthoniê 107
Chthonios 105, 107-108
Chumayel 33-34, 190, 232
Cilicia 205
circle 24, 37, 47-49, 83, 168, 174, 216
circled 134
circles 120
circular 16-17
cities 160, 181, 190
civilized 152, 197
clanlord 38
Classic 35-36, 43, 101, 114, 127, 129, 142, 154, 174, 190, 193, 234
Classical 35, 120, 143, 167, 186-187, 200, 202-203, 210, 216, 221, 225, 232-233, 236
Classicist 117, 212
classrooms 11
clefts 96
Clewlow 17-18, 46, 226
Clifford 103, 222
clouds 37, 94, 168
Cochrane 1-2, 18, 22, 25, 44, 49, 53, 57-58, 60, 89-90, 118, 149, 153, 164, 184, 201-202, 205, 222
codices 44, 49, 173-174
Coffin 11, 30, 32, 123, 134, 141, 149, 200, 224, 229
cognate 77, 92, 95, 104, 121, 133-134, 137-138, 143-144, 146-148, 209, 212, 216

cognates 214, 216
Cognition 28, 36, 38, 148, 173, 227
collage 60
collective 57-58, 80, 159-160, 163
College 65-66, 68, 190, 222, 228
Collision 160, 221
Collon 23-25, 81, 222
Colloquium 74, 233
Colonus 121, 227
Colony 44, 236
colorful 162
colossal 44
Colossus 218
column 110, 133
columnar 127, 134, 136, 144
columns 144
Combat 115-116, 127, 219
comedic 120
comet-like 173
comets 173
communal 153
communis 31
Community 15, 96, 181, 222
Companion 116, 236
company 197
compass 140
compendium 5, 12
compiled 21, 214
complement 189
Complete 54, 121, 178, 184, 211, 227, 229-230
completely 7, 116, 147
completion 67
Complex 39, 60, 205, 233
comrade 5, 151
confusion 56-57
connexion 185
context 53, 77, 88, 90, 107, 112, 117-118, 128, 148, 204, 207, 212, 217, 230-231
conundrum 216
Copernicus 15
copulated 112
Copulco 36
copyright 2
Corinne 205
Corinth 201
cornfield 125

coronation 7, 48, 139-140
Corpus 10, 109, 113
corrigere 143
corroding 202
cosmic 4, 6, 10, 33, 43, 46-47, 49, 55, 57, 62, 68, 101, 103, 109, 112, 116, 128, 140, 142-144, 146-147, 149, 153-154, 156, 166, 175-176, 189, 192, 213, 226, 228, 231
cosmogonic 6, 8, 11-12, 20, 30, 46, 53, 63, 69, 79, 84, 92, 100-101, 103, 105, 108, 127, 129, 132, 135-137, 139-140, 144-146, 148-149, 155, 157-158, 164, 176-177, 180, 186, 189-190, 193, 212
cosmogony 8, 56-57, 66, 98, 101-102, 109-110, 112, 129, 135, 139, 142, 159, 175-176, 182, 212-213, 220, 228
cosmogram 41, 45, 83, 128, 133-134, 139, 141, 144, 180, 191
cosmologie 80, 221
Cosmology 5, 35, 45, 57-58, 67, 96, 107, 125, 127, 157, 169, 181, 190, 227-228, 233-234
cosmos 7, 10, 12, 21, 29, 39, 41, 45, 50-51, 55-58, 78, 83-84, 91, 103, 107, 114, 123, 125-126, 129-130, 132, 135, 137-144, 147-149, 157, 159, 163-164, 168, 188, 190-191, 193-194, 206, 231
cotinga 37
countrymen 217
courage 206
courtesy 33, 137
Crawford 70, 229
Creation 1, 3-4, 6-8, 10-11, 20, 29-32, 35-37, 40-41, 44-45, 51-53, 55-58, 63-64, 66-69, 74, 78, 83, 85-87, 91-95, 97-98, 100, 103, 105, 107-108, 112, 114, 116, 125, 127, 129-132, 134-135, 137, 139-140, 142-148, 154-159, 161-163, 166, 177-178, 180-181, 186, 188, 190-191, 194-195, 206-207, 212, 222, 226-227, 231-232, 234
Creator 58-60, 83, 95, 113, 125, 148, 158, 176, 180, 219, 224
cremation 160, 200, 202-203, 205
crescent 23-24
Cretan 185

crisis   184
Critical   10
Crucible 39-40, 57, 223
cruciform   45, 50, 82, 128, 133, 141, 190-191
cryptic   90, 107, 184
cryptogram   10
cuecueponi   206
cultural   6, 10-11, 36, 38, 58, 71, 96, 122, 157, 164, 173, 220, 223, 227
Culture   8, 28, 36, 43, 46, 57, 69, 104, 153, 157, 159, 167-168, 184, 186, 199, 209, 216, 220-221, 223, 229, 235
cultures   7, 30, 45, 47, 53-56, 60, 65-66, 68-69, 74, 78-79, 83, 93-94, 124, 133, 135, 152, 154, 157, 159, 166, 169-171, 184, 190, 193, 197, 207, 214
Cumont 166
Cuneiform   21, 72, 193, 227, 231
Currie   202, 223
Curtis   16, 78, 223
Cycles   169
cyclonic 149
Cyclopean   118-119, 122
Cyclopes 117
Cyclops 118
cylinder 12, 17, 22-23, 25, 32, 34, 81, 103, 111-113, 119, 128, 171, 212-213, 235-236
cylinders 80, 87, 89, 144

D

Daedala 107, 224
daemon 207
daimoni 207
Dakota   171
Danaids 106
dancing   61, 66, 161, 185
Dandekar   108, 123, 138, 143, 223
dark-blue   187
darkness 14, 36, 52-53, 55-58, 60, 62-64, 94, 99-100, 129, 148-149, 155, 227, 232
Darmstadt   112, 212, 225
database 7, 178
dating   26, 44, 198

daughter 80, 186, 210
daughters   94, 180, 197
daylight   72, 88-89, 210-211, 218
day-light 209
dazzling   163
deadly   207
deathless 102
decipher 207
Decline   83, 219
déesse   80, 221
defeat   53
Deianeira   202-203
Deities   23, 55, 77, 83, 95, 117, 120, 125, 180, 200, 214, 219, 231
Delphi   56
Demarest   193, 223
Demeter 105, 160, 198, 207-208, 224, 236
DeMille 115
demiurgic   95, 131, 142
demonic 14
demons 26, 36, 55, 125, 200, 211, 220, 231
Demophon   198-199, 201-202, 204-208
dérkomai   122
Desana   58
desert   75
Destiny   46, 118, 153, 193-194, 231
deus-dies 211
dharayad 142
Dharma 132, 135, 137, 142-143, 145, 190, 220, 226, 230
dhárma   145
Dharman   142, 221
dhárman 144-145
dharmana   143
dhármana   142
dhármani   145
dharúna 145
dharúno 190
dhruvam 142
Diadem   173, 230
Diadems 38, 230
Dictaean 113, 184-185, 236
dictum   165, 217
diffusion 167, 205
dikeis   143
dinosaur 10

Diodorus 151
Dionysiac 232
Dionysiaca 204, 230
Dionysiaka 204
Dionysos 120, 196, 232
Dionysus 104, 155, 230
Dippie 161, 223
Discourse 147, 219
Disorder 54, 142, 148, 220
Disterheft 149, 223
divine 12, 23, 35, 51-52, 70-71, 76, 78, 80, 85, 103-107, 111, 117, 139, 183, 201, 232
divinities 72
divinity 70, 102, 160, 199, 211
Dodola 107, 224
Dodona 107, 224
dolphin 201
dominion 53
Dominique 23
Doniger 7, 223
Donnerkeil 214, 228
donning 202
doodlings 19
doorposts 137, 187
Dorsey 45, 64, 108, 127, 171, 223
Douglas 71
Dowden 115-116, 120, 209, 211, 215-217, 223
Downer 146, 227
dragon 10, 115-116, 148, 168-169, 235
dragons 116, 211
Dreams 103, 179, 223
Dresden 61, 235
Dronke 106, 223
dti-mu 80
ducklings 161
Dumézil 12, 56, 213, 223
Dumuzi 48, 71-75, 77, 80, 85, 88-90, 110-111, 114, 182, 185, 224, 228, 232
Dumuzid 88
Dundes 7, 223
Durrani 193, 224
dvandva 102
dwarf-god 113
dwarfish 60
dwarves 113

Dynamics 36, 38, 173, 227
Dynastic 11, 23, 29, 86, 109, 113, 213, 232, 236
Dynasty 24, 29, 72, 89-90, 237

E

earmarks 110
Earthborn 4, 183-184
earth-born 177
Earthlings 8, 14, 159-162
earthly 28, 36, 131-132, 136, 141, 157
Eastern 5, 15, 17, 76, 127, 168, 203, 205, 219, 235
Ebeling 76, 86, 226, 228
Ecbatana 151
eclipse 14, 54-56, 63, 148, 153
egersis 200
Eggeling 126, 144, 223
Egyptian 26, 28-32, 41, 47-49, 53, 81, 87, 119, 123, 127, 130-131, 134, 141-142, 146-149, 157-158, 175, 177, 188, 191-192, 195, 214, 219-220, 224, 226, 229, 231-236
Egyptians 28, 146
Egyptology 48, 234
Ekapad 132
Ekapâda 132
electrons 162
Eleusinian 198
Eleusis 120, 202, 223
elevation 130, 192
Eleven 4, 160, 196
Eliade 7, 39-40, 57, 103, 117, 128, 139-140, 159, 162, 189, 207, 213, 222-223
emblem 173
emblems 23
embryo 39, 93, 100, 106, 133, 154
emergence 31, 185
emigrants 65
emission 122-123
Empire 35, 160, 222
E-namtila 80
endless 115
enemies 117
energy 41, 84, 94-95, 117, 141
English 170, 212

enigma 209
Enlil-bani 195
Enmerkar 11, 41, 77, 90-91, 111, 192
Ensink 108, 123, 138, 143, 223
epidemic 66
epigenetic 164, 235
epiphany 12, 29-30, 90, 92, 97, 117, 211-212, 221
epithet 37, 42, 46, 73, 77-78, 80, 88, 94, 96-97, 107, 111, 120, 126, 133, 146, 177, 184, 187, 202, 213
erbetti 46, 49
Erdberg 46, 225
Erdnabel 46, 225
Ergidoupos 211
Erhöhung 80, 226
erklären 30
Eroticism 75, 228
erudite 76, 205
erudition 40, 176
Esarhaddon 71, 153, 230
escape 183
Eshmun 201
essence 12, 90, 148, 207
essense 75
Eternal 57, 187, 232
Ethnology 140, 171, 178, 220-221, 233
Etruscans 199
etymology 120, 137-138, 166, 210, 218
Eubouleus 108
Eudoxus 201
Euripides 9, 101, 104, 106, 116-117, 198, 202, 213, 217, 230, 232
Europe 15-19, 84, 104, 119, 142, 213, 225-226, 235
Europeans 65
euryopa 121
evidence 10-12, 15, 19, 30, 45, 54, 69-70, 74, 76, 78-79, 88-89, 92, 110-111, 114, 120, 122, 133, 147, 159, 164, 166, 169, 184, 200, 210, 214, 216, 218, 227
Evolution 115, 152, 209, 225
Exaltation 111, 226
Excursus 153, 202, 223, 230
existence 7, 52, 56, 104, 158-159

experience 12-14, 20, 34, 109, 117, 129, 160-161, 203, 206, 208, 233
experiment 198
expert 120
Expiation 60, 62, 225
Extremis 202-203, 220
exultation 72
eyelash 159
Ezekiel 200

F

fabled 7, 63
Fabula 106, 202, 223
Fairman 157, 220
falcon-god 28
famine 56
fantasy 19
Farmington 28, 31, 226
Farnell 117, 201, 213, 224
Farrington 215, 224
fascinosum 14, 117, 160
fashion 11, 52, 91, 126, 136, 184
Fastorum 197, 200, 224
father 37-38, 93, 102-104, 106, 112, 168, 185, 197, 202, 210, 212-213
Faulkner 30, 127, 131, 165, 224
Feldman 210, 224
festival 151, 197, 200-201
Festivals 35, 112, 198, 213, 226
filaments 119, 171
Finkel 62, 220
Finnestad 148, 224
Finnish 170
Finsternis 63
fireballs 214
firebrand 198
fire-drill 38, 68
fire-god 3, 37-41, 47, 51, 62, 93, 97, 100, 107, 133, 136, 146, 154, 164, 166, 168-169, 173, 175
Fire-gods 167
fire-like 122
fire-pit 176
fireplace 45
Fire-Star 166-169
firesticks 67-68, 155

fireworks 14
firmament   132
Fischer   22, 224
Fläche   126
Flagstaff 26, 237
flames   53, 145, 178, 196, 198, 200, 203, 206-207
Fletcher   127, 167, 171, 224
floating   126, 143, 149, 186
flocks   185
Floral   33, 75, 81, 204, 228, 234
Florentine   36-37, 41, 53, 55-56, 113, 168, 171, 184, 196, 232
florescent   162
flower   30-31, 33, 81, 86-87, 177-179, 191, 204-205, 226
-flower   32
flowers   79, 178, 205
flutes   72
Folklore   92, 129, 167, 214, 220, 232
Folk-Lore   171, 224
folklorist 7, 170
folktale   7
Folktales 7, 235
footsteps 131
Forbes   154, 224
Forest   181, 190, 232
forests   116
Fossil   44, 49, 53, 57-58, 90, 149, 153, 189, 222
fossilized 16, 179
foundation   21, 137, 142, 145, 153, 169, 187
four-fold 33, 44
four-rayed   25
four-sided   45
Foxvog   89, 224
France   15
Franciscan   36
Frankfort   29, 71, 142, 158-159, 224
Frayne   71, 224
Frazer   68, 71, 152, 155-156, 197-198, 200, 206-207, 224
Freidel   181, 190, 232
French   5, 65, 170
Fribourg 32, 81, 119, 235
Frontiers 194, 231

funeral   62, 151, 200, 205-207
funerary 29
fusion   162
Future   63, 129, 154, 157, 159, 164, 188, 220, 229

G

Gaeffke   108, 123, 138, 143, 223
Gaerte   46, 128, 225
Gagarin   143, 225
garbha   39, 93
garbham 100
garden   3, 32, 67, 74-81, 84-85, 106, 110, 149-150, 181-182, 200, 235
gardener 75
Gardening   37, 226
gardens   74, 85, 149-150
garment 202
Geburt   31, 188, 235
Genealogy   161
generation   6, 8, 54-56, 62-63, 145, 174, 177, 184
generatrix   155
Genesis   11, 31, 74, 97, 127, 129, 146, 219
genetic   164
genetrix   124
genitals   75
genius   52
Geography   46, 49, 83, 95, 125, 149, 180, 213, 219, 226
German 5, 147, 226
Germanic   210
Germans 153
gigantic   40
girin-a   75
Girix-zal 77
girizal   111
gißkiri   77
Gloucester   55, 225
-glyphs   88
Glyptic   44, 236
glyptique   22, 219
goddess 37, 39, 70-71, 73, 76-78, 80, 89, 104, 111, 124, 126, 136, 185, 198-199, 223, 226, 234
goddesses   104-105, 193

247

god-like 197, 207
Gorgonen 118, 232
goslings 161
Göttin 33, 232
Göttingen 77, 231
grammarian 117
gratitude 5, 72
greatness 126, 136
Greece 8, 56, 105, 108, 118, 124, 153, 184, 201, 207, 213, 226, 230-231
Greeks 115, 166, 201, 213, 216
greenery 74-75, 77-78, 85, 110, 185
greening 29-30, 41, 77, 84, 91
greenish 29
greenness 180
greybeard 199
Grinnell 45, 127, 225
Groningen 140, 236
gruesome 35, 67
guardians 154
guzikide 152
Gythium 213

H

Hammurabi 195
happiness 56
Harvard 216, 236
Hathor 29, 101, 220
Hauptstadt 159, 229
headband 173, 175, 230
headdress 67, 78
headgear 43
health 61, 160, 196
hearth 35-37, 39-40, 43, 45, 47, 51-52, 61-62, 67-68, 80, 100, 127, 151-152, 155-156, 166, 174-175, 196-197, 206-207, 234
hearths 55
heartland 65, 69
Heathen 197, 206, 219
heathens 55
heaven 3-4, 8, 10-12, 18, 23, 29-31, 39, 49, 53, 72-73, 77-78, 84-85, 93-94, 101-103, 105-114, 116, 118-121, 123, 126-127, 129-133, 135, 137-138, 142, 145-146, 150, 153, 163, 168, 176-177, 182, 187, 190-193, 195, 210, 212, 214-216, 219, 222, 227, 231-232, 236
heavenly 21, 23, 77, 92, 106, 134, 136, 153, 168, 182, 232
heavens 11, 14-15, 49, 65-66, 72, 109, 132, 135, 148-149, 160, 171, 175, 186, 190, 216-217, 230
Hebrew 170
Heidelberg 74, 142, 146, 166, 229, 233, 235
heirloom 10
heliacal 96
Helios 120-121, 171
Hellenic 113, 185, 236
Helsinki 73, 228
Hephaestus 178
Heracles 160, 201-206, 208, 220
Heracles- 223
Heraclitus 217
Herakles 202-203, 233
herald 164
Hercules 206
herdsman 40, 145
Heritage 8, 35-36, 43, 174, 234
Hermes 31, 220
Heroes 198, 201-202, 205, 207, 223, 230
heroine 104
Hesiod 8, 102-103, 105, 115-116, 121, 124, 143, 183-184, 187-188, 195, 216-218, 224, 227, 236
hestia 155
Hesychius 117
hierodule 111
hierogamic 201
hierogamy 103, 105, 212
hieroglyph 33, 123
hieros 66-69, 72, 74, 77-78, 80, 85, 90-91, 101-102, 105, 110-112, 114, 150, 155, 182, 185, 204, 212-213
hierós 110
Highlands 197
himeros 204
Hinduism 39, 103, 140, 229-230
Hinnom 197
hio-ta 179
Hippolytus 101
Historia 99

historian 59, 87, 151
historians 27
historic 22
history 1, 5-8, 11-12, 16, 23, 28, 36, 38, 45, 60, 62, 64-67, 69, 74, 76, 78, 85, 93, 98-100, 107-108, 113, 116, 119, 128, 131-132, 135, 137, 143, 145, 148-149, 151-152, 161, 164-165, 169, 173, 177, 179, 189-190, 206-209, 220-221, 223, 225-228, 233
Hittite 205
hoarding 148
Holland 190
Hollywood 115
Holmesian 10
Homeric 115, 124, 183, 187-188, 198, 204, 207, 213, 219, 224
Homerica 115, 124, 183, 187-188, 224
ho-pi-rit 167
horizon 15, 29, 32, 49, 69, 109, 168, 227
Horizons 194, 231
horror 35
horses 16, 19
Horus-Re 191
Horus-star 29
household 37, 153
Houston 127, 181, 234
148, 178, 184
Hrußka 80, 226
hubris 217
humankind 10, 12, 15-16, 22, 161-162, 164-165
humans 83-84, 160, 164, 235
Hunahpu 96
Hungaricae 109, 129, 227
Hunger 125, 226
hunting 65
Huracan 94-95, 97, 100, 180-181
husband 80, 105, 199
hybrid 24
Hyenas 135, 227
hypostasis 201
hypotheses 18
hypothesis 15, 33, 41, 69, 109-110, 113, 129
Hypsipyle 35, 221
hysteria 55, 58, 63

I
Icelandic 191
iconic 12, 27, 32, 48
ideogram 22, 173
ideology 38, 40, 138, 153, 158-160, 193, 223
idioms 49, 117, 123
ieh-fu 167
ignorance 209
Ihkawilée 167
imagery 3, 21, 28-30, 33, 45, 75-77, 79, 81, 90, 119-120, 122, 145, 171, 174, 187, 189, 193, 198, 213, 223
images 16-17, 19-20, 22, 24-28, 31-32, 47-49, 70, 82, 84, 119, 128, 213, 229, 232
Imaginary 95, 120, 215, 231
immolation 62, 202, 204-208
immortal 185, 198, 200
Immortals 204, 235
implant 39
Impregnor 154, 156
Inanna 24, 71-81, 85, 87-91, 110-111, 114, 149, 185, 221, 226, 236
Inannas 80, 226
incense 197
inchoate 143
Indian 35-36, 39, 45-46, 57, 63-64, 103, 114, 127, 130, 132, 137, 139-140, 142-143, 145-146, 162, 171, 176-177, 190, 220-221, 223, 225-228, 230, 237
Indians 35, 38, 45, 49, 60, 64-65, 78, 118, 124, 127, 152, 167, 170, 178, 189, 206, 219, 223, 225, 230, 233, 235-236
indigenous 41, 52, 55-56, 60-61, 65-66, 68, 83, 93-94, 96, 114, 118, 152, 173, 190, 196, 207, 214, 223
Indonesia 103
infant 31, 183, 197-198, 201-202, 207
infants 197
initiation 159, 162, 204, 207, 223
insect 179
Insignia 48, 158, 173, 230
instinct 161
integrity 211
intimate 31, 42, 97, 133, 144, 169-170
invention 18
Inversion 7, 223

invisible 121, 126, 170
Iranian 146, 167, 216, 230
Iranica 87, 233
Iroquois 118, 171, 223
irrigation 110
Irstam 152, 227
Ished-tree 191-192
Ishtar 71, 88
Ishtmian 201
island 7, 186-188, 201
isolation 34
Israel 8, 77, 231
Israelites 160
Ißme-Dagan 80, 195
Isthmus 60, 201-202
Italian 17
Italic 134, 143, 235
Ithaca 14, 28, 54, 107, 135, 155, 178, 183, 219, 224, 226-227, 229-230, 234
itheieisi 143
Íumunda 101
Iuppiter 213-214
Ivanov 93, 225

J

Japanese 35
jayamana 176
jealous 117
jeopardy 152
Jeremiah 197
Jeremias 46, 134, 227
Jerusalem 76, 90, 232
Jewish 186, 197
jigsaw 84
Josephus 200
journey 15
journeying 20
Judahite 73, 220
judgment 6, 8, 73, 194-195
judgments 143, 149-150, 195
Junajpu 96
Jupiter 210-211, 213
Jurakán 94, 231
Juraqan 95
justice 121, 142-144, 146-148, 150, 194-195
Justyna 173

K

känastep 140
kanina 114
keraunón 120
Keraunos 107
keraunós 107, 212, 215-217
Kerényi 210, 231
keuthesi 183
keuthmōn 183-184
keuthos 184
kibrat 46
kibrati 217
kibratum 125
kidnap 66
Ki-earth 109, 112, 212
ki-kiri 111
Kingdom 29, 31, 48, 130, 142, 188, 219, 233-234
kingship 11, 28-29, 38, 40, 48, 70, 80, 90, 95, 137, 139, 141-142, 153, 155, 158-159, 163, 169, 173, 175, 192, 224-225
King-star 156
kippat 49
kip-pat 49
kippatu 48-49, 175
Kirfel 126, 227
Kirzal 111
Kißkanu 192
Kitchen 146-148, 227
Knights 198
knowledge 59, 157
Komoróczy 109, 129, 227
ko-ri-tu 167
Kosmogonie 86, 112, 212, 225, 228
Kosmologie 125, 226
Kosmos 134
Kouretes 185
Kouros 113, 184-185, 236
Kronos 44, 183, 185, 234
kudurru 88
kuklos 121
Kultur 33, 131, 232-233
kumaraka 114
ku-miari 123
kusaru 79
ku-tzu 167
Kyeyune 152, 228

L

labors 162
labour 186
lackluster 162
Ladder 18, 222
Ladies 71, 232
landscape 39, 44, 71, 76, 83, 85, 101, 112, 123, 128, 176, 220, 231
Landscapes 194, 231
language 22, 26, 28, 30, 33, 42, 52, 56, 58, 61, 63, 65, 73, 80, 84, 90-91, 106, 111, 116, 123, 140, 145-146, 149, 195, 210, 216-217, 228, 235-236
languages 8, 122, 134, 143, 170, 178, 180, 182, 205, 209-210, 216, 226, 235
larval 174
Lascaux 16, 19, 236
latent 101
Latvian 104, 114
layout 2, 160
lazuli 192
leader 150, 152
leaves 125, 203
legend 53, 61, 183
legendary 63, 155
legends 7, 64, 155, 171, 223
Leiden 11, 29, 41, 46, 53, 62-63, 75, 87-88, 90, 100-101, 106, 108-110, 123, 127, 130, 132, 134, 137-140, 142-143, 147, 149, 152, 154, 157, 168-169, 184-185, 188, 191-193, 198-201, 212, 219-221, 223-229, 231-235, 237
Leipzig 46, 118, 198, 227, 232
leitmotif 78
Letopolis 214, 235
Leuven 49, 60, 80, 221, 225
Leviticus 151
Lexicon 77, 120, 122, 183, 185, 226, 228
Lexikon 46, 48, 198, 227, 229, 232
liability 2
Library 16, 104, 198, 225
license 30, 67
life-blood 202
lifeline 5
lifestyle 65
lifetime 7
lightning 92-97, 103-105, 111-112, 114-118, 120, 122-123, 149, 154, 162, 164, 171, 180, 211-215, 217-218, 233
lights 14, 53, 59, 112
likeness 153
likening 84
likens 89, 178
Lincoln, Abraham 132, 154, 161, 222-223, 225
linguistic 10, 12, 92, 164, 216, 227
Linguists 210
Literature 11, 42, 44, 60-61, 63, 70, 75-76, 78, 89-90, 96, 101, 103, 106, 110, 114, 127, 176, 189, 199-200, 205, 220, 224, 228, 230, 232, 234-236
lithos 213, 216
Lithuanian 92, 104, 216
livelihood 109
location 45, 176
logogram 77, 89, 164
London 7, 9, 16-17, 22, 26, 29, 31, 41, 48, 62, 68, 75, 81, 84, 86, 103, 106, 111, 115, 117, 119-120, 122, 125, 130, 139, 147, 152-153, 155-156, 158, 188, 190, 193, 197-198, 200-201, 206, 209, 211, 214-216, 219-220, 222-226, 228-233, 235-236
Lotusblüte 31
lotus-born 177
lotus-like 31
loveliness 88
lovemaking 121
lovers 70
luminous 43, 78, 90, 171, 181, 210
luxuriance 110
Lycophron 198
Lyctus 183
Lykophron 201-202

M

macabre 104
Macedonian 151
macrocosm 40
Madison 2, 107, 231
madness 7, 201-202, 213, 223

Madrid 16, 221
magical 158, 171, 198
Magnum 5
maiden 104
majestic 14
Majesty 14, 148
Malibu 22-23, 25, 71, 80, 119, 192, 221, 226, 236
mammoths 16
mankind 7, 40, 49, 102
manthana 38
mantle 91
marriage 67, 70-80, 85, 88-90, 93, 101, 103, 105, 107, 112, 200, 213, 220-221, 224, 227-229, 231, 233
Marriages 74, 107, 228
married 60, 66, 107
marrying 92
Martian 22, 66, 80, 201-202, 222
marvel 186-187
masculine 39, 67, 69, 78, 97, 107, 114, 154, 156
Masked 184
matati 49
mating 105
matrix 68, 79, 182
mature 66, 80
Mayanist 34
Mayanists 33, 181
Mayanized 62
Meadow 110, 221
Medieval 9, 197
Megalithic 17, 235
Megistos 113
memoires 128, 229
memorial 56
memory 6, 10, 15, 21, 33, 57, 85, 149, 161, 163, 186, 191-192, 210, 231, 233
merchants 61
messenger 93
Mes-tree 192-193
Metanira 198
metaphor 21, 30-31, 33, 45, 75, 89, 146, 149, 178, 228
metaphoric 178
Metaphors 76, 233
meteor 66, 174, 213-214, 216, 219

meteorite 214, 216
Meteorites 215, 224
meteors 214-215
Mexica 36, 38, 160, 173, 227
Mexican 63, 125, 169, 174
mexicana 173, 230
Mexicanos 41, 99, 122, 220
Mexicans 57
Mexico 36, 38-39, 41, 54, 57, 83, 99, 124, 173, 221, 225, 230, 234
microcosm 40, 160
Micronesia 103
Mictlan 63, 184
midnight 52
midspace 130, 142
Midwestern 65
midwived 105
midwives 197
migration 68
Milano 194, 231
millennia 6, 8, 11, 16, 18, 24, 31, 87, 108, 163
millennium 21-22, 26, 29, 71, 80, 87, 101, 109-111, 127, 150, 200, 212, 228
mimetic 58
Minerva 198
miracle 57, 198, 207
Miranda 19
Mirror 58, 93, 95, 97, 100, 114, 189, 230, 235
mirrored 40
mirrors 62, 195
mißaru 194
missile 215
missionary 7
Mistress 72
Mixe-Zoque 95
Mixtecs 83
mnemonic 189
mnemonics 161
Mnemosyne 110, 202, 221, 223
Mockeries 97, 230
Moctezuma 38, 62, 156, 230
modern 8, 11-12, 19, 22, 26, 31, 49, 59, 64, 67, 74, 76, 92, 97, 103, 107, 112, 114, 116-118, 131, 140, 147-148, 151, 160, 166, 169, 179, 191, 198, 209-211, 213-215, 217, 224, 226

Molech 197
mollify 160
Moloch 160
Molochian 160
monograph 6, 8, 170, 215-216
Monomotapa 152
monster 97, 115
monsters 55
Montreal 73, 220
monumental 197, 210
Monuments 38, 43, 87, 226
moonlight 109
morality 149
Morning 15, 44, 60-62, 64, 66-69, 96, 154-155, 158, 166-167, 215, 228
morpheme 43
mortal 70, 178, 186, 200
mortality 203
Mortals 204, 235
Moteuczoma 38, 43, 226
Mother 29, 38, 66, 70, 78, 80, 84, 89, 92, 94, 97, 100, 102-105, 107, 110-112, 114, 124-126, 136, 155, 168, 183-186, 198, 205, 212-213, 229
mothers 160
mountain 10, 96-97, 114-115, 148, 189, 195, 209, 217
mountains 12, 77, 83, 90, 93, 105, 111, 128, 142
mouths 29
mul-mul 193
mul-mul-e 90
multiform 148
multiple 57, 189
multiplied 70
multiply 72
multitude 72
Mumbai 189, 228
Munster 76, 233
Münster 129, 220
murder 10
murderous 183
muscles 162
Museum 66-67, 78, 93, 228
Musical 120, 223
musings 25, 217
mutilation 162

Mycenaean 203, 230
myopia 217
myopic 74
myriad 14, 134
mysterious 205, 207, 216-217
mysterium 14, 117, 160, 218
mystery 6, 30, 90, 139, 157, 170-171, 176, 189, 205, 228
mytheme 114, 125, 155, 186
Mythic 45, 125, 127, 234
mythical 62, 66, 114, 150, 176, 189, 207
Mythmaker 6, 103, 136, 221
mythmakers 69, 100, 215, 217
mythologem 189
mythologic 64
Mythologie 46, 76, 198, 202-203, 220, 226-227, 232
Mythology 5, 11-12, 33, 54-55, 57, 59, 64, 92, 98, 104-105, 113, 116, 118, 120, 124-125, 129-130, 132, 143-144, 155, 161, 166, 171, 176, 200, 203, 206, 209-210, 212, 216-221, 224-225, 227, 229-231, 236
mythopoeic 191
mythus 205

N

Nachbild 30
Nagaicho 132
Nahuat 96-97, 113-114, 234
Nahuatl 26, 178
Náhuatl 62
naissance 113
nam-lugal 80
nam-ti 80
Nanahuac 59, 113
Nanahuatl 3, 36, 47, 52-53, 58-62, 96-97, 99-100, 113-114, 156, 160, 175, 206-208
Nanahuaton 59, 113
Nanauatl 62, 113
Nanauatzin 52-53, 59
Nanawatzin 97, 114
Nanna-Suen 77, 233
Naqada 28

Narasamsa   46, 133
narrators 114
Narukta 138
nascent 29-30, 50, 91, 146, 148-149, 163, 177-178, 206-207
Natchez 152
nation   152, 181
nations 197
Native   61-62, 64, 84, 96, 118, 206, 219, 227, 231
natural 1, 6, 8, 12, 14, 20, 28-30, 38, 41, 47, 53, 55, 57-58, 66-67, 74, 76, 78, 93, 99, 107-108, 115-117, 120, 126, 131, 139, 145, 148-149, 153-154, 156, 158-159, 163, 167, 169, 174, 177, 206-208, 228
nature   7-8, 11-12, 19, 21, 28-29, 34, 51, 55-58, 69-70, 76-77, 79, 90-91, 102-103, 107, 110, 112, 115-116, 121-122, 124, 129-130, 155, 157-159, 169, 171, 176, 180, 199-200, 209, 230
naucampa   160
nauhcampan   124
Nauhyo 42
nauseam 118
Navaho   45, 133, 225
Navajo   45, 222
navels   128
Naylor   46, 230
Nebraska   65
nebulous 136
Necans   202, 221
neighbors   65, 160
Neolithic   16, 18, 22, 47, 222
Nergal   166
neutrally 75
newborn 196-197
new-born   31, 62
Nietzsche   161
nightfall 36
Nights   112, 132, 225
nihilo   8
ni-si-sá 194
ni-zi-da 194
nomadic 65
nonsense 214
normative   146, 159
northern 15, 19, 118-119, 123, 134

Northwest   65, 171
novice   162, 207
Numinous   14

O

obscure 12, 134, 200
Obsession   4, 157, 159
occlusion   153
Oceania 103
October 151
ocular   123
Odyssey 120, 122, 184
œåb-flower   32
œåœ-flower   32
Oedipus 121, 217, 227
Oetean   202, 223
Offerings   42, 61, 71, 73, 228, 234
officiants 140
offspring 39, 162, 184, 186, 211
O-kee-pa   161-162, 222
okuggyako   152
Olympia 143, 221
Olympian   116, 185
Olympians   116
Olympic 185, 202
Olympus 115-116, 120, 187, 202
omnipotent   157
omukono 152
Omuliro 152
Omutanda   152
one-footed   132-133
one-legged   95
orchard 150
ordinance   142
ordinances   149-150
organic 211
organisms   164, 235
organs   79
orgiasmos   204
Orient   11, 33, 71, 125, 224, 226
Oriental 21, 89, 136, 199-200, 221, 227, 233
orientale 71, 234
Orientalia   56, 70-72, 76, 170, 221, 234, 236
Orientalis   71, 224
ornament   192

Orpheus 204, 230
Orphic 120, 204, 230
Orphism 120, 223
Osiris 31, 71, 158, 199-200, 206, 224
overtones 61
Oxford 9-11, 19, 30-31, 36, 38-39, 41, 45, 61, 64, 70, 84, 89, 93, 96, 101-102, 104-105, 112, 117, 120, 122, 126-127, 134, 136, 138, 140-141, 147, 154-155, 160, 173, 176, 183, 185, 187, 189, 193, 198, 202, 205-206, 209, 212-214, 216, 220-224, 226-236
oxymoron 105

P

Padova 194, 231
paintings 15-16, 19, 236
palace 73, 217
Palenque 95
paltòn 116
Panopolis 204, 230
pantheon 37, 94, 111, 125, 210, 212
pantheons 11
Papyrus 29, 63, 127, 130, 147, 149, 171, 188, 191, 237
parable 217
paragon 146, 194
paramour 185
Paruxti 93-94
Pausanias 213
Pawnee 3, 64-68, 74, 78-79, 85, 93, 106, 108, 155, 167, 171, 175, 223-224, 228-229
pedamentum 134
perception 19, 21
periods 88
Persephone 107
Persian 144, 151
Persians 151-152
petaloid 32
petroglyph 17-19
Phaethon 53, 222
phallus 155
pharaoh 28-29, 157
pharaohs 157

phenomena 14, 16, 22, 28, 55, 76, 97, 123, 158, 211, 214
phenomenon 94, 96, 120, 127, 154, 157, 191, 205
Pherecydes 107
Pherekydes 202
Philology 143, 210, 216, 225, 236
Philosophy 41, 84, 116, 132, 142-143, 145, 190, 221, 225, 229
phobia 57
Phoebus 188
Phoenician 201
Phoenix 204, 216, 227
Phrygian 104
physica 206
pictograph 46
Pillar 133, 140, 145, 161, 189-190
pillars 125, 130, 137, 149, 160, 186, 188
pimples 60
Pindar 8, 116, 143, 186-188, 202, 223, 227, 232
pinturas 99
Plains 49, 65, 69, 85, 167
planet 3, 23-24, 62, 65-66, 68, 70-79, 81, 85, 87-91, 110, 125, 150, 154, 162, 166-167, 169, 172, 175, 182, 215-216
planets 3, 8, 15, 22, 65-67, 69, 74, 85, 162, 175, 206, 222
plasma 161-162, 180, 231
Plautus 74
Plutarch 31, 199-201
Poetic 24, 30, 90, 140, 180, 182, 226, 236
Poetics 54, 149, 155, 161, 227, 230, 232
Poetry 19, 86, 102, 105, 108, 155, 176, 179, 187, 204, 209, 212, 220, 224, 227, 236
pointed 22, 29, 40, 75, 79, 82, 84, 86-88, 96, 105, 113, 126, 145, 159, 200, 205, 213
poison 202
Political 142, 220
Polomé 210, 231
polytekton 2
Portland 180, 234
Portugal 15
post-Vedic 176
pot-hook 197
pottery 82

255

Praenestan 198
Praeneste 155
Prague 82, 166, 222
prathamânâ 126, 136
prayer 23, 37, 63, 105, 181, 232
prehistory 65, 161, 164
Priests 33, 36, 57, 66-67, 74, 78, 94, 142, 146, 229, 233-235
primal 29-30, 33, 36, 40-41, 47, 49-50, 84, 105, 110, 128, 131, 133-134, 136, 141, 144, 147, 153, 156, 164, 170-172, 191
primeval 30, 54, 58, 67, 104, 106, 108, 110, 112-114, 125, 129, 142, 158, 161, 191, 196, 213, 222
primitive 17, 64
primordial 4, 7, 33, 80, 96, 100, 102, 109-111, 113-114, 124-128, 130-132, 136-139, 142-145, 148, 150, 176-177, 186-187, 192, 212
prince 41, 61, 77, 204
Princeton 39, 171, 177, 198, 204, 223-224, 228, 232, 235, 237
prithivi 126, 136
Problemata 206
Profane 117, 224
progenitor 154
Prometheus 116, 121, 178, 184, 229
Propheten 77, 231
Prosecky 166
prosperity 77, 79, 91, 111, 126, 136, 152, 180-182
prothales 204
prototype 41, 45, 49, 51, 69, 78, 87, 107, 113, 119, 144, 153, 156, 160-161, 173, 193
provenance 17, 81
proximity 109, 113, 191
Prthivi 123, 125
prthivyah 93
Psalms 124
psychology 161
Ptolemaic 29, 187, 227
Ptolemy 21
Pueblo 26, 237
Puhvel 12, 105, 143, 149, 210-212, 216, 223, 231
puzzle 84

Pyramid 29, 34
pyramids 158, 162
Pyroeis 166

Q

quadrants 46, 124, 139, 160
quetzal 63
Quiché 113
Quichean 95
Quichés 59, 113
quincross 42, 45
quincunx 43, 49, 83, 160
quipped 105
Quirke 48, 231

R

Rabbit 98, 193
radiance 80, 133, 147-148, 185, 192, 195
radii-like 139
Ragavan 10, 123, 153, 219, 231
rajamsi 139
rájamsi 132, 136
rajan- 138
rajasi 145
Rajasuya 139-140, 193
rasta- 144
rawhide 162
ray-like 139
reality 7, 11, 15, 19, 21, 29-30, 33, 47, 63-64, 79, 95, 118, 120, 135, 139-140, 215-217, 223, 228
reason 14-15, 19, 45, 47, 54, 56-57, 60, 74-75, 77, 82, 107, 110-111, 136, 138, 149, 164, 166-167, 169, 171, 173, 178, 185-186, 193, 209-210
rebirth 57, 199
reddish 175
redemption 158
reflection 56, 129
Reflex 10, 234
Religion 10, 12, 14, 28-29, 31, 38, 48, 53, 56-57, 62, 67, 70, 74, 76-77, 87, 92, 96, 103, 107, 117, 120, 124, 130, 146, 156-157, 166-167, 169, 183-184, 188-189,

198-199, 205, 209-211, 213-216, 218-223, 226-227, 230-232, 235
Religions 19, 62, 127, 135, 161, 219
religious 15, 19, 28, 31, 36-38, 44, 64-65, 71, 78, 97, 103, 106, 117, 128, 137, 139, 142, 149, 161, 177, 185, 201, 213, 222-223, 225-226, 236
remains 13, 22, 65, 69, 80, 109, 121, 138, 146, 165, 200, 205, 209
remnants 92
rendition 62, 136
replica 140, 153, 176
Requiem 165, 224
revolution 12, 15, 164-165
riddle 9, 163
ritual 9-11, 19, 36, 39-41, 54-55, 57, 63-64, 67-68, 70-74, 86, 90, 94, 106, 125, 133, 139-140, 145, 152-154, 160-162, 176-177, 199, 202, 204, 208, 219-220, 230-232
rituals 8, 37-38, 43, 58, 78, 138-139, 145, 151, 153, 158, 161-162, 197, 205, 207, 226
rivers 55, 65, 128
Rochelle 201, 213, 224
Rochester 18, 221
romadico 61
Romans 166
Rosetta 11
rosette 33, 71, 81-82, 86-88, 191, 221, 229, 232
Royalty 48, 139, 226
rulers 28, 37-38, 47, 51, 63, 193-194
Rulership 127, 141, 234

S

Sacrality 135
sacred 6-7, 10, 38-39, 43, 45, 47, 49, 54-55, 61, 66-80, 83, 85, 88-90, 92, 94-95, 99, 106, 112, 117, 125, 139, 151-152, 160, 163-164, 167, 180, 191, 200, 207, 213, 219-221, 224, 226-229, 231, 233, 236
Sacrifice 35-36, 43, 60, 62, 64, 66-67, 78, 100, 160-162, 176, 197, 201, 206, 222, 225-226, 228, 231
sacrifices 52, 54, 59, 160-161, 196, 201
saeculum 199
Sahagún 36-38, 41-42, 52-56, 58, 62, 113, 168, 171, 196, 207, 232
sailors 187
samrajya- 40
sanctuary 70, 212
sandal 100
sandstone 132-133
Sanskrit 93, 133, 136-139, 143, 146, 221, 229
Santayana 165
Saturn 5, 46, 83, 134, 175, 234
savage 197
scaffold 67, 79
scenes 19, 48, 140, 173, 236
scholia 201
scholiast 198, 201
School 136, 221
science 8, 10, 21-22, 26, 59, 131, 148, 153, 162, 169, 180, 231
sciences 22
scientific 15, 20-22, 102, 117, 147, 209, 226, 230
scientists 6
Scorpio 167
Scotland 197
Scroll 89, 167, 224
Seattle 108, 130, 220
Secret 86, 101-102, 104, 109, 112, 183-184, 204, 220, 233
Sefati 76, 88, 90, 193, 227, 232
semantic 138-139, 147, 149, 178, 182
semantics 149, 210
Semele 101, 104-105, 116, 154, 212-213
seminal 94, 162
Semitic 56, 71, 217, 236
senile 199
Senses 122, 139, 220
serpent 63, 95, 169, 171, 173-174, 228
sew-ta 178
sexual 38, 66-68, 70, 72-76, 79, 88, 90-91, 102, 104-106, 169, 180
shadow 9-10, 90, 140, 236
shadows 168
shafts 215
shaman 178
shamans 19

shards   84
sheepfold   88
shen-bond   47-49, 175
shen-sign   49
shepherd 88, 192
Shield   44, 222
Shields   26, 185, 237
Shilluk   152
shorthand   23, 27
showers   106, 214
shrine   103
shrines   135, 191
Siberia   65
sickness   56, 206
signal   51, 56, 152
silence   113
silent   60
simile   76
similes   193
Singing   54, 66, 205, 230
Sirius   44, 234
-si-sa   194-195
skambha 130, 190
skambhana   130
skepticism   215
sky-father   101
Sky-god   4, 101-102, 104-105, 107, 110, 119, 209, 212-214, 216
sky-prop 133, 190
sky-props   127, 134, 136-137, 145
Slavic   104
sloughs   203
societies   17, 159
society   28, 89, 96, 152, 157-158, 189, 222, 227-228
Sonnengott   31, 191
Sophocles   121, 202, 217
Southwest   26, 44-45, 65, 178
sovereign 40, 62, 97, 102, 105, 139, 141, 145-146, 153, 156, 169, 175
Spanish   59, 65
sparks   122
spectacle 118, 123
sphere   71, 201
spinner   124, 234
spirit   52, 170, 197
splendor 14, 77, 90, 111, 185

spouse   80, 89
springtime   92, 97, 212
square   11, 96, 116
Squire   122, 220
ßamßatu 23
ßaqlata   49
ßarurußu   217
stability   15
star-disc 23
star-flung   120
star-god   96
star-like   51, 88
Statue   143, 182, 211, 221
statuettes 203
stellar   15, 26, 40, 45, 47, 55, 81-83, 87, 157, 185
sticks   38, 152
stimulus 161, 180, 216
Stockholm   152, 161, 227
stone-like   213-214
stones   18, 213, 215, 221
storm-god   76, 89, 127, 211, 218-219
storms   95, 149, 164
Strassburg   125, 130, 132, 229
strata   71, 82
strategy   11
stratum   213
streamers 46-47, 128, 130, 172, 180-181
strongman   202, 204-205
Students 69, 189, 214
Subartic 118, 227
sublime   14, 205
suicide   202
Sumerian   5, 11, 41, 70-71, 73-81, 84-88, 90-91, 101-102, 108-110, 112-113, 140, 149-150, 159, 164, 170, 182, 185, 192-195, 212-213, 215, 220, 226, 228-229, 232, 235-236
Sumerians   74, 101, 112, 220
Sumerica 71, 234
sumérienne   80, 221
Summer 112
summit   93-94, 177
sunbeams   134, 195
sun-cross 180
sun-discs 24
sun-disk   29

Sun-father 140
Sun-Folk 131, 233
sun-god 11, 22, 25, 30-31, 33, 41, 46, 49, 89-90, 118, 120-123, 127, 134-136, 141, 144, 146, 153, 164, 188, 191, 193-195, 222, 224, 231
Sun-Gods 18-19, 84, 119, 140, 225
sun-images 19
sunlight 109, 131
sunrise 12, 30, 47-49, 53, 96, 146, 148-149, 171, 193-195
supergod 185
Suppliants 106, 184, 230
surface 58, 84, 116, 137, 181
survival 161
swaddling 197
Swansea 211, 221
Swedish 170
sycamore 191
Sydney 169
symbol 15, 24-26, 31, 39, 43, 47-48, 71, 81, 83, 87, 97, 147-148, 152, 158, 173, 219, 222, 224
symbolic 17, 41, 68, 76, 79, 87, 134, 153
symbolical 214
symbolism 10, 33, 38-39, 41, 75-76, 80, 87, 89-90, 134, 140-142, 144-149, 153, 170, 189, 193, 219, 231, 234
Symbols 15, 18, 23, 26-27, 43, 48, 71, 125, 134, 159, 162, 177, 189, 191, 207, 220, 223-224, 237
Symposium 7, 235
syndrome 161
Syrian 32

T

Tablet 21, 89, 192, 224-225, 232
taiyin 168
Tamoanchan 61, 113
Tartarus 216, 227
taßiltu 77
Technology 154, 224
tecuhtli 173
Tekizikira 152
te-kuh-tli 62
teletê 204

temple 7, 39, 56, 61, 75, 78, 80, 84, 87, 89, 100, 126-127, 143, 150, 182, 200, 223, 227, 234
temples 10, 54, 71, 135, 158-159, 231
Templo 42, 184, 228
Tenacity 180, 182, 226
Tenedos 201
terror 162
Testament 146, 197, 200, 208, 227
testimony 7-8, 10, 12, 15, 20, 30, 38, 55, 58, 71, 77-78, 89, 100, 106, 108-110, 115, 117-118, 120, 130-131, 134, 146, 149, 163, 167, 171, 177-178, 194, 204, 215
Teteoinnan 124
teuctli 42
Teutonic 55, 225
thalos 205
theogonic 102
Theogony 101-103, 109-110, 115-116, 143, 183-184, 187, 212, 228, 236
theology 14, 28, 65, 111, 191, 232
Theseus 201
Thessaly 217
Thracian 104-105
thunder 12, 78, 92-95, 97, 104, 106, 111-113, 115-116, 132-133, 211-212, 214-215, 217, 225, 228
thunderer 212
Thundergod 3-4, 54, 92-97, 100, 105, 107, 110, 112, 114-115, 117-118, 130, 135, 154, 164, 180, 209, 211, 216-218
ti-mú-a 80
Tirawa 93
Tirawahat 65
Titans 116
Tlaloc 160
Tlalocan 171
tlalxicco 37
tlalxico 124, 160
Tlillan 100
toh-mel 95
tonalli 83-84, 180
Topcuoglu 22, 235
Topheth 197
Topiltzin 61, 230
topography 47
Torture 10, 161, 228

tortures 162
toruses 162
Trachiniae 202
tradition 38, 58, 79, 84-85, 93, 102-108, 110, 118, 125-127, 132, 142, 148-149, 166, 168, 171, 177, 180, 183, 186-187, 190, 205, 208
tragedies 101, 106, 201, 217, 225
trappers 65
trauma 160, 164
traumatic 58, 160-161, 164
travel 162
treasure 14
Treasures 14, 227
tremendum 14, 117, 160, 218
tribes 45, 57, 65, 162, 190, 207
tropes 77, 120
Trophonios 108
Tsimshian 171, 220
Tübingen 232
tubuqat 49
Tucson 63, 95, 98, 113-114, 220, 226
Tuesday 210
Tullius 155
turbulence 149
Türkis 29-30
Turkiß 191
Turquise 163
turquoise 1-3, 29-30, 35-38, 41, 43, 47, 49-51, 62-63, 83-84, 149, 163-164, 166, 168, 173-175, 180-181, 184, 191-192, 206, 230, 234
Turtle 44, 170, 219, 222
Tuscaloosa 37, 44, 226, 231
Twilight 22, 224
Twohig 17, 235
Typhon 115-116
Tyranny 107, 229
Tyrian 200, 204
Tzitzimime 55
Tzotzil 190, 228

U

Ueueteotl 37
Uganda 152
Ugaritic 127, 219
-ul-é-a-ta 86
Umbilicus 33, 228
unammaru 217
underworld 97, 107, 113, 148, 160, 184, 192
universe 7-8, 40-41, 47, 51, 64, 67-68, 79, 94, 103, 106, 108, 118, 123, 138, 140, 143, 146, 154, 160, 192-193, 204, 216-217, 223, 227, 235
u-pirikucu 66
Urania 201
Urbana 36, 79, 83, 201, 226, 230, 236
Ur-Namma 195
Urnammu 153
Ur-Nammu 48
urqitu 77
Urstätte 191
urucaksas- 121
ußkaru 23
Utrecht 95, 225
utujil 96
Utukku 192, 225

V

vagina 114
vaincue 80, 221
Vaisvanara 146
Valley 17-19, 46, 152, 197, 219
Vancouver 13, 58, 129, 181, 233
Varuna 142
Vaticanus 55, 168, 232
vegetable 76
vegetation 75, 77, 86, 102, 110, 149-150, 185
vegetative 75
Venusberg 148
Venusian 80, 155
Venus-star 23-24, 80
Veracruz 60
vessel 199
Vessels 11, 86-87, 232
Vestal 57, 151, 155, 220, 231
victim 35, 66-67, 78
Victorian 115, 209
victory 53, 116
village 66-67

villagers 35, 55
villages 151
vineyard 149-150
Violence 35, 113, 222
virgin 12, 110, 154
Virginity 155, 220
virgins 155
virtual 113
virtually 15, 26, 58, 60, 76, 83, 89, 117, 119, 125, 128-129, 141, 159
virtue 156
Vishnu 131-132, 136, 144
Visnuism 95, 225
vispátni 39
visvatah 190
vitality 196
voices 54
Volcanus 155
voyage 165

W

Waiyungari 169
walking 131, 133, 157, 159, 188, 229
walnut 61, 235
Wandering 186, 229
war-god 166
Warminster 116
warrior 35, 66, 72-73, 80
warriors 66
Warsaw 38, 71, 230, 234
Washington 33, 43-45, 83, 95, 103, 144, 149, 167, 171, 178, 184, 190, 210, 219-220, 222-223, 231-234
watershed 11
wealth 15, 81, 94, 114, 127, 159, 166, 189, 197
weapon 10, 116-117, 173, 216
weaver 124, 234
wedding 103, 106
Weltecken 125, 134
Weltfish 64, 67, 79, 106, 154-155, 235
Weltgegend 170
wheel-like 18, 25, 121, 164
wheels 18
whirlwind 149
Wiederkehr 47, 219
Wiesbaden 30, 48, 125, 148, 220-221, 224, 226, 229
wildlife 16
window 6, 64
Windrosen 134
Windstrich 170
wine-j 185
Winter 112
Witness 14, 24, 54, 58, 62-63, 75, 88, 90, 100, 102, 106, 111-112, 117, 121-123, 126, 137, 141, 143, 149, 154-155, 168-170, 181, 185, 187, 190, 193, 195, 197, 204, 209, 215
wnb-flower 32
wn-glyph 191
womb-like 79
wonder 14, 217
wordplays 10
Worlds 44, 49, 53, 57-58, 86, 90, 123, 139, 144, 149, 153, 160, 180, 182, 221-222, 226, 231
worldview 64, 158
worship 14, 19, 71, 185, 221
worshipped 28, 70, 213, 216
Wörterbuch 131, 226

X

Xiuhcoatl 168-169, 173-174
xiuitl 43
Xocbiltun 33
xo-tla 178

Y

Yajurveda 144, 225
Yankee 215
Yggdrasil 191-192
Yucatan 43, 95, 234

Z

zagindaru 192
-zal-am 78
-zal-e 111

-zal-gin   77
Zenobius   201
Zeus-like 117
ziggurats 162
zoïstic   107
Z-Pinch 162, 180, 231

Made in United States
Orlando, FL
11 February 2025